ENGLAND'S
100
BEST VIEWS

D023227

First published in Great Britain in 2013 by
PROFILE BOOKS LTD
3A Exmouth House
Pine Street
London EC1R 0JH
www.profilebooks.com

Copyright © Simon Jenkins, 2013

1 3 5 7 9 10 8 6 4 2

Designed by James Alexander

Butl...

...ed and bound in Great Britain by
Tanner & Dennis Ltd, Frome and London

The moral right of the author has been asserted.

All rights reserved. ...ts rights under copyright reserved
above, no part of this publication may be reproduced, stored or introduced into
a retrieval system, or transmitted, in any form or by any means (electronic,
mechanical, photocopying, recording or otherwise), without the prior written
permission of both the copyright owner and the publisher of this book.

A CIP catalogue record for this book is available from the British Library.

ISBN 978 178125 0952
eISBN 978 184765 9484

MIX
Paper from
responsible sources
FSC® C023561

Extract on p.39 from 'Dart', from Alice Oswald's *Dart* (Faber & Faber, 2010) reproduced
courtesy of Faber & Faber Ltd; extract on p. 54 taken from 'Tregardock', from *The Collected
Poems of John Betjeman* (John Murray, 2006), reproduced with permission of John Murray
Publishers, Ltd; extract on p. 235 from 'Crown Point Pensioners', from *The Collected Poems
of Ted Hughes* (Faber & Faber, 2005) reproduced courtesy of Faber & Faber Ltd. While every
effort has been made to contact copyright-holders of illustrations and poetry extracts, the
author and publishers would be grateful for information where they have been unable to trace
them, and would be glad to make amendments in further editions.

'With the exception of love, there is nothing else by which people of all kinds are more united than by their pleasure in a good view.'

Kenneth Clark

INTRODUCTION
11

THE HUNDRED BEST
21

ENGLAND'S TOP TEN VIEWS
24

DEVON & CORNWALL
Botallack; Carrick Roads; Clovelly; Dartmoor;
Dartmouth; Hartland Quay; Kynance Cove; Minack Theatre;
Plymouth Sound; St Michael's Mount; Tintagel
25

THE WEST COUNTRY
Bath, Royal Crescent; Bath, Prior Park; Bristol;
Castle Combe; Chesil Beach; Corfe Castle; Creech Hill;
Dunster; Exmoor, Barna Barrow; Exmoor, Dunkery;
Glastonbury Tor; Little Bredy; Lulworth Cove; Lyme Regis;
Salisbury; Shaftesbury; Stourhead Gardens
55

THE SOUTH

Arundel; Ashford Hangers; Coombe Hill; The Chilterns;
Dover; The North Downs; Oxford, The High; Oxford, Radcliffe
Square; Seven Sisters; The Solent; Stowe; White Horse Hill;
Windsor Great Park

105

EAST ANGLIA

Cambridge, Backs; Flatford Mill; Holkham; Lavenham;
Sheringham; Snape Marshes

147

WEST MIDLANDS

Bibury; Broadway Tower; Chipping Campden; Clee Hills;
Clyro Hill; Hawkstone; Ironbridge Gorge; The Long Mynd;
Ludlow; The Malverns; Peckforton; The Stiperstones;
Symonds Yat; Tyndale Monument

167

EAST MIDLANDS

Chatsworth; Dovedale; Kinder Scout;
Mam Tor; The Roaches

209

YORKSHIRE

Bempton Cliffs; Gordale Scar; Hebden Bridge;
Ribblehead; Richmond; Rievaulx; Roseberry Topping;
Saltaire; Swaledale; Whitby Harbour

225

THE NORTH WEST

Borrowdale; Buttermere; Castlerigg; Derwentwater;
Gummer's How; Langdale; Ullswater; Wasdale Head; Wrynose
and Hardknott; Hartside Pass; High Cup Nick; Liverpool

255

THE NORTH EAST

Coquetdale; The Cheviots; Durham; Hadrian's Wall;
Lindisfarne; Newcastle

291

LONDON

Greenwich; The City; Parliament Square;
Primrose Hill; Richmond Hill; Waterloo Bridge

311

EPILOGUE
337

ACKNOWLEDGEMENTS
344

PICTURE CREDITS
345

INDEX
346

INTRODUCTION

This book is a celebration of the hills, valleys, rivers, woods and settlements that are the landscape of England. I came to marvel at them while seeking out the best of England's churches and houses. I realised that a building's appeal is not intrinsic, but is a collage of the contexts from which it draws historical and topographical reference. They might be a churchyard, a garden, a stand of trees, an adjacent village or other buildings in an urban setting. Mostly it was just countryside. Such background became an ever more important component of my appreciation of a building, until background became foreground and I was captivated.

The English landscape is traditionally divided between town and country, the product of mankind's struggle to wrest a living from the earth over thousands of years. None of it remains truly 'wild', but a diminishing amount is what we call countryside, land between built-up areas that still answers to nature's moods and seasons. This is the England that English people profess to love. It is among the crown jewels of the national personality.

My intention is to examine not so much the landscape as our emotions in responding to it, the impact it makes on the eye and the imagination. I am not just presenting a picture of Buttermere's pines, Snape's marshes, Beachy Head or Tintagel, I am there on location, experiencing and trying to articulate the beauty of these places. This awareness is what distinguishes a picture from a view, which to me is an ever-changing blend of geology and climate,

Windermere from Gummer's How, Morecambe Bay in the distance

seasons of the year, time of day, even my own mood at the time. It is the soothing dance of sun across a Dorset pasture, the flicker of light on the Thames, the tricks of rain clouds over a Yorkshire dale.

A view is a window on our relationship to the natural and man-made environment. The experience can be uplifting, some say spiritual. It prompted William Hazlitt to tell his readers always to walk alone (though afterwards to dine in company). To him other people were a distraction from the presence of nature, almost a sacrilege. Much of the greatest poetry and painting emanates from the solitary experience of landscape. Yet it is an experience that can also enrich our relations with each other. The art historian Kenneth Clark wrote, 'With the exception of love, there is nothing else by which people of all kinds are more united than by their pleasure in a good view.'

The modern writer on landscape Robert Macfarlane likewise remarks, 'Every day, millions of people find themselves deepened and dignified by their encounters with particular places . . . brought to sudden states of awe by encounters . . . whose power to move us is beyond expression.' I understand this concept of awe 'beyond expression', but in my view we must struggle to express it. If we do not, what we love will be taken from us. Awe needs champions. The landscape is a garden of delights but one as vulnerable as any garden. England is among the most intensely developed of the world's leading countries. Yet it is a country whose landscape has for half a century been the most carefully protected against insensitive development. I regard that landscape as a treasure house no less in need of guardianship than the contents of the British Museum or the National Gallery. This book is a catalogue of its finest contents.

My approach is to list the best views in England. I accept that such a list is personal, and that there are hundreds of other equally glorious candidates. But I defend the concept of best, contesting the idea that beauty of any sort, especially of landscape, is subjective. The history of civilisation is of the search for a community of terms, for definitions of beauty that have general meaning, leading to discussion and conclusion. If visual beauty were purely subjective, conversation about art would cease and custodianship and conservation would have no basis. We must find agreement on what is lovely in our surroundings if we are to know what we are trying to protect. That agreement must start with a common terminology.

The language of landscape begins in geology. The rocks and earth of the British Isles, of which England comprises roughly a half, are more varied within narrower confines than of any country in Europe. The planet's primal eruptions left England itself neatly divided by the long limestone spine of the Pennines and Cotswolds. To the west of this spine, volcanic rocks spewed up through sedimentary layers, mostly of old red sandstone, to produce the lumpy uplands of the West Country, the Welsh marches and the Lake District. The glaciation of subsequent ice ages eroded these mountains into the rounded hills and smooth-shaped combes we know today. To the east is a different geology, that of softer carboniferous limestone in the north and chalk and clay in the south. It yielded the gentler contours of the wolds and downs, the alluvial plains shaped by great rivers and the erosion of the coast by an invading sea.

England at the dawn of human settlement was mostly covered in woods. Pollen analysis shows post-glacial warming that pushed birch and pine northwards in favour of oak, elm, lime and ash. For all the claims of guidebooks, no truly wild woodland survives. The arriving Romans would have found an already managed landscape, cleared of much of its forest to meet the need for fuel, grazing animals and building materials. England's last wild woodland is believed to have been the old Forest of Dean, and it was gone by the early Middle Ages.

Beside or replacing the woods were the fields. Their origins and geometry can seem as mysterious as Stonehenge, shaped into oblongs, lozenges, ovals and triangles. Swaledale and Langdale are a crazy paving of walls, a possible legacy of some Saxon or Viking family settlement or dispute, or perhaps the wayward course of a drunken ploughman or rebellious ox. To this day fields remain secrets that the English countryside keeps locked in its heart.

By the eighteenth century the balance between wood and field had drastically tipped towards the latter. Forests were devastated by the need for heating, iron smelting and ship timbers. Landowners enclosed open country for grazing and common land for agriculture. Uplands were torn apart for minerals and building stone. At the same time much of the countryside was viewed with a new eye, not just as a source of sustenance, whether farmed or hunted, but as a place that might be visited for recreation. The concept of landscape as beauty was born.

Such awareness was not wholly new. Horace and Virgil expressed a deep attachment to their rural homes. Petrarch famously climbed Mont Ventoux 'for pleasure'. Landscape appeared in the background of medieval altarpieces and tapestries, emerging as a subject in its own right in the Renaissance. Its presence in the paintings of Poussin and Claude was reflected in the gardens of kings and noblemen.

This appreciation came late to England. It was imported largely by the Grand Tour, an experience that educated the eye of the rich and informed the management of their country estates. It extended from enclosed gardens and parks to an awareness of the wider landscape. The poet Alexander Pope commanded the designers of the age, 'Let nature never be forgot . . . Consult the genius of the place.' Horace Walpole wrote of William Kent that he 'leapt the fence and saw that all nature was a garden'. If art could copy landscape, landscape could copy art. By the late eighteenth century English writers and painters moved beyond such fabrications to honour nature as such. In 1768 William Gilpin defined the picturesque, as he called it, as 'that kind of beauty which is agreeable in a picture'. He particularly championed the Wye Valley, where he advised travellers to carry an empty frame or a tinted mirror, through which to view his recommended views. The resulting craze was satirised by Rowlandson's Dr Syntax.

Apotheosis of the picturesque: Dr Syntax captures a view

Soon rural design became a profession in itself. Capability Brown and later Humphry Repton were wealthy entrepreneurs, much in demand. During the eighteenth century they prevailed upon their clients to move thousands of tons of earth, to upheave villages and plant forests. They were not borrowing from nature but creating facsimiles of it. The artificial had to 'look natural'. Vision became slave to fashion. The poet and landscapist William Shenstone advised his contemporaries 'to see directly, but then lose the object, and draw nigh obliquely . . . The foot should never travel by the same path which the eye has travelled over before.' The course of a footpath, the lie of a slope, the curve of a lake, became matters of obsessive attention. At Rievaulx Abbey in Yorkshire and at Stourhead, a view was reduced to a series of keyhole scenes observed from the terrace above.

What had begun as a leisure pursuit soon acquired a moral

dimension, that of the Romantic movement. As early as 1755 John Dalton wrote of Derwentwater,

> Horrors like these at first alarm,
> But soon with savage grandeur charm,
> And raise to noblest thoughts the mind.

Edmund Burke's *Enquiry into the Origins of the Sublime and the Beautiful* concluded that the 'terror' of mountains should be that of 'exultation, awe and delight rather than dread and loathing'. Wordsworth, Coleridge, Shelley and Keats saw nature as ethically superior. Beauty, said Keats, was truth. To Wordsworth on the Wye, nature was 'the anchor of my purest thoughts, the nurse, the guide, the guardian of my heart, and soul of all my moral being'.

Thus enhanced by morality and truth, natural beauty was more than ready for the turbulence of the nineteenth century. The Napoleonic wars stalled continental travel and crowded the Lake District and the West Country with tourists. By the 1820s the English countryside was suffused with religious symbolism. To William Blake and Samuel Palmer it was a place fashioned by God, to be shielded from the hideous works of man. When criticised for including workaday scenes in his pictures, Constable declared loftily, 'I never saw an ugly thing in my life.'

This led in turn to the controversies of the Victorian age and the conflict between aestheticism and industrialisation. Enraged by the intrusion into the countryside of the railway, Ruskin followed the Romantics to the Lake District, to be joined by the Pre-Raphaelites. They were followed by Hardwicke Rawnsley and Beatrix Potter, who was to use her fortune to buy thousands of Lakeland acres and give them to the National Trust. There followed the promoters of rambling, bird-watching and climbing. The peaks and the lakes saw the birth of English mountaineering.

The twentieth century, especially its second half, brought a trauma to the landscape, urban and rural, that even the industrialising

Victorians could not have imagined. Slow evolution over centuries now erupted in brutal change. In cities war was the great destroyer, to be followed by a civic obsession with urban demolition and rebuilding, stronger in England than anywhere on the Continent. In the countryside, town and country planning after 1947 sought to delineate the boundary between urban and rural development. It 'listed' for protection urban historic buildings and in the countryside it gradually extended protection to some fifteen per cent of England's land area, designated as national parks, green belts and areas of outstanding natural beauty.

Yet even planning could do little to halt the impact of modern agriculture on rural England, aggravated by public subsidy. The countryside was coated in prairie fields, silos, power stations and, at the turn of the twenty-first century, wind turbines. A landscape that had revelled in diversity became widely monocultural, taking its toll on flora and fauna alike. In half a century over a third of the hedgerows in England were grubbed out, and the area of deciduous woodland halved. As a result, whereas average woodland cover in continental Europe is forty-four per cent, in England it is less than ten per cent.

In the 1950s, the historian W. G. Hoskins set out to chart and record what he sensed was the result of this physical upheaval to the surface area of his nation. Mankind's use (and abuse) of rural England had lowered a membrane of obscurity between him and the natural environment. He wrote, 'I felt in my bones that the landscape was speaking to me in a language that I did not understand.' Hoskins dug deep and, in *The Making of the English Landscape*, revealed the history embedded in his surroundings. He ended appalled at the destruction he saw around him, mostly by twentieth-century development insensitive to beauty. It was rarely in any sense 'necessary'. I return to Hoskins and his alarm in my epilogue.

Yet we can still escape and find beauty in the countryside. From the right viewpoint we can look out over the Severn Vale, the Somerset Levels or the Weald of Kent and marvel at how much that is rural remains varied, informal, unmistakably old. There are places where England looks as it has for centuries and where people in their thousands gather to find and declare it beautiful.

I have often wondered what lies at the root of this powerful response to natural landscape, however much it has been managed over the centuries. Evolutionists intriguingly claim that it harks back to the survival ethic of *Homo sapiens* in the savannahs of Africa. We instinctively welcome the sight of open grassland, with water holes for sustenance, vegetation to hide animals and high points from which to see enemies. In England that means fields, lakes, woods and hills: each feature has its evolutionary purpose.

This may explain why, for many people, a view is an exercise in nostalgia, a craving for a more ordered, secure and predictable past. Though reassuring, nostalgia has dangers. It can fuel resistance to a democratic wish, indeed a need, for wealth and progress. Equally it is a caution, a corrective to reckless change that in the countryside is by its nature irreversible. I do not regard an appreciation of landscape as nostalgic but rather on a par with a love of art or music. The difference is that it is constantly vulnerable, to seasons, to weather, to varying patterns of land use and to changing human needs and responses. I am acutely aware that what we find beautiful today, those in the past found terrifying, ugly or boring, and those in the future may do likewise. But I am encouraged by the manifest fact that public appreciation of environmental beauty seems to increase with time.

As Clark stated, the enjoyment of landscape is the most popular of shared delights. The *Michelin Green Guides* give as many stars to views as to buildings. The crowds that gather at viewpoints are voting for beauty with their feet. But we must beware of overanalysing their motives. I do not agree with the poet Wallace Stevens that we are puppets of culture, that 'we live in a description of a place and not in the place itself'. We are more instinctive in our likes and dislikes than that. We should also heed Wordsworth's warning not to over-analyse our appreciation, lest 'our meddling intellect misshapes the beauteous forms of things'. People need only to be encouraged to open their eyes and see. As the seventeenth-century divine Thomas Traherne remarked, 'You never enjoy the world aright, till you so love the beauty of enjoying it that you are covetous and earnest to persuade others to enjoy it.'

A more immediate danger than nostalgia is cliché, and my listing the 'best of' risks such criticism. Beautiful places invite superlatives, but I have tried to avoid words such as idyllic, iconic, sensational, incomparable, stunning and picturesque (other than in its art-historical sense), though I refuse to abjure the word beautiful. I am equally on guard against personal likes and dislikes. However objectively we seek to champion the landscape, championship can evoke strong feelings, and when dealing with just a hundred views, favouritism is hard to avoid.

I also confess to biases. In gazing on a view I cannot rejoice at grim spruce plantations, intrusive warehouses, waving turbines or random city towers. They may have an inner loveliness, but they jar on a prospect, just as ill-planted trees can obscure it. I have a preference for bare mountains to forests, hedges to fences, winding roads to motorways. I delight in natural materials and the patina of age. I apologise to those who disagree and find these biases irritating. They will have theirs. What is crucial is that we concentrate on what matters. I have tried to find ground on which we can agree.

I am often asked to name my favourite view. This is hard, for as I said above, any view is conditioned by the experience of it. I shall never forget the sea storm I watched at Hartland, or Borrowdale bathed in sun, or the thrill I get every time I reach the top of Primrose Hill in London. But I confess that nothing quite matched a late-summer afternoon on Gummer's How in Cumbria. Windermere was glistening at my feet. The heights of the Lake District and the Pennines were spread on either side and the Lancashire plain lay as a foil to the south. It is surely the classic English view. It made me feel I never wanted to be anywhere else, in a landscape exhilarating, consoling, desperately precious and, above all, alive.

Salisbury: nature at peace with architecture

THE HUNDRED BEST

I have spent my life exploring England. Many of my views may not seem imaginative choices, since they have been favourites of so many people across time. Locations such as the White Cliffs of Dover, the tors of Dartmoor, Windermere and Dovedale are embedded in England's personality. They are depicted on a thousand prints, posters and calendars. I chose other views for their artistic associations: Salisbury, Flatford Mill and Snape Marshes. Many I discovered in my ramblings and at the suggestion of friends, the more rewarding for being less well-known, such as Hartland, Little Bredy, High Cup Nick and Coquetdale.

I sympathise with Gilpin's idea of composition, of foreground, distance and character. This was reflected in Constable's 'rearrangement' of his landscapes as he transferred them from sketch to finished canvas. But I gave up wasting time shifting this way and that to get 'just the right' angle, Gilpin-style, reminding myself that a view is not a picture but the act of looking at one. That said, many places have a 'good' side, and in such instances I have chosen my viewpoints accordingly. In some cases there was a tussle between angles on the same scene – Greenwich from above or below, Derwentwater from either end, or the long Cotswold escarpment. In each case many vistas offered themselves. Indeed the Lake District is entirely composed of views.

Scale alone was not enough. The fact that a dozen counties could be seen from a summit added little by way of appeal. I also ruled out the difficulty of access, such as views from mountain tops. I therefore set a limit of a half-hour walk from a public road. In my experience, most views gain in contrast and perspective from being 'halfway up', whereas views from a great height tended to be more like maps. Hence I prefer Ullswater from Gowbarrow, Kinder from Mam Tor and the City of London from The Monument.

I realise that most of my choices are either along England's limestone spine or from points west of it. This is simply because most views benefit from contour. I am aware I have short-changed the Lincolnshire Wolds, the Essex marshes and the East Midlands among others. England's low-lying eastern regions are beautiful and much loved, but their views rely heavily on sky, sea and light. They fulfil my earlier-noted criterion of atmosphere but generally lack the sweep and variety to constitute a great view. That said, I plead in my defence Lindisfarne, Bempton, Sheringham and Snape.

Since I have written elsewhere about individual buildings, I decided to treat them as views only where they formed part of a wider prospect, such as at Stowe, Holkham and Chatsworth. Urban landscapes were more difficult. Dorothy Wordsworth chided her brother for not treating man-made scenery as a legitimate source of beauty. He was prompted to write 'Upon Westminster Bridge', in which he maintained that 'Earth has not anything to show more fair' than London seen from there. I regard London's modern skyline, and therefore most of its views, as largely a 'ruin' of a landscape. But it undeniably embraces some of England's best known and most cherished prospects. So, with a critical eye, I have included them.

Elsewhere I have included Liverpool, Durham, Bath, Oxford and smaller towns such as Lavenham and Chipping Campden. Some might seem overly 'chocolate box', but that is because chocolate box makers know what is popular, and popular for a reason. As for other cities, the wreckage inflicted on their streetscapes and skylines by post-war planning and architecture is the most glaring comment on the cultural decline of the English in matters visual. Future generations may come to see today's Bristol, Birmingham, Manchester and Sheffield as beautiful. I can only doubt it.

Any journey across the English landscape is bound to be conditioned by weather. Few people are immune to sun and blue sky, which bring nature to life and raise the dullest spirits. What is little realised, especially by those who holiday abroad, is how rarely it rains in England for any extended period. A 'rainy day' is more typically just a rainy hour. This book was researched for the most part in the exceptionally wet years of 2011 and 2012, but not one day was wiped out by rain. Indeed, I found a constant source of delight in the changeability of the English climate, the chasing clouds, the sudden squalls, the shafts of sunlight.

I have tried to choose views that can be appreciated throughout the year, though some will naturally be better in certain seasons, or even at certain times of day. Kynance is not much fun in winter and Hartside is best in a storm. Distant Helvellyn likes snow. The view from Waterloo Bridge may be painful to those schooled on the London of Canaletto and Wordsworth, but it comes alive at night. I have mostly avoided illustrations that fall for the clichés of garish sunsets and moody mists, despite their unarguable photogenicity.

To list a mere hundred English views is a stern discipline. I must apologise if many a reader's favourite is not on the list. I have discovered, to my initial surprise, that views arouse fiercer passions than buildings. When I asked friends to nominate their favourites, I was surprised yet delighted at how many began with 'the view from my back garden'. It shows the depth of feeling this subject inspires. Views are no trifling matter.

ENGLAND'S TOP TEN VIEWS

BORROWDALE
From Castle Crag looking towards Derwentwater

CAMBRIDGE
The Backs and King's College

CHESIL BEACH
From Abbotsbury along the coast to Portland Bill

GLASTONBURY
The Tor from the Mendips over the towers of Wells

GREENWICH
The Royal Hospital with Canary Wharf in the distance

GUMMER'S HOW
Windermere panorama of the Lake District, Pennines and
Morecambe Bay

HAYTOR
Dartmoor and the Exe Valley

THE MALVERN HILLS
The Wye Valley and across the Severn Vale to the Cotswolds

MAM TOR
Panorama from Kinder Ridge to Stanage Edge

SEVEN SISTERS
From the Cuckmere Meanders to Beachy Head

DEVON & CORNWALL

———

Botallack: Towards Cape Cornwall 27
Carrick Roads: From Trelissick 30
Clovelly 32
Dartmoor: From Haytor 35
Dartmouth: From Dyer's Hill 37
Hartland Quay 40
Kynance Cove: Towards Lizard Point 42
Minack Theatre: Towards Logan Rock 45
Plymouth Sound: From the Hoe 47
St Michael's Mount: From Newlyn 50
Tintagel 52

BOTALLACK

Towards Cape Cornwall

The landscape of St Just is Cornwall apart, a bleak, dramatic grave-yard of a place, as if County Durham had come south to die. Small groups of plain houses, chapels and workaday shops sit in an infertile terrain. Behind the village of Botallack a lane leads down to the sea, where the coast is a wilderness of bare rocks and beating waves. Vegetation thins and battered ruins appear, often through a thick sea mist. The ground heaves and dips towards the shore. Granite gives way to rusty shale. This is the land of tin.

The rocks of Botallack are a geologist's paradise. Layers of copper, quartz, garnet, cobalt, uranium and arsenic were here 'exhaled' through volcanic fissures. Lodes of molten earth ran vertically and diagonally, requiring an impenetrable nomenclature of metapelite hornfels and pegmatite dykes. The ground at our feet shimmers with metallic colour.

Celts and Romans mined these parts. In 1539 the historian John Norden wrote that Botallack was 'a little hamlet on the coaste of the Irishe sea most visited with tinners, where they lodge and feede'. The need of the industrial revolution for tin and copper led to a boom in the eighteenth and nineteenth centuries, with Botallack at its peak in the 1860s. The famous Boscawen diagonal shaft drove 400 feet down and half a mile out to sea from the Crowns mine.

The engine house and chimney of Crowns are reached by a ver-tiginous path down the cliff. Miners told of their terror at the sound of rocks rumbling in the surf above their heads. The experience attracted tourists, including Queen Victoria in 1846. The writer

Wilkie Collins admitted to being petrified. Such was the popularity of the place that visitors were charged the then huge entry of half a guinea, to be used for the much-needed relief of deceased or incapacitated miners' families.

The arrival of cheap tin from Australia in the 1870s made Cornish tin less profitable. By the turn of the century Botallack had all but ceased production, its engines having to work ever harder to pump water from the shafts. The gaunt buildings began to disappear and

St Just coast to Cape Cornwall: shrines to the gods of rock

today just thirteen engine houses survive. The Botallack group includes the old counting house, the ruin of an arsenic works with
sheds and trackways. The Levant mine over the hill to the north
lived on into the 1960s and Geevor until 1990. The latter is now a
museum.

The best view of Botallack is from the cliff top a quarter of a mile north along the coast path, with a scramble down onto a cliffside slab. From here we can see the two cliffside engine houses of Crowns immediately below, with behind them the coast to Cape Cornwall and its offshore islands. The view is dotted with engine houses and chimneys, disused shrines to the gods of the rocks, reminding me of parts of Norfolk where ruined churches stretch to the horizon.

Here even the ubiquitous cliff heather seems meagre and half-hearted, as if admitting its defeat by geology. The rocks offshore are equally unforgiving. The marine floor along this coast is thick with wrecks, rich pickings for future archaeologists. Only the sky is alive, with cormorants circling like vultures, feeding on the history of the place.

CARRICK ROADS
From Trelissick

At Carrick Roads every prospect pleases. The Scots would call this a sea loch, an enclosed expanse of calm water across which boats scurry in safety and the sea seems far away. At its entrance we can stand astride the battlements of Pendennis and look down on Falmouth. On its eastern shore we can walk the shoreline of St Mawes to the sub-tropical gardens of Roseland. We can snooze in the sun in Mylor churchyard.

Carrick Roads vies with Rio de Janeiro and Halifax, Nova Scotia, for the title of largest natural harbour in the world. It is a classic ria, or deep glacial valley, flooded after the ice age by the incoming sea. The outer bays have long offered refuge from Atlantic storms to sailing ships rounding the Lizard, guided by the lighthouse on St Anthony Head. Though steam mostly brought an end to this role, the Roads were used to shelter convoys in two world wars. Falmouth harbour has become the terminus for round-the-world sailors such as Sir Robin Knox-Johnston and Dame Ellen MacArthur.

The inland reaches become more intimate and exciting. The Roads dissolve into Restronguet Creek and the fjord-like inlet of the King Harry Ferry. These creeks are steep-sided and deep, ideal for mothballing container ships and tankers. An adjacent coastal lane offers surreal glimpses of maritime superstructures seemingly suspended in the trees. I have seen tankers moored here in a line astern, like victims of some bizarre GPS malfunction.

The best view of Carrick Roads is south from the Trelissick peninsula, where a meadow sweeps down to the water's edge, its convex curve creating a distant illusion of cows grazing amid bobbing

Grass meets water meets sky: Trelissick towards Falmouth

masts and sails. Sky and glistening water are framed by tall trees. This is a place of peace.

From here the lie of the land has the Roads drifting out towards the sea, its shore bending gently from one side to the other like the shoulders of the ria it once was. To the right is the Feock peninsula, to the left Camerance Point. Next on the right is the creek of Mylor village, with the misty outline of the Fal estuary beyond. Each promontory slides easily into the water, crowned by trees. The only sign of life is the occasional yacht, attended by egrets, herons and grebes. Nothing is in a hurry.

On either side of the meadow lie the gardens of Trelissick House, oaks, beeches and pines interspersed with dense rhododendron, camellia and azalea. The garden is home to the national collection of photinia. More exotic species such as banana, palm and tree fern flourish inland.

CLOVELLY

Clovelly is famously attractive. A single cobbled street, known as Up-along, Down-along, stumbles down an isolated coastal ravine to a bay and small harbour. Public access is on foot (or donkey) and requires good legs and flat shoes. Residents have to haul their goods on sledges. They must have strong lungs.

Credit for preserving Clovelly goes to Christine Hamlyn, a former owner who restored the cottages in the 1930s and installed plumbing and lighting. Her initials adorn many of the buildings. The main street is attended by tiny courtyards through vaulted passages. There is no room for a square or church, other than a tiny

Clovelly before its restoration, painting by Anna Brewster, 1895

chapel. Village business takes place where it always did, round the harbour below.

Confronted by the popularity that Hamlyn's preservation brought in its train, her descendants (now the Rouses) decided in the 1980s to turn its car park and access point into a large supermarket. Visitors now enter, pay to visit and leave Clovelly through a shopping mall. It has become a gift shop with a village attached. This is dismaying, yet nothing can detract from the intrinsic charm of the place. It has the quality of a Greek island settlement while remaining unmistakably English.

Halfway downhill, the street reaches a small plateau from where there is a view both up and down. Upwards, the curve of the street is defined by cottage walls, lime-washed white, cream, lemon and pink. Devon slates cover the roofs and windows are wooden casements. From every crevice erupt petunia, geranium, hydrangea and fuchsia. As the eye travels upwards, the street line is broken by an intimation of courtyards and alleys, everywhere backed by the trees of the surrounding cliff.

The view downhill to the harbour is quite different. The village's existence depended on fishing and sea rescue, its harbour built in Tudor times. As the only haven along this stretch of coast its accessibility to the herring grounds of Lundy brought it prosperity. By the late nineteenth century the Red Lion hotel was already attracting seaborne tourists from Bristol and Wales. On my last visit, the harbour was hosting a crowded shellfish festival.

The harbour is set against the backdrop of the obscurely named Bight a Doubleyou, curving round to Bideford Bay. It is a Mediterranean prospect, contrasting starkly with Hartland Point to the south-west with its crashing Atlantic rollers.

There is an undeniable tweeness to Clovelly. Houses are called Crazy Kate's Cottage and Rat's Castle. Residents warn, Beware: Grumpy Old Women, or Remove Your Choos. But for all the complaints about 'Disneyfication' such places are alive. Their industry may be tourism rather than fish and smuggling, but a quarter of a million visitors a year are real. The goods they buy may seem down-market, but that does not invalidate the enterprise. Above all, Clovelly continues to please the eye.

DARTMOOR
From Haytor

Haytor is Dartmoor accessible: popular, touristy, anything but Dartmoor *profond*. I was warned to shun its coach parties and head west, to the bogs and mires of the interior, to Conan Doyle's

Granite Haytor, Dartmoor in the distance

Baskerville country and Princetown's notorious jail. But while they may be more remote, Haytor has the most commanding view, a 360-degree sweep of moorland and sea, hill and valley. Its tor is the finest on the moor.

Dartmoor is England's biggest dome of volcanic granite, heaving up through the Devonian sandstone to form the highest land in the south-west. On the peaks, erosion has worked on the fissures in the granite to create tors of rounded rock. These now stand as such distinctive features that it was once thought they were carved by hand, familiarly described as cyclopean. There are some 120 of these tors, among the strangest geological formations in England, surrounded by some 250 square miles of mostly peat moorland. Local churches made of this granite are rough-cast and crude, blunting the keenest chisel.

Haytor was long a granite quarry. The old workings can be seen to the north east, a landscape of smashed megaliths and deep pools. Rail tracks are still visible in places. The stone was much prized for its durability, used for many London bridges, and best seen in the hard grey base of Nelson's Column.

The tor's car park may be crowded, but the walk to the summit sorts out the strong from the weak. The final scramble onto the crowning boulder is by no means easy, up smooth slabs of unyielding granite. I must admit to getting so stuck I needed help to get down. The view from the top embraces a sizeable expanse of south-west England, a panorama from Dartmoor and Exmoor in the north to the inlets of the Devon coast and the English Channel in the south.

Dominant is Dartmoor itself, a rolling wilderness that seems to extend for ever. Each prominence is topped by its own distinctive boulder, as if the landscape had been furnished by Henry Moore. The ground is largely blanket bog, among the wettest in England. The vegetation is mainly cotton-grass, sedge, sphagnum and moss, often lying thin over pools of water unable to penetrate the granite. This creates the notorious mires into which people and horses can sink.

The landscape is bare of trees other than a scattering of birch and pine. Sheep and ponies eke out a living, helped by the occasional dark combe where a watercourse has slashed its way into the granite cap. Loveliest of these is due west of Haytor, at Widecombe-in-the-Moor, where the barren hillside swoops down in a fertile valley, marked by a superb Perpendicular steeple.

The view east is wholly different from the moor, showing the lush woodlands of the Exe valley with Exmoor's Dunkery Beacon in the far distance. To the south lies the sea, flanked by the expanse of Lyme Bay, Chesil Beach and Portland Bill, the celebrated Jurassic coast. In the foreground, the Haldon Hills shield Exmouth and Dawlish from view, but we can make out Newton Abbot and the suburbs of Torquay.

Haytor is in the manner of a border fortress. For centuries after the Roman withdrawal, it defied the invading Saxons and guarded a distinctive Celtic language and culture to its west. This culture vanished from all other parts of England, from Cumbria and the Scottish border country, surviving only across Offa's Dyke and Hadrian's Wall. Cornish – Kernewek – lasted into the eighteenth century and is now being revived. To this day some Cornish flirt with independence, and refer to the English as outsiders.

DARTMOUTH

From Dyer's Hill

This is ocean-going England, a coastline that looked not to Europe but to the Atlantic and the world beyond. Of its many deep-water shelters, Plymouth was the grandest and Falmouth the biggest, but the lesser havens of Salcombe, Helford and Dartmouth served the same purpose. Each has its champions, but to me Dartmouth is the most appealing.

JMW Turner's evocation of Dartmouth Cove from Dyer's Hill, c. 1822

Two cliffs guard its steep, wooded entrance, with medieval castles on either side. These were once linked by chains laid under the narrow estuary entrance, to be raised in emergency to obstruct attackers. It was here that the mischievous 'historian' Geoffrey of Monmouth claimed Brutus, grandson of Aeneas, landed from France to become first king of the Britons. If you believe this you can go to Totnes and see the stone on which he declared himself monarch.

It was at Dartmouth that crusader fleets mustered in the twelfth century to sail for the Mediterranean. Here was the base of the medieval wine trade with Bordeaux. Dartmouth was also the departure point for the Pilgrim Fathers to America, before they were driven into Plymouth Sound by a storm. There are as many Dartmouths in America as there are Plymouths.

The viewpoint overlooks the first elbow of the Dart river creek, from Dyer's Hill above Warfleet. From here we can see down what is almost a ravine to one of the entry castles. On the slope opposite thick trees give way to smooth meadows on the hill crest. The swirling tides below are where Alice Oswald's epic poem, *Dart*, has Proteus guiding the seals out to sea, asking

> Who's this moving in the dark? Me,
> . . . the shepherd of the seals,
> Driving my many selves from cave to cave.

Inland the river opens out into the protected basin of Dartmouth harbour, with the town on the left and the answering village of Kingswear on the right. The latter's houses climb uphill in shades of white, pink and cream, architecture imitating watercolour. The harbour teems with sailing ships, the masts and spars a filigree against the trees. For once an English riviera is reminiscent not of an aquatic caravan park but of ancient sailing ships.

Piracy was to the south coast of Devon what smuggling was to the north. The town's larger-than-life mayor in the fourteenth century, John Hawley, 'always kept the law because he made it himself'. Chaucer visited Dartmouth as inspector of customs and his pilgrims included a Dartmouth captain, who 'of nyce conscience took he no keep'.

The church's tower is prominent, its interior nautical in furnishings, as if built by ship's carpenters. A ferry fusses round the same quay as was used by the Crusaders and later by a large flotilla gathered for D-Day. Above rises the palatial Edwardian building of the Royal Naval College, the shades of empire drawing inspiration from the buccaneering history of the port below.

The Dart valley wanders upstream through charming meadows past Agatha Christie's holiday home of Greenway, high on the east bank. The tidal reach goes as far inland as Totnes. Queen Victoria called this England's Rhine.

HARTLAND QUAY

Hartland is X-certificate coast. It craves bad weather, leaden skies and tumultuous waves. Facing due west, it is the first land the Atlantic has encountered since America, and it is not pleased. The cliffs and rocks are irresistible force meeting immovable object. They are best seen in a swirling mist, disappearing and re-emerging with added menace. Hartland is always a good view, but it rages into life in a storm.

Irresistible Atlantic meets immovable rock at Hartland

The road to the quay from inland seems headed for the end of the earth. Trees shorten to stumps, hills empty and the few farms look like desperate survivors of a climatic disaster. We pass through the village of Stoke, its tall church tower supposedly a beacon to sailors, before dipping down to the isolated manor of Hartland Abbey and on to the coast at Hartland Quay. It is an unfrequented spot.

Hartland Point, two miles to the north along the 'iron coast', was notorious in the days of sail. A ship failing to round it into Bideford Bay in a sou'westerly was usually doomed. Admiralty advice to sailors was, if wrecked, to stay aboard as 'there is little or no chance of saving life by taking to the ship's boats'. The Victorian vicar of neighbouring Morwenstow, Robert Hawker, recorded that 'so stern and pitiless is this iron-bound coast' that a parishioner had witnessed eighty wrecks in just fifteen miles 'with only here and there the rescue of a living man'.

There was a Tudor harbour here, but it fell into ruin and collapsed in the nineteenth century, battered to pieces by the surf and considered not worth replacing. The settlement now comprises a single, strangely urban lane called 'The Street', housing the Wrecker's Retreat pub. Opposite are a museum and rental cottages. The best views are either from the folly on the cliffs above or, especially in rough weather, from the grassy platform and lookout by the quay. There is no better place to sense the fury of sea, with the foreshore stretching on either side under the cliffs.

Hartland is England's version of Ulster's Giant's Causeway, well described in a guide by a local geologist, Peter Keene. Its sedimentary mudstone and sandstone were compressed, buckled, fissured and folded into corrugations by tectonic collision some 300 million years ago. The resulting layers are embedded in the cliffs, fashioned into waves, arches, zigzags and chevrons.

Immediately north of the quay lie Warren Beach and Bear Rock, an upward stack with saw-like teeth stretching out into the waves. The rocks seem twisted in agony, piled against each other like corpses at the mouth of hell. To the south is Well Beach. Here erosion has left smooth wave-cut platforms of rippled rock sliding into the water, ideal for landing small boats. Behind it are the rockfalls of a so-called storm beach, patiently awaiting their turn to be crushed to sand. In the distance lies Screda Point, its lofty slabs of sandstone so smooth as to look man-made.

Along the tops of these cliffs clumps of thrift and sea campion cling where trees have long given up the ghost. In one thicket I heard a stonechat chirping defiance at the elements.

KYNANCE COVE

Towards Lizard Point

Kynance is picture perfect. Open heath slopes down to sandy shore. Elegant rocks do not enrage the surf, as at Hartland, but soothe it. The beach abounds in streams, rock pools and windbreaks. A discreet café causes no offence. Acquired by the National Trust in the 1990s, Kynance is perpetually posing for a photograph.

The secret of the Lizard peninsula, of which Kynance is part, lies in its geology, in ancient volcanic rock taking the form of green or red serpentine stone. This stone, unique in England, is cut and polished for jewellery and trinkets. Serpentine also yields a unique Cornish heathland, and lends a deep turquoise to the surrounding waters.

Kynance bay is divided into two beaches by Asparagus Island with its prominent Lion Rock and, to the right, by Sugarloaf Rock.

Asparagus Island from Tennyson's look-out

They are joined to the shore by a tombolo, a sandy spit covered at high tide. Facing them on the cliff is a grassy promontory from which the best view of the whole bay is obtained. I once sat here surrounded by heather, thyme and thrift in bright sunlight after days of miserable weather and could hardly believe myself in England.

It was here in 1860 that the Pre-Raphaelites Holman Hunt and Val Prinsep sat sketching Asparagus Rock on a holiday visit with Tennyson and Palgrave. Hunt wrote of looking down on 'the emerald waves breaking with foam, white as snow, on to the porphyry rocks . . . The gulls and choughs were whirling about to the tune of their music, with the pulsing sea acting as bass.' Palgrave was desperate lest the elderly Tennyson go too near the cliff, infuriating the poet by his attentiveness. Tennyson eventually relaxed and imagined an eagle on the rock:

He clasps the crag with crooked hands
Close to the sun in lonely lands
Ring'd with the azure world he stands.

The wrinkled sea beneath him crawls;
He watches from his mountain walls,
And like a thunderbolt he falls.

The rocks compose a complete gallery of natural sculpture, formed of cones, cubes and triangles. At high tide they emerge from the water like floating mountains in an oriental print. From each angle, and especially in moonlight, they take on new shapes, as faces, volcanoes, lions and dolphins' heads. The seaweed underwater floats like fish in shoals. Lesser rocks litter the beach, forming pools of childhood delight. This is a beach of clean sand and privacy, a monument to the variety and intimacy of England's shore. In the distance are the cliffs of the Lizard, the country's southernmost point.

MINACK THEATRE
Towards Logan Rock

The cliffs of Minack form the most exciting natural amphitheatre in England. In 1929 Rowena Cade, a thirty-six-year-old Derbyshire woman, came with her widowed mother to live at Porthcurno. A troupe of amateur actors were performing *A Midsummer Night's Dream* in a local meadow. So entranced was Cade that she suggested next year they do *The Tempest* on a cliff ledge at the foot of her garden at a spot called Minack, Cornish for rocky place. A rudimentary stage was built and lighting supplied from car batteries and a wire from the house. As the moon rose on the setting that first evening, Cade knew she had found magic.

Cade and her gardeners slowly transformed the cliffside into a Greek theatre. Granite boulders were levered into place, concrete poured and timbers hauled up the slopes, Cade doing much of the work herself. The result is not just a feat of engineering but the most dramatic of theatrical backdrops. The actors perform in front of two great rocks and a backdrop of wave-capped sea. Gulls cry overhead. The birds are distracting for the audience at first, but they and the setting gradually fuse nature and drama into one experience. Only during the war did performances cease.

By the time Cade died in 1983, the Minack was an established summer festival. Companies now visit from across the world, performing mostly Shakespeare but also local favourites such as *The Pirates of Penzance*. I recall an Oxford student troupe returning from a summer appearance, spellbound by the experience.

The auditorium, which borders the South West Coast Path, is open daily to visitors and offers a sweeping view east over Porthcurno bay. The precipitous slope to the stage, beautiful as it may be, is not for acrophobics, giving the impression of the sea rising vertically as a giddy backdrop. In the distance is Logan Rock, a 'rocking boulder' of eighty

Porthcurno and Logan Rock as backdrop to Minack's drama

tons of granite. It used to move to the touch, but was toppled by a group of drunken sailors in 1820. They were forced by local villagers to restore it, which they did, but the rocking is now harder to achieve.

Among other interests, Cade was intrigued by the botanical challenge of her site, sunny most of the time and sheltered from the prevailing south-west wind. Exotics were imported to see whether they could survive the salt-laden air, planted in among the theatre's seats and tiers. They include bird-of-paradise trees from South Africa, Californian poppies, aeoniums from the Canary Isles, agaves from Mexico and Madeiran geraniums.

The only threat to the Minack is from Cornwall's planners. They have allowed rows of holiday homes to break the cliff horizon in almost every direction, bringing intimations of suburbia to what should be a wild, open coast. Such development could at least have been pushed a hundred yards inland.

PLYMOUTH SOUND
From the Hoe

———

I can't love it, I can't hate it. The post-war devastation of Plymouth was unparalleled among English towns. What the Luftwaffe left standing, Plymouth's city fathers set about destroying. Even where old buildings remained, as in the Barbican neighbourhood, planners forced setbacks and realignments that spoiled the rhythm of the streets and alleys. Plymouth seems a far cry from Thomas Hardy's 'marble-streeted town' and nearer to Geoffrey Grigson's post-war lament, 'Dirty concrete rises and replaces/ Your town's stuccoed dignities and maritime graces.'

Nor did Plymouth spare its most notable feature, the Hoe, from which generations of seafaring families had watched their ships sail, first from the Barbican and then from the naval base at Devonport. Today its Regency terrace is punctuated by a bland slab and a tower. A Ferris wheel has been deposited on the Hoe's summit, while the descent to the waterfront is crowded with modern leisure facilities. In 2008 the council published a plan boldly proposing the removal of buildings of 'negative quality'. They are still there.

For all that, the Hoe remains the hub round which the Plymouth landscape revolves. It ranks in England's historical geography with the white cliffs of Dover, testified by the cluster of memorials on its summit. It was here in 1588 that Sir Francis Drake supposedly played bowls while waiting for the tide to turn before confronting the Armada, a happy tale now discredited. Below on the Barbican quayside, the Pilgrim Fathers embarked in 1620 to found the colony of New Plymouth in America, having been forced by a storm to come ashore after leaving from Dartmouth.

The Hoe remained strategically important into the seventeenth century, when Plymouth rallied to Parliament during the Civil War and was besieged for four years. On the Restoration a star-shaped citadel was built on its summit, its guns pointing both out to sea and inland over the town. Local regicides were imprisoned on Drake's Island, a prominent rock in the Sound. This island was later converted into a naval fortress, last fitted with guns in 1942. Since then the defence ministry and Plymouth council have vied with each other in failing to find a use for it.

The view out over the Sound is refreshingly sylvan. The west side is occupied by the woods of Mount Edgcumbe, green, lush and preserved. Here in the 1550s Sir Richard Edgcumbe built a mansion to complement his 'country' seat up the Tamar at Cotehele. The house survived, much altered, until hit by a German incendiary bomb in the war. The seventh Earl of Mount Edgcumbe rebuilt it within the old walls in neo-Georgian style. After his death the estate passed to a succession of New Zealand relatives who dutifully returned to occupy it. The house passed to the local council in 1987.

Opposite to the east is Mount Batten, site of the first prehistoric settlement of the area. Archaeologists have revealed the possible remains of a trading post with links to Iberia and the Mediterranean. The round tower is a seventeenth-century artillery base. Mount Batten was later used for flying boats, a mode of transport now sadly almost defunct, with the Sound as an ideal landing strip. Covering its entrance is a breakwater, used to stage the British firework championships since 1997.

In the 1870s the Hoe played host to the relocated Eddystone light, known as Smeaton's Tower, removed from the notorious rock out at sea. It now stands prominent on the slope, and can be climbed for a better view (though curiously not after 4.30 or on Sundays).

Gracious Great Western: flying boats over the Hoe,
poster by Claude Buckle, 1938

Behind, at 3 Elliot Terrace, is the house that once belonged to Nancy Astor, Britain's first sitting woman MP, who represented Plymouth after her husband's resignation. She famously came out onto the Hoe during the blitz to dance with the sailors.

ST MICHAEL'S MOUNT
From Newlyn

St Michael led the army of God, defended Christians against Satan and is patron saint of high places. His Cornish 'home' rises from the sea to gaze across Mount's Bay towards Penzance, oozing legend and tourist appeal in equal measure. St Michael appeared to local fishermen in 495. The rock was used by the giant Cormoran, eventually slain by Jack the Giant Killer, and again by the hermit Ogrin to buy dresses for Queen Isolde. It was also the scene of yet another of King Arthur's incessant battles. St Michael's is a plot of land entirely surrounded by myth.

The rock was certainly an Iron Age trading post for Cornish tin. A chapel is said to have been founded here by Edward the Confessor and later given to the celebrated Normandy abbey of Mont Saint-Michel. Confusion surrounds a report in the Anglo-Saxon Chronicle that the rock was originally five miles inland, surrounded by sea only in 1099 after an inundation of the Penzance plain. If so it can hardly have been a prehistoric port. Either way, after the conquest it passed to the Benedictines, who founded a priory on the rock in 1135.

History has rarely left St Michael's in peace. As a French foundation, the priory saw early dissolution by Henry V in the Hundred Years War, but it remained as a powerful fortress. It was held against the Yorkists in the Wars of the Roses and against Henry VII by the pretender, Perkin Warbeck. Elizabeth I gave it to her loyal aide, Robert Cecil, and it was later held for the king in the Civil War. It then passed to Colonel John St Aubyn, whose descendants live there to this day, under lease from the National Trust.

The mount forms a triangular profile, its rocks turning into the ramparts of the castle and priory buildings that form its summit. The stone causeway over the beach to its quay is usable only at low tide. The monastery's military, religious and domestic ranges are reached up a winding path through richly exotic semi-tropical gardens. It is a peaceful spot with little of the 'industrial' tourism of its French sister at Mont Saint-Michel. Whatever the weather it seems an island of calm.

The most photogenic view of St Michael's Mount is from the shore and the narrow streets of adjacent Marazion. I prefer a wider setting, across the bay from the lanes above Newlyn harbour. From here the whole shoreline is visible along a twenty-five-mile sweep to

Workaday Cornwall: The Mount from Newlyn harbour

Lizard Point. The mount rises dark across the water in the middle distance. To the left are the uplands of Mulfra Hill, with the remains of the remarkable Iron Age village of Chysauster, which must once have traded tin through the port at St Michael's.

In the foreground lies Newlyn, once home to a school of landscape artists and bustling with maritime commerce. The mount is thus seen rising through the masts of workaday fishing boats, surrounded by quays, warehouses, cranes and seamen's missions.

TINTAGEL

Dark headland hovers over massive rock. Round them crash seas of a turquoise colour produced by light acting on copper embedded in slate. This slate is one of the few sure things about Tintagel. It is a place where history has conceded victory to myth. The castle's website is stuffed with Arthur, Merlin, Guinevere, Tristan and Isolde, not to mention advertisements for £170 chain-mail tunics. The small village is surrounded by a rampart of hot-dog stalls and an outer bailey of caravan and camp sites.

The exploitation of Tintagel is not new. The link with Arthur derives from a twelfth-century cleric, Geoffrey of Monmouth, who wrote a work of fiction with the unhelpful title *History of the Kings of Britain*. He told of someone called Arthur, conceived at Tintagel by Uther Pendragon of Igraine, wife of the local warlord, Gorlois. This was achieved by Merlin magically transforming Uther into the form of Gorlois, and thus getting him into the castle to impregnate Igraine.

The result of this unseemly congress was a saga of romance, chivalry and tomfoolery of timeless appeal. The story consumed all Europe throughout the Middle Ages and beyond. During the

Hundred Years War, Edward III had his courtiers dress as Arthurian characters, and welcomed his treacherous mother, Isabella, back to court as Guinevere. By the time Caxton printed Sir Thomas Malory's *Morte d'Arthur* in the 1480s, the legendary monarch was a world celebrity.

As usual the Victorians trumped the pack. Tennyson and Swinburne rewrote the legends at length. The Pre-Raphaelites and William Morris added copious depictions. In 1899 a Tintagel entrepreneur built a mock-medieval hotel called Camelot on the headland overlooking the island. It now claims Ava Gardner, Noël Coward and Winston Churchill as guests who came to see 'the birthplace of King Arthur'. Hollywood continues to bolster the genre.

There is evidence that the rock and adjoining cliff may have been occupied in the Dark Ages, possibly by a lord of the Cornish kingdom of Dumnonia. The first known castle was built by an English earl, Richard of Cornwall, in 1233, apparently to identify himself with Geoffrey's Arthur and ingratiate himself with the locals. He

Arthurian Tintagel, Samuel Palmer, c. 1848

found Tintagel a miserable spot and the castle was ruinous by the fourteenth century. Were it not for Geoffrey it would have been forgotten. Tintagel should thank him, not Arthur.

The best place from which to see Tintagel rock is from the cliff-edge to the north, directly in front of the Camelot hotel – if only because no other view can avoid it. The rock is linked to the mainland by a tenuous causeway, now crossed by a footbridge. It is worth a view if only for the way it rises majestically from the sea in defiance of the elements. Some scattered ruins, enhanced by the Victorians and English Heritage, can be made out on the inland side of the island. Others on the mainland are partial reconstructions. As so often I would love more of this, to convey some sense of place and purpose.

The setting is tremendous, a vista of brutal rocks and head-lands stretching in either direction along the Atlantic shore. The most vivid monument along this shore is not the castle but Tintagel church, standing wild on its cliff top defiantly gazing out to sea like a lighthouse. This is a Norman building with all the antiquity the castle lacks. It appears Roman Catholic in its fixtures and dressings, as ignorant of the Reformation as Tintagel is of the truth.

This has long been an inspiring place. The composer Arnold Bax wrote his surging tone poem, 'Tintagel', after a secret visit with his mistress, Harriet Cohen, in 1917. The theme is taken from Wagner's *Tristan* and the words include, 'For all my heart's warm blood is mixed/ With surf and green-sea flame.' A few miles to the south, the young John Betjeman likewise sat on a cliff, contemplating suicide after his poems were ridiculed by the press. He gazed over the edge where

Gigantic slithering shelves of slate
In waiting awfulness appear,
Like journalism full of hate.

THE WEST COUNTRY

Bath: Royal Crescent 57

Bath: From Prior Park 59

Bristol: Avon Gorge from Clifton Bridge 62

Castle Combe: The Street 64

Chesil Beach: From Abbotsbury 66

Corfe Castle: From Kingston 70

Creech Hill: Towards the Somerset Levels 73

Dunster: From Conygar Hill 76

Exmoor: From Barna Barrow 78

Exmoor: From Dunkery Beacon 81

Glastonbury Tor: From the Mendips 85

Little Bredy: The cricket field 87

Lulworth Cove 89

Lyme Regis: The Jurassic Coast from the Cobb 92

Salisbury: From the Avon water meadows 95

Shaftesbury: Towards Gold Hill 98

Stourhead Gardens 100

Avon Gorge

Swindon ●

Castle Combe ◎

Bristol ◎

Bath ◎

Barna Barrow ◎

SOMERSET

WILTSHIRE

Dunster ◎

Dunkery Beacon ◎

Stourhead ◎

Glastonbury Tor ◎

Salisbury ●

Creech Hill ◎

Shaftesbury ◎

Taunton ●

DORSET

Bournemouth

Little Bredy ◎

Poole ●

Lyme Regis ◎

Chesil Beach ◎

Corfe Castle ◎

Lulworth Cove

BATH
Royal Crescent

Bath's marriage of architecture and landscape is as happy today as it was when first brokered by the Georgians two and a half centuries ago. The town was a scruffy spa visited by Queen Anne in 1702 and 1703 seeking to cure her gout. This stir of fashion was seized on by the town's self-appointed 'master of ceremonies', Beau Nash, at a time when England was becoming more mobile and the bonds of society were eroding.

Aristocrats and commoners alike arrived on supposedly therapeutic holidays and felt licensed to disregard some of the conventions of back home. But they were expected to obey Nash's own 'rules', which reassured them that they, and especially their children, could mix with people they did not know, at least for the duration of the season. Nash's assembly rooms became a focus of style, money and plots for Jane Austen novels.

Nash's success was exploited in turn by the quarry owner and builder Ralph Allen, and by his architect John Wood. They supplied him with a set for his revels, a series of avenues, squares and circuses laid out on the slopes overlooking the spa. Bath became England's most desirable resort, declining only under the Regency with the rise of Brighton and sea-water cures. It is a monument to an extraordinary social enterprise, a place of carefully modulated leisure and social intercourse.

Everything in Bath reflects Nash's plutocratic egalitarianism. There were few individual mansions, but rather terrace houses for rent. Everything took place behind a monumental facade. Behind the ashlar front of a Bath house are usually cheap rubble walls and a pokey garden.

The Bath of Nash and Wood is best appreciated by climbing from Queen Square up Gay Street to the Circus. An honour guard of Bath stone flanks the route, stone that seems to drink in the sun by day and radiate it back after dusk. The Circus, composed of three equal segments, was Wood's fantasy of a Druidical stone circle in architectural form, a Romano-British Colosseum.

Three avenues lead off the Circus, one of them, Brock Street, appearing to vanish into thin air. Only as we turn the corner does the astonishing spectacle of Royal Crescent unfold to the right, a terrace of immaculate proportion and rhythm curving away from the eye. Every time I see it I gasp. As Bath's historian David Gadd remarks, 'Here familiarity breeds only delight.'

Royal Crescent was completed in 1767 by Wood's son after his death and was intended to create a sense of *rus in urbe*, the pretence of the country come to town in a tightly articulated sequence

Wealthy egalitarianism: The Royal Crescent *by Thomas Malton, 1777*

of thirty-seven town houses. Each resident enjoyed the illusion of coming home to a palace and, when looking from its windows, might enjoy the illusion of a private park. The plan is not semicircular, but semi-elliptical, a dazzling composition of town planning with the perspective seeming to drift into the middle distance. The facades are adorned by 114 attached Ionic columns, paired only on the middle. One house (a smart hotel) has been permitted a magnolia, spoiling the rhythm.

The best vantage point is from the steps outside No 1, its pillared facade giving prominence to the turn of the corner from Brock Street. This house was rented during the season for £140, taken initially by the Duke of York on a timeshare basis. The view from this corner embraces the whole west of the city, dropping sharply down into the Avon valley. On all sides are thickly wooded hills, guarding what is still a town of gentility and calm.

BATH
From Prior Park

Ralph Allen was a Victorian before his time. He began his working life as a postal innovator and stone merchant of Cornish extraction. Born in 1694, he came to Bath with the idea of setting up a postal service so its holidaying visitors could keep in touch with home. He also wanted to promote his local quarry and its soft oolite stone, warmest and most malleable of limestones. He went on to become Bath's principal developer, one of the triumvirate, with Beau Nash and John Wood, on which the town's wealth was built. A philanthropist and entertainer of artists and writers, he was also Bath's mayor.

Allen opened a quarry on Combe Down with an early tramway down to the Kennet and Avon canal, along which he hoped to transport his stone to London and the world. He was mortified when London's builders preferred the more durable Portland stone from Dorset, as had been used by Wren for Greenwich Hospital and St Paul's. London became a city of silver, while Bath, like Oxford, is a city of gold.

Allen occupied a house that still stands in the city centre, but in 1733 he commissioned Wood to design a Palladian mansion on

Bath's swirling terraces, from Prior Park

the downs above Widcombe. Prior Park was located near his quarry and gave a view down a steep and narrow valley to the town below. A contemporary called it 'a noble seat, which sees all Bath, and which was built for all Bath to see'. To Pevsner it was 'in the grand manner, the most ambitious and the most complete re-creation of Palladio's villas on English soil'.

Here Allen entertained Pope, Fielding, Gainsborough, Garrick and Pitt, indeed anyone of distinction who came to Bath for the season. His dinner table was crowded and his local donations generous. Fielding used him as model for the saintly Squire Allworthy in *Tom Jones*, remarking that Prior Park was the only house in the kingdom 'where you are sure to gain a dinner by deserving it'.

After Allen's death the house was gutted by fire. It later became a Catholic boarding school and is now a college. But the prospect over central Bath is as Allen would have known it. We see his terraces swirling along the contours opposite, rising to Royal Crescent in the distance, like regiments manoeuvring before battle. The old quarter round the abbey is clearly visible below, marked by church spires and the Victorian town hall and hotel.

An added delight of the view from Prior Park is the immediate foreground, where parkland sweeps down the valley to the river. On the left of this descent, Alexander Pope laid out a 'wilderness' in honour of his maxim, 'Let Nature never be forgot . . . Consult the Genius of the Place.' Above all he consulted contour.

The wider park was later redesigned by Capability Brown as a tumbling slope of grass between flanking woodlands. It culminates in two lakes framed by a colonnaded bridge, all now owned by the National Trust. This is one of three bridges in England copied from Palladio's bridge at Bassano del Grappa in Italy (the others are at Wilton and Stowe). Another characteristic view is from below, looking up through the silhouetted bridge to Prior Park above. In mist or snow, when the surroundings slip into the background, it seems to float on the hillside.

BRISTOL
Avon Gorge from Clifton Bridge

Why the River Avon cut through a steep fold in the southern Cotswolds, instead of finding an easier path through Somerset to the Bristol Channel, has long been a geological conundrum. It is possible an ice sheet of some sort may have blocked its easier way, forcing the river to create a gorge a mile long and some 300 feet deep. Another more prosaic suggestion (according to geographers Andrew Goudie and Rita Gardner) is that the river always went this way. When upper tiers of rock eroded, the river's path was already established. Either way, the gorge is a true English Grand Canyon.

At its bottom is the fiercest tide in England, forty-nine feet high. Since the gorge was just three miles from the sea, this tide brought sea-going ships far inland, to make Bristol one of Europe's greatest medieval ports. Even in the eighteenth century prints show the gorge crowded with ships, a turmoil of masts, tugs and tow ropes.

To surmount this gorge a Bristol wine merchant, William Vick, in 1753 envisaged a stone bridge of what would have been unprecedented scale. He left £1,000 to be invested and spent on such a crossing, as and when interest had grown it to the £10,000 he estimated it would cost. Progress was slow. The first iron bridge, in Coalbrookdale in Shropshire, was built in 1780. Not until 1829 was the Bristol project begun, with a competition judged by the leading engineer of the day, Thomas Telford. He rejected all twenty-two entries and declared a design of his own the winner, based on his recent Menai suspension bridge.

The decision was thought so outrageous that the competition was re-staged, and won by the twenty-four-year-old Isambard Kingdom Brunel. His 1831 design was for a suspension bridge with towers in an Egyptian style then much in vogue. The towers were supposed to be crowned with sphinxes. Constant delay left

Stately portal: Clifton bridge in 1840

the project unfinished and it was completed, after Brunel's death in 1859, by the Institution of Civil Engineers as his memorial. The bridge finally opened in 1864. To reduce the expense, chains and ironwork from Brunel's demolished Hungerford Bridge in London were used for the job.

From below, the bridge looks light and beautiful. It does not tame or diminish the gorge but acts as a visual unifier. From above, the view downstream shows the muddy River Avon flanked by the snaking path of the A4. The speed of the tides made the gorge difficult to navigate, and the phrase 'ship shape and Bristol fashion' referred to the need for cargoes to be made fast when hulls might have to rest on the bottom at low tide. On the steep sides, trees find scant grip. The withdrawal of sheep has led to woods crowding the cliff tops, home to peregrine falcons.

On the Bristol side of the bridge is a whitewashed windmill, once used for grinding snuff and then as an observatory. It now houses a camera obscura with views of the surrounding hills. Below is the gallery of a cave dug into the cliffside, with more views of the gorge. Upstream are intimations of suburban Bristol. The dignified Regency terraces of Clifton are tiered down the hillside to the river bank. Disused wooden quays indicate where ships were moored to await the tide. Neither the city nor its docks are visible, except in the form of three red-brick Victorian warehouses.

Bristol cannot hope to recapture the excitement of fleets of sailing ships moving up the gorge into the heart of the city. But it still has the bridge as its symbol. It is much used for bungee-jumping and shares with Beachy Head a grim reputation for suicides, now made harder by the fitting of barriers. Its walls carry prominent notices for the Samaritans.

CASTLE COMBE
The Street

The English village ranks with Big Ben and the white cliffs of Dover as an emblem of English picturesque. Nowhere better embodies it than Castle Combe. It has the reassurance of soft sun on limestone walls, the gentle curve of gabled cottages, a humpback bridge and a market cross. Petunias and begonias deck creamy houses against a backdrop of oak-clad hills. It is the England of 'All Things Bright and Beautiful'.

Strip back the sentiment and this remains a place of visual delight. Castle Combe's main street stretches just two hundred yards, but in every direction the townscape offers lessons in informality, intimacy, proportion and surprise. An hour spent sitting on its market cross is worth a dozen lectures on modern architecture.

The village is set above a stream in a well-watered fold of the Wiltshire hills. The castle stands at a distance and the manor, now a hotel, is hidden in its park behind the church. There is one street, running from a bridge over the Bybrook stream up to the cross. Off the square is the church, its graveyard filled with clothiers' chest tombs. The population is just 350.

Almost everything about these limestone villages is attributable to the wool boom of the fifteenth and early sixteenth centuries. Compared with most of Europe, peace reigned and England supplied the troubled markets abroad with wool cloth. The Cotswolds were rich in sheep. Wealth flowed down the streams to where villagers carded, spun, wove and dyed the wool. Castle Combe produced a popular red and white chequered cloth and claims to have invented the blanket.

This was a community as wealthy as any in the country. Its church was rebuilt with tall perpendicular naves. The lord of the manor was Sir John Fastolf, who financed a troop at Agincourt and was one of many 'Falstaffs' credited as Shakespeare's original. He would have presided over its ceremonies and patronised its civic institutions.

Castle Combe high street from market cross

These institutions would seem lavish today. They included a school, a constable's house, a manorial court, a pound, two inns and a cockpit. The local economy embraced millers' and weavers' cottages along the stream, shops and a market hall. This last stood adjacent to the present market cross and is marked by a mounting stone. Castle Combe was a 'one-stop shop' of local welfare. Only the church and the pubs remain.

The view south down the main street from the cross is a casual yet immaculate composition. Stone facades curve towards the bridge, one- or two-storeyed, their roofs of differing pitches, some gabled, some with dormers. One house on the left is half-timbered. Each has a distinctive floral dressing. Thickly wooded hills crown the view.

North from the square the church gate offers a glimpse of the churchyard and tower, neatly at arm's length from the village's former commercial focus. The gatehouse to the manor is memorable for hosting the escape of Dr Doolittle in a 1960s film. The village also featured in *Poirot* and *War Horse*, epitomising antiquity and serenity as a contrast to the dark horrors of crime and war. As a result Castle Combe is rarely free of that signature of the English picturesque, wandering clouds of tourists. Mercifully the view is kept free of parked cars, albeit at the price of aggressive yellow lines.

CHESIL BEACH
From Abbotsbury

Dorset is perfect for views, a county of rolling downs, wide bays, beaches and sea. Chesil Beach is the queen of them, though its interminable shingle is both hard on the feet and hard to appreciate at close quarters. Its full extent is best seen from the coast road west of Abbotsbury, a panorama unique in England. Eighteen miles of uninterrupted beach, the longest 'storm barrier' in Europe, stretches to a climax at Portland Bill, separated from the coast by the Fleet lagoon. The spectacle is overlooked by a circular mound on which stands St Catherine's Chapel. The best view is 200 yards below the car park at the top of the hill, which gives the chapel greater prominence and renders the contours explicit.

Chesil Beach is a bulwark of flint shingles driven by submarine waves from deep offshore, some of it arriving at the end of the last ice age from the decomposing cliffs of Devon to the west. Wave upon wave piled the shingles twenty feet high to the west and forty feet to the east, moving it steadily towards the shore and with wind and tidal drift shifting it eastwards at a rate of some six inches a year. Ambitious geologists have estimated its weight at 50–100 million tons.

Wave action has sorted the pebbles, with the smallest to the west the size of peas and the largest to the east the size of hen's eggs, beautifully graded as the beach sweeps eastward. The bank runs in one glorious uninterrupted arc from near Bridport to its climax at the limestone promontory of Portland. There is nothing else like it in Europe.

The Fleet lagoon shelters a large population of migratory birds. Swans are joined by geese, divers and grebes, while the shingle protects the delicate nests of plovers and terns. The landward bank of Chesil Beach is rich in sea kale, sea pea, yellow horned poppy, campion and eel grass. I am told it is home to the rare scaly cricket, which does not fly, sing or hop, a bleak existence.

The beach's eerie sense of desolation has proved an inspiration for many writers. Ian McEwan's *On Chesil Beach* bathes it in 'a grey, soft light and a delicate mist drifting in from the sea, whose steady motion of advance and withdrawal made sounds of gentle thunder'. To McEwan the beach becomes a metaphor for a doomed relationship. Raymond Friel's poem of the same name concludes, 'We are

Queen of Dorset views: St Catherine's towards Portland Bill

made creatures on this bank of time,/ Longing to hear the voice of the creator.'

In the distance is the jutting outline of the Isle of Portland as it defies a sea that continues to sculpt this coast. Its quarries have been sought throughout history, used by Wren to rebuild London after the Great Fire. While its stone easily blackens with city soot, it

reverts to brilliant white when washed. Thanks to Portland, I have been privileged to see London turn from black to white in my life-time. From afar the promontory is like a capsized ship, its hull up-turned towards the shore. A lighthouse on Portland Bill guards its southern tip.

In the middle distance is St Catherine's Chapel on its mound. It was built in the fifteenth century as a pilgrim chapel of the local abbey, of blackened local stone, heavily buttressed and with a stone roof to withstand the south-west winds. St Catherine was patron saint of spinsters, making this a favourite shrine for women hoping for husbands. One prayer pleads:

> A husband, St Catherine,
> A handsome one, St Catherine,
> A rich one, St Catherine,
> A nice one, St Catherine,
> And soon, St Catherine.

Of the abbey little remains except its huge tithe barn, one of the largest medieval secular buildings in England. The chapel survived dissolution by serving as a landmark for seafarers.

To the left of the mound lies the village of Abbotsbury, of the most beautiful tawny Dorset stone. Beyond rolls the Dorset heathland, protected from over-farming by poor soil and studded with plantations. It is an exquisite landscape. To watch clouds play cat and mouse across it on a sunny day is a special Dorset delight. In the distance stands the Hardy monument, with Dorchester beyond, while to the east lies Weymouth and its harbour, protected from the south-westerlies by Chesil and Portland alike.

CORFE CASTLE
From Kingston

Corfe is a castle of romance. Begun by William the Conqueror soon after the 1066 invasion, it was rebuilt in Portland stone to guard the hills overlooking Poole and Weymouth. The castle passed to the

Corfe: citadel of Royalist romance

Bankes family in the seventeenth century and was the last Royalist castle in the south to fall to Parliament.

For three years Lady Mary Bankes, wife of Charles I's attorney-general, held out against a parliamentary siege, defeated only when betrayed by treachery in 1643. Her stance became the stuff of feminist legend. The attackers were afterwards so impressed they allowed her to keep the castle's keys, though they blew up its walls. The Bankes family moved to Kingston Lacy and the castle was left a ruin. Lady Mary's statue stands at Kingston, the famous key in her hand.

The castle survives today as little more than a jumble of cubist shapes piled above its adjoining village, the rocks of its walls seeming to grow from those of the hillside. Its village lies cosily in a defile beneath. Seen down East Street on a moonlit night, Corfe looks like a gothic film set, adorned with owls and bats.

My favourite view is from further off, two miles south on the Worth Matravers road beyond Kingston. From here the castle stands proud on its hillock, strangely sandwiched between two limbs of the Purbeck hills. The site was regarded as impregnable. It had an inner and outer bailey and attackers needed to brave a long defensive wall curving up the slope. During the Bankes siege just two defenders were lost, against over a hundred attackers. I know of few castles that would so benefit from a latter-day Viollet-le-Duc, to reinstate its romantic magnificence.

Behind the castle and its hills stretches Dorset heath, the earth chalky and the fields sparsely enclosed. To the north lies Wareham forest, the intervening valley blessedly free of conifers, pylons and visible settlement. To the east we get a glimpse of Poole harbour and its inlet from the sea. When the sun is on them, its white high-rise flats are a shock, like aliens creeping from a distant shore.

Closer to hand is the tower of Kingston's Victorian church. This was built by the pious Earl of Eldon, despite the village having a perfectly good medieval church already. Eldon commissioned the architect G. E. Street to erect a large cruciform building and not to worry at the expense. No architect balks at such a commission. The tower dominates this flank of Purbeck, as if echoing the heights of Corfe across the vale.

CREECH HILL
Towards the Somerset Levels

Where best to view the Somerset Levels westwards from the Wiltshire downs? The prospect is drenched in English history. Here legend put one of Arthur's capitals, at Cadbury above the River Cam, and thus perhaps Camelot. Here too is the possible site of the battle of Mons Badonicus, a last British triumph over the invading Saxons, fought circa 500 by a Romano-British leader who just may have been called Arthur.

It was in these Levels that the finally victorious Saxons founded an abbey, possibly as early as the sixth century, enveloped in myths of the Holy Grail. It was to this country that Alfred the Great retreated in 878 to plan his resistance to the Vikings, then pressing south into Mercia and threatening to conquer all England. Here Alfred is said to have burned the famous cakes in a local hut while absorbed in his preparations, returning none the less to defeat the Viking Guthrum at the battle of Edington near Marlborough. As part of the settlement, Guthrum agreed to become a Christian, with Alfred as his godfather. Had the battle been lost, English history would have been different, though whether, as some suggest, this book would be written in Danish must be moot.

The view over the Levels from Alfred's Tower on the Stourhead estate supposedly captures this mix of fact and fiction. But for me it is too high, flattening Cadbury Hill and the surrounding contours. Creech Hill stands seven miles to the north and is closer to

the Levels. It looks up to Stourhead behind it, and looks across to Cadbury to the left. It directly overlooks the golden limestone town of Bruton, deep in the Brue valley and with only its church and dovecot visible from a distance. Creech is recognisable for the two groves of trees, mostly ash, that crown it like a Mohican haircut. It is a mysterious place, home of a 'bull-beggar' or bogeyman, and of black wildcats often 'sighted' in these parts, usually after pub closing time. An Iron Age fort crowns the summit.

The view north from Creech Hill over the valley of the Frome and the Avon rivers is of the southern outliers of the Cotswolds, marked in the distance by Beckford's Tower above Bath. This is a geographical fulcrum of England, where the north–south limestone spine ends and the country turns south-west towards the sandstone uplands of Devon.

Behind us to the east and south are the fringes of Salisbury plain, an expanse of rolling wildness, desecrated through decades of use as an army training ground and now being extensively sold for building development. Next to it lies the open horizon of Cranborne Chase and the woodlands of three great estates, the Marquis of Bath's Longleat, the Hoares' Stourhead and the Bradley estate of the dukes of Somerset. Stourhead is the closest and most prominent, a ridge of solid forest, planted by the Hoares over two centuries as a belt of protective woodland around their Palladian mansion.

To the south-west is the ancient acropolis of Cadbury, a rectangular plateau on the crest of a hill above a garland of trees. Whatever its association with Arthur, it is one of England's most dramatically sited Iron Age forts, dating from 1000 BC. It was clearly more than a castle, probably a substantial centre of population. How little we know of these places is frustrating.

West of Cadbury stretch the Levels themselves, bounded by the Quantocks, the Bristol Channel and, to the north, the low ridge of the Mendips. Composed of wetlands and peat bog moors, the

Peaceful and inviolate: the Levels from Creech Hill

Levels were, like the East Anglian fens, a place apart. Their inhabitants lived on islands or lake villages, with only Brent Tor and Glastonbury Tor offering any serious contour. Today the landscape of fields and hedges seems peaceful and inviolate, though battles continue between farmers eager for drainage and the biodiversity of wetland enthusiasts. A project to re-flood part of the area was fiercely resisted, and abandoned in 2010.

DUNSTER
From Conygar Hill

From the coast road to Minehead we could have stumbled on a Robin Hood film set. A tower peers from the top of a wooded hill with, across a small valley, a red sandstone castle on a crag. Everywhere are turrets and fluttering flags. We need only armoured knights to come riding through the trees. This is Dunster, castle-village buried in tumbling forests, once guarding the approach to the royal hunting ground of Exmoor.

Dunster is what the Germans call romantic and the English picturesque. The village is spread along a dainty high street from the gates of the castle towards the old yarn market. Cottages run up hill on every side, enveloped in flowers and greenery. This is a lush valley, a haven for walkers descending from the moors above.

Though the view from Dunster Castle is excellent an even finer one is of it from across the village opposite. A path leads up Conygar Hill directly behind the market cross, but there is little point in climbing the path through the wood to the 'lookout' tower. The landowner, the Crown Estate, has ensured that the tower looks out

Dunster's castle-village on the flanks of Exmoor

only onto adjacent trees. A tiny 'window' has been cut in the foliage, but what should be a magnificent panorama from the coastal plain to the heights of Exmoor is obscured.

That said, the view from the field halfway up the hill is an adequate substitute. A meadow of grass and flowers fills the foreground. Dunster's main street rises beyond, straight to the castle, overlooked by the wooded flanks of Exmoor. Red sandstone is everywhere, in the walls, roofs, footpaths and earth, with just the odd splash of white. The deep pinks of the stone and pale greens of the trees are offset by the russet of an occasional copper beech and the dark green of a pine. In autumn it makes a wonderful palette.

Dunster Castle was built by the Norman Mohun dynasty and passed to the Luttrells in the fourteenth century. It was held for the king in the Civil War and its walls were slighted afterwards as a result. Rebuilt and enhanced for the Luttrells by the Victorian medievalist Anthony Salvin, it passed to the National Trust in 1976. Salvin's work is an elegant composition of towers, turrets and garden terraces, perfectly proportioned for its location on the hill.

Such places are lauded when genuinely medieval yet often derided as pastiche when Victorian. Yet Tudors and Jacobeans were no less 'revivalist' than those of the nineteenth century. The intention was to create a chivalric effect, to pack a romantic punch. Dunster does it on a grand scale, and with respect for the genius of the place.

EXMOOR
From Barna Barrow

The north coast of Exmoor is a scenic feast. An upland of peat and heath on a cap of sedimentary sandstone reaches the sea in cliffs punctuated by deep wooded valleys. To the west of Lynmouth these cliffs take the form of a row of jagged peaks known as the Valley of the Rocks. They offer a fine prospect, overlooking an exquisitely sited cricket field. But my favourite view round Lynmouth is to its east from above Barna Barrow car park, between County Gate and Countisbury.

This offers the Bristol Channel in one direction with, inland, a plunging view down into the Lyn river valleys, known in these parts as combes. These are steep indentations, created by water cutting furiously into the sides of Exmoor's impermeable sandstone. The rivers are not the sluggish streams of the chalk country but impatient, angry cascades. There are some 300 miles of such combe rivers across Exmoor.

At our feet is a canyon, that of the East Lyn river as it descends from the central Chains plateau to Watersmeet. It passes Oare, the country of Lorna Doone. The feud between the Doone bandits and the respectable Ridds at the time of the Monmouth rebellion formed the backdrop to one of the great romances of nineteenth-century fiction, a West Country *Romeo and Juliet* by R. D. Blackmore.

The river feeds into the network of combes radiating from the coast. From above they are like the tentacles of a green octopus. It was from here that a flash storm in 1952 sent a wall of water crashing down on Lynmouth, destroying much of the town and killing thirty-four people.

On a calm day it is hard to imagine these valleys harbouring such menace. Today the channels through Lynmouth have been widened and the conduits are better managed. But the dark oaks in the valley seem from above to be as dense and menacing as an Amazon rain forest. They make the bare moors seem almost friendly.

Behind us out to sea lies the Bristol Channel. Here the heath runs directly down to the shore, with a backdrop of the Brecon Beacons across the water. East lies the wooded inlet of Glenthorne, where it is believed a German submarine came ashore for water during the war. Beyond it are the woods of Culbone. This was a sad place, where history's outcasts, heretics, criminals, lepers and freed slaves

The Lyn combes 'betwixt two Isles of purple shadow'

were dumped ashore from Bristol and left to fend for themselves. They were served intermittently by what claims to be the smallest church in England, St Culbone's. It sits alone in a forest glade near the sea, at last a place of peace.

It was on this stretch of coast that Coleridge, temporarily lamed in an accident, imagined his friends walking without him, through

> The roaring dell, o'er wooded, narrow, deep
> and only speckled by the midday sun.

They emerged onto what might be our view:

> [a] tract magnificent
> Of hilly fields and meadows, and the sea
> With some fair bark, perhaps, whose sails light up
> The slip of smooth clear blue betwixt two Isles
> Of purple shadow!

EXMOOR
From Dunkery Beacon

The view from Dunkery can be windy and dull. It lacks foreground and, in all but the finest weather, the horizon disappears into haze. But no list can omit this grandest of English views. It doffs its cap in all directions, to Haytor in the south, north to the Brecon Beacons and north-east to the Cotswolds. At 519m Dunkery is the highest point on Exmoor, surrounded by a typical moor ecology of dense heather with occasional scrub oak. In autumn this turns into a

kaleidoscope of pinks, mauves and purples, a Persian carpet rolled out beneath our feet in all directions.

To the north the view is down through Horner Wood to the combes flanking Porlock. This might be a promised land, a place where fields of green and yellow give way to the shore of Porlock Bay.

Grand old man of views: bracken and heather on Dunkery

Porlock itself is out of sight round the corner, home of the anonymous 'person' who interrupted Coleridge in his composition of 'Kubla Khan', to become a euphemism for unwanted interruptions.

The valley forms a serene visual foil to the surrounding moor.

To the east of Porlock rises Bossington Hill and Selworthy Beacon. Selworthy's white church peers above the surrounding wood. On the hill to its left, clearance has left a circle of trees surrounded by grass, making the whole outcrop seem like a one-eyed whale, basking on a shore.

This flank of Dunkery is the Holnicote estate of the Acland family, last royal wardens of Exmoor in the eighteenth century. They gave it to the National Trust in 1944 and it was one of the last places in England to practise stag hunting. Much controversy surrounded the Trust's decision in 1997 to ban such hunting on its estate. On adjacent land, the largest known land animal in England, a 9 foot-tall stag known as the Emperor of Exmoor, was killed by a (wisely anonymous) hunter in 2010.

To the north of Dunkery lies the coast of Wales, with the Gower to the left, followed by Swansea, Port Talbot and Llantwit Major. This last was the site of the monastery where Christianity is believed to have lived on after the departure of the Romans, keeping alive links between Wales, Ireland and Cornwall, while England reverted to paganism. These waters are thus a historic thoroughfare of Christian faith. To the right runs the Severn estuary and its bridges, but in a mist they vanish into what appears open sea, giving Wales the appearance of an island.

Due east lie the Brent and Blackdown hills, followed by the Quantocks. These are gentler slopes described by Wordsworth as hills whose 'murmurous woods,/ Give a curious feeling to the mind/ of peopled solitude.' Round to the south is a moor that seems to stretch for ever, cut only by the valley of the Exe. Lacking the rugged outcrops of Dartmoor's granite tors, Exmoor's undulating expanse is a savannah. Across it we expect to see not native ponies and the occasional hiker, but drifts of mammoth, giraffe and sabre-tooth tiger, an English Serengeti.

GLASTONBURY TOR
From the Mendips

There are few sights lovelier than Glastonbury Tor at dawn. The Isle of Avalon rises above the mist of the Levels, a ship of mystery on a sea of legend. Is that Joseph of Arimathea, landing from the Holy Land with the Crown of Thorns? Is that Arthur sporting with Lancelot and Guinevere? Is that a monk burying the Holy Grail? Over the centuries, Glastonbury has mutated from Christian mission to pagan shrine to hippie hang-out, while also hosting one of the world's most renowned music festivals.

My own holy grail was to find the exact spot where the Tor could be seen floating between the towers of its magnificent neighbour, Wells Cathedral. After much searching I found a field at the end of Beryl Lane on the flank of the Mendips above Wells. The convex curve of the meadow fell away to the roofs of the town, above which the cathedral's towers seemed close enough to touch. Behind them across the Levels lay Glastonbury, its turreted mount perfectly silhouetted behind the towers of Wells. It was a satisfying moment.

Glastonbury was a medieval foundation dating from the invading Saxons in the eighth century. Whereas Wells became the seat of a bishop and survived the Dissolution, Glastonbury soon degenerated into ruin. Its monks fled to Strata Florida in Wales, supposedly taking with them the Holy Grail. Since the Second World War the site has become home to a bizarre procession of mystics, new-agers, Druids, hippies and folk-singers. Glastonbury high street wafts with incense, spices, bells and chants, an oriental souk come to Somerset. In the churchyard a battered thorn bush claims descent from the Crown of Thorns.

The vista from above Wells is over the whole of west Somerset. To the left are the hills round Crowcombe, with beyond them the golden Hamstone outcrops of the Wiltshire border. This is the

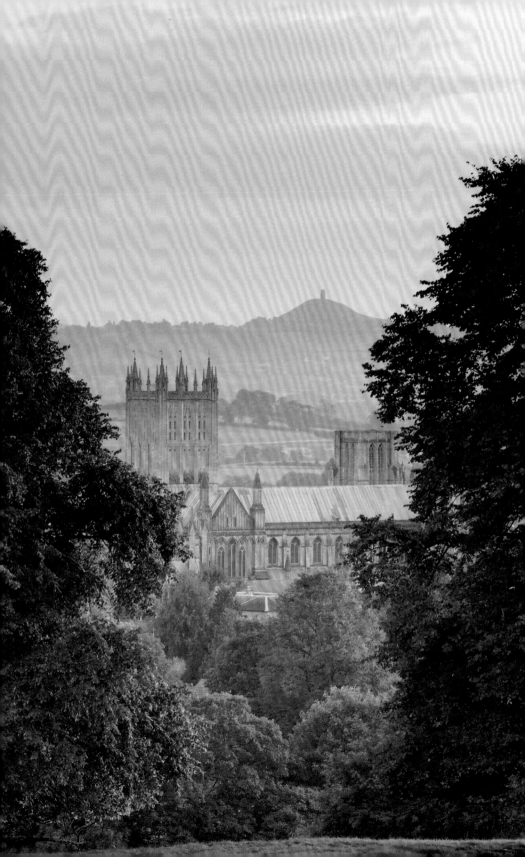

The power of myth: Glastonbury above Wells cathedral

loveliest stone in England, a limestone glistening with crustaceans that the sun can turn from pink to crimson to gold. Ahead are the Levels, interrupted by the Polden Hills and behind them the Quantocks. To the west lie the Bristol Channel and Wales, with the mound of Brent Knoll in the middle distance.

At our feet lies Wells, the 'smallest city in England', tucked busily beneath its cathedral. From where we stand we see only its roof-ridge, with the fourteenth-century crossing tower and the twin west towers. Across town they are answered by the tower of St Cuthbert's, noblest of Somerset steeples. Yet always the eye is drawn to the Tor as along a flare-path to a citadel of magic. There is force in those myths after all.

LITTLE BREDY
The cricket field

Then there are the secret views. They appear on no lists and may at first seem of no matter. I first became aware of this spot on a warm summer day when I was lying on the grass waiting to bat in a village cricket match. Dizzy from the heat, I felt the slopes begin to shimmer and shift. Three dimensions became two, hill and vale advanced and receded, fields and trees seemed mere patches of colour. I later found David Inshaw's painting of this view, exactly as I remembered it that day. Little Bredy was landscape paying back a debt to art.

The village hides itself discreetly in a cleft below the Dorchester plateau, at the upper extremity of the valley of the Bride, a chalk-land stream that reaches the sea at Burton Bradstock. The village is little more than a hamlet, with the eighteenth-century Bridehead manor and park next to a lake that doubles as the river's source. Beyond lie Jacobean stables, a medieval church, rectory, village hall and a scatter of cottages.

The cricket pitch must be the loveliest in England. The configuration of the enveloping hills is that of a glacial scouring, forming a hollow bed round which pillows are arranged for comfort. In the bottom is the cricket field, the central playing area flat but the outfield turning up at its corners, making boundaries hard to score. The field ranks with Arundel and Lynton as most beautiful venues for England's most decorous sport.

The appeal of the hills lies in part in the regularity of their elevation (all are between 170 and 180m). Behind the pavilion rises White Hill Wood, a classic chalkland beech wood above a meadow. To its right a second down takes over, with Heart Clump Wood on its summit. The horizon then breaks into open heath at the twin humps of Old Warren, dotted with cows and sheep. These humps are intersected by the crest of a lesser ridge, creating an effect of rising and dipping curves, an immaculate geometry. At one point

Little Bredy's immaculate geometry: painting by David Inshaw, 1976

the dip of Old Warren meets the rise of the ridge in a perfect cusp.

The slopes are peopled by random trees, some standing alone, some in groups, like oratorio singers in an amphitheatre. Here stands an oak, there a pair of chestnuts, there a spreading sycamore, there a chorus of beeches. Such is the incline of the slope that the trees to the south-west create evening shadows fifty yards long, as in Inshaw's painting.

To the west of the cricket field and house is the village. Every step through it offers a Dorset view: the thatched cottages of Church Walk, the old schoolhouse enveloped in flowers, a field of ornamental trees. Finally a lane leads out of the combe past a Victorian lodge toward Long Bredy. The vista opens over the Bride valley, with Bridport, the coast and the sea in the distance.

LULWORTH COVE

The Dorset shoreline is a wreckage of a rampart. A wall of old and battered limestone ill-protects its interior of fragile chalk, greensand and clay. Everything has been buckled by time and eroded where the sea has broken through. A few ruined bastions survive at the isles of Purbeck and Portland. Fragments poke up elsewhere along beaches and headlands.

Nowhere is the wall's degeneration more apparent than on the stretch from Lulworth to Durdle Door. At Lulworth a glacial stream must once have rolled down the hill and punched a hole in the limestone to reach the sea. The tide raced in and scoured out a bay from the soft greensand rock before hitting a firmer cliff of chalk. The movement of the waves eventually described a circular lagoon.

The road to Lulworth descends through isolated artillery ranges. The village itself is set back from the coast in a scatter of cottages

and Victorian villas. On its fringe is an intrusive car park that should have been placed further inland. The best view of the cove is from directly above the car park on the western promontory enclosing the bay.

From here we look down into the breach in the wall, some 200 yards across, with the tide racing in and out. The cove is surrounded by steep chalk slopes, except where the stream and the road make their entry. Fishing and tourist boats are drawn up on the shore but, praise be, not one building has been allowed. The water has the deep blue of submarine chalk.

The vantage point looks east along Kimmeridge Bay towards St Aldhelm's Head. The coast here has been colonised for half a century by the army, leaving a deserted landscape of ruined buildings and old tanks which has at least preserved a precious ecology. At its centre is the ghost village of Tyneham, taken by the army as part of a training range in 1943 when its 250 inhabitants were evicted on

A rampart breached: Lulworth Cove at dusk

the promise that they could return at the war's end. The promise has never been kept. Back from the shore is England's oldest working oil well at Kimmeridge, still nodding after half a century.

To the west, almost at our feet, is Stair Hole, a so-called infant cove where the sea has again broken through the limestone to create a series of caves and arches. It intrigues geologists as a vision of how Lulworth might once have begun. Its twin 'entrance' rocks were referred to by Thomas Hardy as 'the pillars of Hercules to this miniature Mediterranean'. On one side is the remarkable 'Lulworth crumple', a formation covering an entire face of the cliff, similar to that at Hartland Quay in Devon. Layers of sedimentary rock, limestone and shale are buckled and corrugated like folded blankets. Parts rise vertically. Rarely have I seen geological forces so vividly displayed. The soft cliff edge is in perpetual erosion and has to be barricaded.

Behind Stair Hole the South West Coast Path rises up the cliff towards Durdle Door, with more astonishing limestone outcrops. A quarter of a million people tramp this path a year, but the view beyond has been spoiled by caravans sited up to the edge of the cliff above. I would like to believe a special place in hell is reserved for the planners who permit this sort of vandalism on the English coast. There is no reason for not moving the caravans a few hundred yards inland. Whatever income their intrusive presence generates is surely inadequate compensation.

LYME REGIS
Jurassic Coast from the Cobb

Some views are of yesterday, some of today and some of all time. Lyme demands an imagination of when seas were coming and going, ice forming and dissolving, and strange creatures roaming Dorset's wastes. At some point the English Channel is formed and the sea slices through the sedimentary layers. Geology solidifies and the time-lapse camera halts, leaving a cross-section through these cliffs for those who care to read.

One such was Mary Anning of Lyme. She was born in 1799, a Dorset working girl who died forty-seven years later a national celebrity. Left fatherless at eleven, she and her brother earned a living selling ammonite fossils from Lyme beach to Regency tourists. Intrigued by what she was finding, and armed with a chapel education, she became the first serious amateur palaeontologist. Her souvenir business prospered. Enthusiasts would come from far and wide to follow the Lyme lass in her smock and hat, hammer in hand,

Anning's apostles: Jurassic treasure-hunters on Lyme beach

along the foot of the cliffs. Her discoveries were to include the first ichthyosaur and the first plesiosaur.

Anning's laboratory is now called the Jurassic Coast and is a world heritage site. It stretches for ninety-five miles on either side of Lyme, from the Exe estuary to Poole harbour. Its geology is young, the Cretaceous, Jurassic and Triassic ages dominant in southern England. But while the cliffs at Dover and Beachy Head are pure chalk, Dorset offers a richer palette: the marls and clays of blue lias, limestones and shales, and the brown, red and yellow sand-stones, all interspersed with chalk. Exposed by the eroding waves, these layers have become a wonder of the world, a prehistoric zoo sunk in a preserving bog. From the ammonite shells falling onto the beach to the dinosaur parts regularly excavated from the cliffs, the Jurassic Coast is a cornucopia of prehistory.

The best prospect is from Lyme's ancient jetty, the Cobb. The harbour was built out from the shingle beach in the thir-teenth century, there being no natural haven for miles around. Breakwater boulders were floated into position, lashed to empty barrels, giving Lyme a prosperous port into the eighteenth cen-tury. This prosperity was overtaken by the resort of Lyme Regis on land immediately to the east, first patronised by tourists holidaying at home during the Napoleonic wars. The Cobb saw a pivotal scene in Jane Austen's *Persuasion*, when the heroine, Anne, comes to the aid of an injured friend and thus revives the ardour of Captain Wentworth. Local youths use the boulders for a lethal form of mountain biking.

In the foreground of the view from the Cobb is the port, busy with boats and boatmen, fish restaurants and crowds, overlooked by exotic gardens on the cliff above. To the right lies the main resort of Lyme with its church tower rising above tiers of Georgian cottages, painted in whites, reds, blues and ochres. It carries its fame with gentility. There is a discreet Dinosaurland fossil museum. Shops still sell souvenir fossils as in Anning's day. Ammonites are depicted in the streetlight brackets.

This is a mere prelude for the cliffs. Beyond Lyme they rise and fall along the beach, an echo of Sussex's Seven Sisters. Each cliff is different, the most dramatic being the layered rampart at Charmouth. The climax, the highest point on the south coast, is Golden Cap (191m), named after the outcrop of bright greensand at its summit. The beaches below are usually alive with fossil hunters, the present craving a glimpse into the past.

Turning west we see a different mystery. Here the view is closed by the thickly wooded slopes of the Undercliff, a unique feature of the English coast. It was caused by a series of landslips, the most dramatic being the Bindon Slip on Christmas Eve 1839. A hundred yards of chalk broke away and slid towards the sea, leaving an island on the beach and a five-mile-long chasm between it and the mainland. The slip was an immediate tourist attraction, and has since developed as an isolated nature reserve, accessible only from each end. This lost world was evoked in the novel and film *The French Lieutenant's Woman*, by a local writer, John Fowles.

SALISBURY
From the water meadows

The view of Salisbury from across the Avon meadows is a perennial favourite among 'England's best views'. Its celebrity rests on John Constable and his 300 depictions of Salisbury. Constable was drawn there by his friendship with a canon at the cathedral, John Fisher, whom he first visited in 1811 when he was thirty-five.

Salisbury soon supplanted Flatford as his inspiration. He viewed it from every angle, from Old Sarum to the north, from Leadenhall to the south, from the adjacent Bishop's Garden and from the Avon and its water meadows. Usually the cathedral steeple was

accompanied by wild skies and blowing trees, a work of man set amid the always grander works of nature.

Constable's most finished masterpiece of the scene, *Salisbury Cathedral from the Meadows*, was painted at the height of his powers in 1831, preceded by numerous drawings and oil sketches. It embodied the message of his lectures on art. As Constable's biographer Charles Leslie wrote, 'his nature was peculiarly social, and could not feel satisfied with scenery . . . that did not abound in human associations'. His paintings were therefore replete with 'villages, churches, farmhouses and cottages'. In this work we see a placid group of people going about the daily round, with carthorses drinking in the stream. But we also see a darker symbolism, of an Anglican church in turmoil, under attack for opposing the 1832 Reform Bill. Constable, like Fisher, was a supporter of reform and his storm clouds were those of looming trouble.

The most prominent feature of the painting is the rainbow, symbol of the covenant between God and man. The bow lands on Fisher's house, a shaft of heavenly light contrasted with clouds enveloping the cathedral. Constable even appended a verse by James Thomson to his painting:

> As from the face of heaven the scattered clouds
> Tumultuous rove, th'interminable sky
> Sublimer swells, and o'er the world expands
> A purer azure.

An anonymous critic put it more prosaically: Constable 'almost imparts the wish for an umbrella'.

The viewpoint is unmistakable today, a hundred yards south from the footbridge by the Crane Street car park, looking across to the cathedral's west front. There may now be no horses in the stream and the Crane Street car park is too close. But sheep make

A church in turmoil: detail of Constable's Salisbury from the Meadows, *1831*

a suitable substitute for horses, and the red brick of Constable's Georgian houses still peeps through the greenery. The cathedral steeple is crowned by a graceful spire. Constable depicts it at an angle from the north-west, with the nave west front at an angle to the viewer. In front is a now over-abundant rampart of trees, alder, willow, copper beech and pine.

I have never seen Salisbury with such a rainbow, but on my last visit, blustery clouds were forming behind the darkened steeple. Rain was in the air and I prepared to depart. Suddenly the sun broke from the clouds behind me, raced past me across the meadow and lit up the trees and the roofs of the close. Finally, it caught the cathedral and set the steeple ablaze. I wished for Constable at my side.

SHAFTESBURY
Towards Gold Hill

In 1973 the town of Shaftesbury was chosen as location for a Hovis bread advertisement by the director Ridley Scott. Filmed in old-world colour, it showed a boy puffing his way up the town's Gold Hill, pushing his bike to reach, 'last on the left, Old Ma Peggotty's house'. A chord wails implausibly from Dvořák's New World symphony and a Somerset voice says, ''Twas like taking bread to the top of the world.'

Gold Hill never looked back. It featured in the film of Hardy's *Far from the Madding Crowd* and on calendars, guidebooks, jigsaw puzzles and biscuit tins galore. Ma Peggotty and the boy are the subject of a bawdy YouTube satire and the cobbles seem to spend half their time covered in movie maker's mud, straw and prop manure. The hill even has a small museum in its honour. A memorial to Hovis stands on the high street above, a large bronze loaf.

The reason is that the street embodies 'Ye Olde England', a row of apparently tumbledown cottages with steep eaves and walls draped in flowers. Each dwelling has its own personality, yet is part of a communal whole. Such townscapes convey a security, comfort and good neighbourliness wholly absent from hard-edged modern design. We can preserve these qualities from the past, yet seem unable to replicate them.

While such scenes are familiar in France and Italy, England

Hovis reaches 'Old Ma Peggotty's house' on Gold Hill

offers few streets to equal Gold Hill's charm. Shaftesbury is an isolated town on an outlier of the Wiltshire downs. Steep roads lead up from the plain. The old high street is lined with eighteenth-century buildings, with the site of the Saxon abbey on a dramatic prominence at its south-west corner. The abbey is recreated 'virtually' in a small museum but its garden survives, its wall looming over Gold Hill down an alley next to St Peter's church. The wall is massively buttressed and seems in perpetual danger of collapsing into the street.

From the top of the hill the line of cottages curves down a cobbled pavement. Though clearly medieval in origin, most have windows and roofs no earlier than the eighteenth century. Each is a composition in itself, a facade of stone or whitewash and a roof of thatch or tile. There is no clutter of modern vehicles or street furniture.

Seen from above, Gold Hill has a backdrop of rolling Wiltshire countryside. Such backdrops, a leitmotif to many of my views, are critical to the composition. They are the frames, the garlands, the adornments of the landscape.

STOURHEAD GARDENS

Stourhead's creator, Henry Hoare (1705–85), banker, tourist, connoisseur and designer, appears in Michael Dahl's portrait in his former house astride a rising white steed like Marlborough at Blenheim. He epitomises his nickname, 'the Magnificent'. He inherited his father's home at the age of thirty-three and in 1744 began to reorder the estate above a valley in the Wiltshire downs. How far his inspiration was William Kent's contemporary work at Stowe is not known, but both were clearly inspired by the early Georgian fascination for classical gardens in an English setting.

Wealthy Britons at the time were returning from Italy imbued with an education, that of ancient Greece and Rome, that is obscure to most people today. At first it was reflected in a landscape of formal avenues, glades, temples and statues. At Stourhead and later at Stowe and elsewhere it evolved into something quite different, an English informality and asymmetry. Hoare took as his theme a painting of his by Poussin, of Aeneas at Delos.

He intended the walk round a new lake to represent Aeneas's journey from Troy to Rome. It passed temples and grottos, culminating in a pantheon where lived the gods of the underworld. All this was to be viewed through 'the shades' of trees from a terrace of firs across the lawn from the house. It was a woodland of serpentine walks and surprises, as if straddling the boundary between this world and the next.

Hoare's successors swamped this erudite message with hundreds more trees and shrubs which now threaten to turn Stourhead into a jungle. Even with vigorous National Trust pruning, Stourhead is more an arboretum than Hoare's sylvan metaphor for Arcadia. But we can appreciate his desire that 'greens should be ranged together in large masses as the shades are in painting . . . to relieve each dark mass itself with little sprinklings of lighter greens here and there'.

In late autumn this vision is so transformed that October is now the busiest month for visitors to Stourhead. The view west up the lake becomes a billowing cornucopia of yellows, golds, browns and reds, each overwhelming the next. The gods of the ancient world are upstaged by those of nature.

Hoare did not demolish Stourhead village, as many grandees would have done at the time, but employed it to visual effect. His allegory might be a pagan legend but his composition was thoroughly English. A classical bridge and pantheon are balanced by a village green with gothic cross, a parish church and a farm. The scene is overlooked by part of the old village street.

Overleaf: Ancient gods upstaged by nature: autumnal Stourhead

This composition can be perfectly appreciated from the slope of the churchyard. The view is down a grassy slope to the stables and inn. The medieval cross was moved to the green from Bristol in 1765. Beyond, the eye is drawn over the lake to the pantheon, designed by Henry Flitcroft, domed and porticoed and set at an angle to the view, almost engulfed by trees. Inside is a sculpture gallery of the deities Aeneas would have encountered in the underworld, including Diana, Ceres, Isis and Hercules. A curved slope of grass leads down to the water, from where can be seen the other temples around the lake.

I cannot better Pevsner's reaction. Rarely given to effusive reflection, he says of Hoare's creation, 'English picturesque landscaping of the eighteenth century is the most beautiful form of gardening ever created, superior in variety and subtlety to the Italy of Frascati and the France of Versailles.' Most remarkable to Pevsner was that such gardens were inevitably being 'created with a view to later generations than one's own'. Hoare himself would never have witnessed his work in its maturity. We are lucky to be among his beneficiaries.

THE SOUTH

―――

Arundel: From Crossbush   107

Ashford Hangers: Towards Steep   110

Coombe Hill: Towards the Vale of Aylesbury   113

The Chilterns: Stonor Valley from the Turville hills   116

Dover: From the white cliffs   118

The North Downs: From the Devil's Kneading Trough   121

Oxford: The High   125

Oxford: Radcliffe Square   127

Seven Sisters: From Cuckmere Haven   131

The Solent: From Hurst Spit towards the Needles   135

Stowe: The Gardens   137

White Horse Hill: Towards the Vale of the White Horse   140

Windsor Great Park: The Castle from Snow Hill   143

Stowe

BUCKINGHAMSHIRE

Aylesbury

OXFORDSHIRE

Oxford

Coombe Hill

Stonor Valley

Reading

Windsor

BERKSHIRE

White Horse Hill

SURREY

Devil's Kneading Trough

Maidstone

HAMPSHIRE

Guildford

KENT

Winchester

Ashford Hangers

WEST SUSSEX

Dover

Chichester

Arundel

EAST SUSSEX

Lewes

Cuckmere Haven

Hurst Spit

ARUNDEL

From Crossbush

———

Grey, sombre Arundel lies on the flank of the downs like a cat waiting to prey on the valley below. In the Sussex volume of Pevsner's *Buildings of England* Ian Nairn declared it one of the finest town views in England, though he reflected mid-twentieth-century taste in complaining that this was chiefly due to the Victorians. Arundel is indeed a marriage of Middle Ages and nineteenth century, a monumental expression of the aristocratic pomp and Catholic faith of the Howards, dukes of Norfolk.

The tightly packed town at the foot of its castle appears at first more French than English, a lofty citadel on a defensible cliff on a bend in a river. But from across the fertile flood plain of the Arun from Crossbush, the scene acquires the softer outlines of Sussex and the South Downs. From here, Arundel could only be in England.

A motte and bailey castle was begun in 1067 by Roger of Montgomery immediately after the Norman conquest. It was to command the south coast and guard a crucial gap in the downs. The castle then passed down the female line of Fitzalans and Howards to become the principal seat of the dukes of Norfolk. Nothing better illustrates the flexibility of the English constitution than that the Howards should remain hereditary heads of the peerage and earls marshal of England despite being Roman Catholic. The family lives at Arundel to this day.

Arundel's outer defences were demolished after the Civil War but extensive rebuilding took place under the Georgians, including the creation of one of England's finest private libraries. The castle

was drastically enlarged, in 1846 for a visit by Queen Victoria and again by the fifteenth duke in the late nineteenth century. Arundel became the Windsor of the south coast, a sequence of halls, state rooms and private apartments surmounted by battlements and fortifications. They start out from the side of the hill, dominating the town below. The castle has stood in for Windsor in films such as *The Young Victoria* and *The Madness of King George*.

The adjacent cathedral is almost more prominent than the castle, built at Norfolk expense in 1868 to celebrate the Catholic emancipation of forty years earlier. The architect was the eminent gothicist Joseph Hansom, who also designed the Hansom cab. Though lacking the florid detail of most gothic structures, it is a superb stage

Arundel: Victorian variations on a medieval theme

set, rising on buttresses, transepts and pinnacles to profess its faith across the valley.

These two great buildings are attended by an immaculate small Sussex town, a packed cluster of tiled roofs and red-brick walls surrounding a high street that winds round the castle mound. The downs above extend west towards Goodwood, where the prominent racing stadium of another Sussex grandee, the Earl of March, intrudes on the horizon. To the east is the Arun gap, punched through the downs towards Pulborough.

The foreground of the view comprises water meadows so smooth they might have been rolled for cricket, interspersed with dikes and punctuated by an occasional tree, barn and church tower. The prospect is specially blessed when a mist lies on the meadow and the castle rises in the sun beyond. Victorian does not clash with the Middle Ages, but rather plays variations on a medieval theme.

ASHFORD HANGERS
Towards Steep

In the distance we can see the long ridge of the South Downs floating comfortably across the horizon. To the south the contour softens towards the coast at Portsmouth. But above the village of Steep, the hills seem to lose all discipline. The greenside ridges of the Hampshire Downs argue with each other. Escarpments bunch and jostle. Beech woods cling to the slopes in dramatic clumps known as hangers, from the Old English *hangra*, or wood on a slope.

It was here that the young Edward Thomas came with his family in 1906 to pursue a struggling career as a writer and naturalist. Here the American poet Robert Frost encouraged him to turn to poetry before he enlisted for the trenches in 1916 at the advanced age of thirty-eight. Thomas was a depressive who found solace in communing with his surroundings. He would run the soil through his hands and say the England he so loved 'was not mine unless I were willing and prepared to die' in its cause. Die he did, at Arras in 1917.

The Thomases lived in a number of houses beneath and above a bend in the Ashford Chase escarpment known as Shoulder of Mutton. From here, he claimed, he could see 'sixty miles of South

A land worth dying for: Thomas's Ashford

Downs in one glance'. To commemorate Thomas's birthday each March, the Edward Thomas Fellowship organises walks in the area, observing the folds of hill, the beech, yew and elm, the buzzards and the rich birdsong, as he did. Ashford Hangers was to Thomas's pen what Flatford Mill was to Constable's brush.

The viewpoint from Shoulder of Mutton towards Steep is reached along Cockshott Lane past the gallery of the Edwardian Arts and Crafts woodworker Edward Barnsley. Next door is the Red House, one of Thomas's local homes. The path passes through thick woods which narrowly avoided clearance in the 1950s and opens out through a gap in the trees. The valley floor presents a picture of clusters of woods and fields, with the downs rolling into the distance, blue-grey in the summer gloaming. Boundaries intersect in a geometry of curving lines. To left and right the hangers seem literally to hang from the slopes.

The landscape is dotted with affluent Hampshire villas. The area is known from its contours as Little Switzerland (an epithet shared with Church Stretton under the Long Mynd), though Little Tuscany might seem more appropriate. It was colonised by the Arts and Crafts movement in the early twentieth century, stimulated by the arrival of Bedales school. We can see through the trees the sloping roofs and gables of houses by Ernest Gimson, Raymond Unwin, Baillie Scott and W. F. Unsworth, with Barnsley up on the hill working their wood.

Thomas was little recognised in his life, but in 1937 John Masefield commemorated him with the Poet's Stone halfway up the Shoulder of Mutton slope, looking out across the valley he knew well. The stone is, curiously, a sarsen brought from Avebury. The inscription from Thomas is typically gloomy: 'And I rose up and knew I was tired, and I continued my journey.'

These hills have a strange atmosphere. The Hampshire hangers are unlike the comforting beech woods of the Chilterns. As Thomas sensed, they are more restless and mysterious in their evocation of nature:

The Combe was ever dark, ancient and dark.
Its mouth is stopped with bramble, thorn, and briar;
And no one scrambles over the sliding chalk
By beech and yew and perishing juniper
Down the half precipices of its sides, with roots
And rabbit holes for steps. The sun of Winter,
The moon of Summer, and all the singing birds
Except the missel-thrush that loves juniper,
Are quite shut out.

COOMBE HILL

Towards the Vale of Aylesbury

The Chiltern escarpment rises above the Vale of Aylesbury as if intended to guard the approaches to London from a wilder west. Today it guards the wilder west from the approach of London. Housing estates expand from High Wycombe, Chesham and Amersham, bringing the metropolis ever closer. Yet the ramparts and moats of the Chilterns seem a match for such assault. They form a series of rolling chalk hills and secluded valleys as quiet as any in southern England, the more precious for being just half an hour from London.

Nowhere are the Chilterns more prominent in the landscape than along the ridge either side of the gash of the M40 cutting. Like the North Downs, they form one of the folds that hold London's clay soil as in a saucer. Their emblem is the beech wood, lover of dry, alkaline hillsides, noble in summer and unequalled for splendour in autumn. Then the woodland lanes round Coombe Hill seem overlaid with a filter of blazing gold.

Here the Ridgeway path from White Horse Hill walks the

escarpment in tandem with the South Bucks Way, both holding to the high ground while the Roman Icknield Way trudges along the valley below. The summit is marked by the Coombe Hill monument, one of the earliest war memorials in England, erected in 1904 in honour of the Buckinghamshire dead in the Boer War. The site is exposed, the beeches giving way to moorland, with hardier grass, gorse, holly and turkey oak.

The character of this view changes with the hour and the season. South-west along the escarpment the folds of the Chilterns bulge and recede towards Bledlow almost like a cliff. These are hills of mood and temperament, the more sinister when the recesses are deepened by a late sun and the valley immediately below can become near invisible. Here lurks the red-brick Jacobean mansion of Chequers, weekend retreat of prime ministers since the 1920s. The old house is suitably surrounded by protective uplands, the Chiltern flank on one side and the outliers of Pulpit Hill and Beacon Hill guarding it from the vale on the other.

Beacon Hill, with its single tree and the ghost of a motte and bailey in its meadow, is the legendary site of Cymbeline's last stand against the Romans. Below it is the village of Ellesborough and the church where prime ministers sometimes worship on Sundays, notably Margaret Thatcher during the Falklands war.

Directly below Coombe is a large, bare field, now arable. Over the centuries this would have been an intensively worked landscape, open grazing giving way to hedged enclosure and then reopened in the twentieth century for heavy ploughing, as it now is. Part has recently been taken for a golf course, its immaculate greens and dotted trees rising up the hillside, surreal in an evening light. Meanwhile, to the north, the Vale of Aylesbury displays the irregular rural landscape of what the landscape historian Oliver Rackham calls 'mindless' field systems, the pattern seeming to defy origin or understanding. Aerial photographs reveal traces of strip-and-furrow farming, surviving from the Middle Ages despite centuries of deep ploughing.

Coombe Valley Looking over Ellesborough *by Anna Dillon, 2012*

To the west rise the twin hills of Brill and Waddesdon, the latter crowned by the turrets of the Rothschild mansion of that name. The Rothschild dynasty colonised the Vale of Aylesbury in the nineteenth century, with seven houses and some 30,000 acres, including Waddesdon, Ascott and Mentmore, the better to visit and hunt with each other. (Their London colony was Rothschild row on Piccadilly at Hyde Park Corner, mostly demolished in the 1960s.) To the south-west lie the hills round Oxford, with the misty Cotswolds just visible in the distance. South is the valley of the Thames.

The view is pockmarked by the sprawl of London's commuter belt, telltale of the erosion of rural planning at the turn of the twenty-first century. Yet on a clear autumn day, this is still gilded England, a countryside changing from green to yellow to ochre, pink, crimson and gold. Overhead is performed the ceaseless ballet of the Chiltern red kites. They soar and swoop, mocking not just the contours but their fellow raptors embattled in Chequers below.

THE CHILTERNS
Stonor Valley from the Turville hills

The folds of the southern Chilterns are crowned by dense woods from Stokenchurch down to the Thames at Henley. Their hidden valleys have dry, chalky bottoms, once heath but now enclosed as pasture and arable. Their slopes alternate in convex and concave contours, yielding an abstract geometry of intersecting lines. Almost all are garlanded by beech trees.

In the Middle Ages these hills were harvested for oak, hornbeam and hazel, felled to heat London. As they were supplanted by coal, faster-growing beeches took their place. Beech is a straw-coloured wood, easily bent, moulded and turned, and the trees were coppiced so the trunks grew tall and straight to supply the furniture trade that became the Chilterns' staple industry. The effect was to render the undergrowth mostly barren of other trees, though a rich habitat for bluebells and wild garlic. In summer these beeches are a soft green, but in autumn they take fire. Their leaves create a diaphanous canopy of colour that falls to fashion a quilt of gold over which it seems a privilege to walk. There is no finer autumnal experience in England than to traverse these woods. The Chilterns are reputedly cobwebbed with some 1,500 miles of footpaths.

Over the hill from Turville Heath, the path near Balhams Farm looks across the Stonor Valley at the eastern flank of the main Chiltern ridge. The view is of a vale criss-crossed by boundaries, each field in differing shades of green and brown. Hedges are of hawthorn, oak and holly, miraculously spared by twentieth-century hedge-destroyers. This is poor clay soil, where the winterbournes erode the chalk and leave the fields strewn with flints after a storm. They reappear embedded in local walls.

The Balham slope offers the perfect Chiltern view up and down the valley. To the left is the ordered parkland of the Stonor estate,

Chiltern repose: Stonor Valley

with its great house and church beautifully set on the flank of a side valley. Opposite lies the hamlet of Pishill, with its fine Crown Inn. To the right the view buries itself in the 2,500-acre Wormsley Park estate, bought by John Paul Getty in 1986 as what now seems a private glen. It plays host to the twin pleasures of cricket and opera.

On all sides are the Turville ridges, guarding affluent weekend and commuter cottages. We must imagine these fields once populated with sowers, harvesters and flint-pickers, while carters and drovers crowded the lanes. Today these byways and fields are unpeopled, other than by walkers and the occasional 4x4, shepherding a daughter on a horse. The skies overhead are more crowded, with the brown and white undersides and forked tails of the red kites, introduced in 1989 from Spain. These birds were instantly at home and form one of England's most successful conservation projects. They hover over the adjacent M40, feasting on the road kill below.

DOVER
From the white cliffs

Here stand the defensive walls of Shakespeare's sceptred isle, his 'demi-paradise/ This fortress built by Nature for herself,/ Against infection and the hand of war.' At Dover, England comes closest to abroad, and thus embodies resistance to invading foreigners, to Romans, Normans, French, Dutch and Germans. The cliffs breathe national defiance, from Henry V through Pitt to Churchill.

The chalk hills of southern England began as a soup of micro-organic crustaceans deposited on the ocean floor. They were heaved upwards into ridges and domes of limestone interspersed with layers of hard black flint, that formed the North and South Downs. These ridges extended into Hampshire and Dorset and across the Channel into northern France.

Guarding England: Dover Castle above the white cliffs and Channel port

Then came the sensational day, probably some 400,000 years ago towards the end of the ice age, when the North Sea broke through the land bridge joining Dover to Calais. Recent underwater archaeology has revealed signs of massive scouring some fifty metres deep, suggesting a catastrophic release of water from a lake formed in the south end of the North Sea. This tsunami would have hurtled down the Channel from Dover, leaving mighty scars along its path. What once had been part of mainland Europe was thenceforth an 'offshore island'. I therefore prefer to see the cliffs not so much as chauvinist bastions but rather as geological survivors, gazing over the scene of that primeval catastrophe and weeping chalky tears over its shattered partnership with France.

Painters of the Romantic movement mostly depicted Dover from Shakespeare Cliff to the west of the port. This view is now dominated by Dover town and lacks a sight of the cliffs. A better one is from the east, above the visitor centre by the coastguard station. Here the view is of the cliffs towards Dover's castle and church on their hill, neatly hiding the town and looking much as they must have done for centuries. France is visible across the straits. The wildness of this place was best captured by Shakespeare in *King Lear*, with Edgar's peering over the cliff:

> Come on, sir, here's the place. Stand still.
> How fearful and dizzy 'tis to cast one's eyes so low!
> The crows and choughs that wing the midway air
> Show scarce so gross as beetles . . .
> The murmuring surge
> That on the unnumbered idle pebbles chafes
> Cannot be heard so high. I'll look no more;
> Lest my brain turn.

The first structure on the castle hill was an Iron Age fort, built against enemies unknown. This was followed by the Roman pharos, a relic of ancient navigation unique in England. Some sixty feet of the original structure still stands. The adjacent church of St Mary in Castro is Saxon, much restored in the nineteenth century.

Next to the church and alone on the crest is Dover's great Norman keep. It was begun in 1168 by Henry II and recently restored by English Heritage, with its Norman interior and contents boldly replicated and reinstated. They look as if delivered from IKEA, but we are told that is indeed how they looked. Below runs a curtain wall with eleven towers, forming a prodigious citadel with attendant outbuildings and barracks. The full extent of Dover's defences are underground, notably those built in the nineteenth and twentieth centuries to repel Napoleonic and Nazi invasions. The surrounding cliffs are honeycombed with grim weapons of war buried beneath miles of chalk. The Dover area is a theme park of national defence, probably the most extensive military monument in Europe.

Directly behind the visitor centre was an 1880s prison, reused as a barracks for soldiers on their way to the Great War. Gun emplacements were located here with an arc of fire across the Channel. During the Second World War the area was known as 'hellfire corner' for the intensity of bombs that landed on Dover and its surroundings. The landscape remains ravaged by tunnel entrances and the bumps and defiles of bomb blasts.

Dover's chalk lacks the 'clean cut' look of the Seven Sisters along the coast. The cliffs are here less white and bear the scars of their history. To the east towards St Margaret's is Langdon Hole, a quarry for chalk used in the building of the port in the nineteenth century, once with its own railway. Today the old military walls have been tamed by scrub oak, gorse and wild roses, while the thin cliff-top soil is home to a wealth of chalkland flora. In one small patch a botanist friend found zigzag clover, yellow saxifrage, lady's bedstraw, thyme and rock rose. These are tended by some thirty species of butterfly, including the famous chalkland 'blues'. Gulls, kittiwakes, linnets and skylarks skim overhead. Dover is fast recovering its ancient past.

Below the visitor centre is something of a shock. Matthew Arnold wrote of Dover beach as a 'darkling plain/ Swept with confused alarms of struggle and flight/ Where ignorant armies clash by night.' He could say the same of Dover port today. Here is one of the world's busiest shipping lanes and a foreshore dominated by the modern port. Lorries load and unload in a choreography of commerce, tending a procession of ferries crawling back and forth across the water. I could hear health and safety warnings in French, carried upwards on the wind like the cry of a seagull.

NORTH DOWNS
From the Devil's Kneading Trough

I visited Wye Down one warm July afternoon across a road lined with lilac to a meadow coated in wild flowers and herbs. Up from the valley came the sound of church bells announcing a wedding. It reminded me that a view can be not just a matter of sight but of all the senses, of touch, sound and smell.

This final escarpment of the North Downs as they reach the coast once overlooked a salt-water lagoon extending from Romney Marsh to Tenterden and the Low Weald. Medieval Tenterden, now far inland, was a ship-building port. The silting up of the lagoon yielded rich farmland, but the chalk ridges remained above. Into these are cut a series of dry valleys or combes of which Goudie and Gardner have defined nine, the most dramatic being the Devil's Kneading Trough behind the village of Brook.

The trough is a simple concave scoop out of the down formed at the end of the Ice Age by a process known to geologists as

Overleaf: Ashdown Forest over the Low Weald

solifluction. A sequence of freezing and thawing loosens sections of chalk slope which become unstable and slide down into the valley beneath, creating a chalk 'fan' of hummocky debris at its mouth. The best view of the trough is from the ridge a few hundred yards south of its summit, where the meadow opens to reveal its continuation towards the coast in a series of humps and similar scoops, undulating into the distance.

Far off to the south lies Romney Marsh with its terminal stub of Dungeness power station and wind turbines behind Rye. Ahead, as if across the old lagoon, lies the ridge of the High Weald, a dark horizon of wood and heath now designated as Ashdown Forest. The valley below contains the smudge of development round Ashford, the M20 and the Channel Tunnel rail corridors, but the view is overwhelmingly rural. At the foot of the Kneading Trough stands Brook church, a sturdy Norman defensive tower on what once was a sea shore. It is the typical countryside of southern England, what Orwell returning from the Spanish Civil War called 'probably the sleekest landscape in the world'.

We are standing here on the Wye nature reserve, one of the 284 such reserves listed for conservation in 1915 by Charles Rothschild, an early champion of conservation. They formed the basis for today's protected areas and 'sites of special scientific interest'. Some thirty species of butterfly flit over drifts of orchid, horseshoe vetch, autumn gentian and a national rarity, the dwarf or Kentish milk-wort, across which float the scents of marjoram, basil and thyme. This part of Kent is still visited by nightingales.

Sheep have long damaged the ecology of these uplands, nibbling vegetation to a smooth lawn. Here they have thankfully been replaced by white cattle, which aerate the soil by tearing up grass by the roots. They are tended by the admirable Wye community farm. The sole jarring note is a notice board ordering us to be 'stunned' by this 'prized and protected jewel'. We can do that unaided, but would prefer a guide to nature's rich feast on this glorious spot.

OXFORD
The High

I have searched in vain for a view of Oxford's 'dreaming spires' un-polluted by strings of pylons or the crude high-rise of the Radcliffe Hospital. As it is, seekers after views of this exquisite city must find them within. I have known Oxford High Street, 'The High', in all its moods and in all of mine, and still find it the most visually satisfying thoroughfare in England. The informal urbanity of its gently curving line contrasts with the avenues and boulevards of dirigiste town design. It follows some ancient track running west from Magdalen Tower past colleges, shops and inns to the Carfax crossroads, a perfect walking view, an unfolding vista of delight.

The best vantage point is at the apex of the curve, outside

Curve of satisfaction: The High Street *by JMW Turner*

Queen's College and opposite the Examination Schools. The road here widens, allowing the facades to spread themselves to view, all the finer for the recent removal of traffic and most of the street clutter. Sadly the black tarmac was not replaced at the same time with Thames gravel, to match the ochre of the facades.

The High commences at the east end with the medieval tower of Magdalen, built in the fifteenth century outside the city wall on the bank of the Cherwell. The tower, of soft Headington stone, dates from 1492, slender and elegant overlooking the bridge and the road at the old entry to the city. The lower stages rise to a richly embellished bell-chamber, where a choir greets the spring each year on May Day.

The view from Queen's towards Magdalen is flanked by the Eastgate Hotel on the right and shops fronting St Edmund Hall on the left. These were all rebuilt at the end of the nineteenth century in the much-favoured Jacobean revival style. While the colleges were of stone, The High's commercial buildings are mostly timber-framed and fronted in coloured paint and stucco. This gives the street a pleasant variety, gown conversing with town in the language of architecture.

The High's junction with Merton St brings the Examination Schools of 1887, the first substantial work by the architect of much of late-Victorian Oxford, T. G. Jackson. He turned against the high French gothic of Alfred Waterhouse and William Butterfield (architects of Balliol and Keble), professing 'haunting visions of Elizabethan and Jacobean work'. His style was dubbed Anglo-Jackson and it well matched the character of a still-conservative university. It also fused perfectly with the seventeenth-century buildings of The High.

The view's foreground is supplied by Queen's College and its celebrated screen. This was built by a Paris-loving provost at the start of the eighteenth century, its design unashamedly based on the Palais du Luxembourg. Two bold ranges crowned by classical pediments front the street, linked by a formal screen and gatehouse, completed in 1736 on 'advice' from Nicholas Hawksmoor. A cupola covers a statue of the college's most recent patron, George II's Queen Caroline. Though starkly classical, Queen's respects the street in scale and materials. It is a model marriage of new architecture to old.

To the west the anonymous facades of University College and All Souls on either side of the street are interspersed by colourful commercial buildings. The western climax is the spire of St Mary's church, a wedding cake of Perpendicular battlements and pinnacles as if struggling to compensate for its constricted site. Pevsner enthused that the tower was 'one of the most spectacular in all England'.

Nor is the tower the sum of St Mary's delights. In 1637 when Oxford was briefly the capital of Stuart England the carver Nicholas Stone graced the old church with a high baroque porch. It has an open pediment and barley-sugar columns, possibly copied from the Raphael cartoons recently acquired by Charles I. The porch might be facing a piazza in Rome. The contrast with the gothic of the church round it is as daring, and as satisfying, as that of the Queen's screen down the road.

OXFORD
Radcliffe Square

Two views within a hundred yards may seem excessive. But while The High is a typically informal streetscape, Radcliffe Square is an essay in eighteenth-century equilibrium. The eye feasts on crumbling yellow/grey stone set amid cobbles and grass. Drifts of undergraduates and tourists wander across it as in a deer park. This is Oxford's answer to Cambridge's Backs, great architecture in a minor

rather than a major key. Oxford's historian, Geoffrey Tyack, called Radcliffe Square 'one of the most romantic pieces of urban landscape anywhere'.

The centrepiece is the Radcliffe Camera. Oxford at the turn of the eighteenth century was eager to transform itself 'from training, clumsily enough, a parcel of uncouth youths to be clergymen', in the words of a contemporary. It needed to attract the sons of the wealthy and the aristocratic, to become the 'academy of the nation'. For this the university needed a central presence beyond the scatter of its component colleges.

The authorities commissioned Hawksmoor to propose what

Architecture 'in a minor key': the Camera and All Souls

amounted to an academic campus. This would lie between the official university church of St Mary's on The High and the Sheldonian Theatre, the assembly hall already built by the young Christopher Wren in 1669 on Broad Street. The campus would encompass the old Bodleian library, a rebuilt Brasenose College and a new university church on the site of what is now Hertford College. At its centre would be an open square with a column in the middle, a true *forum universitatis*.

This vision was drastically altered in 1714 with the receipt of an enormous bequest of £40,000 from the royal doctor, John Radcliffe. It was for a university science library and infirmary. Radcliffe insisted that his library be prominently located in the centre of town. He was known to have no time for books and the endowment was derided 'as if a eunuch should found a seraglio'.

But money talked. The job of designing the library went to the young James Gibbs, working in the brief period of English baroque associated with the followers of Wren. A grand circular drum sat on an arcaded base, crowned by a parapet and dome. The style is unrelated to its surroundings, yet its material, soft yellow Headington stone, merges perfectly with them. The Camera opened in 1748.

The best viewpoint is from the north-west of the square outside the private garden wall of Exeter College (from the top of which is an even better view). From here the planes, curves and perspectives of the various buildings all harmonise with each other. On the left is the modest entrance to medieval Bodleian library. Ahead is the neo-gothic screen of All Souls College, designed by Hawksmoor in 1715. He outspokenly advised that it be gothic, in the character of 'antient durable Publick Buildings . . . instead of erecting new, fantasticall, perishable trash'. Rarely was the eighteenth century's battle of styles so emphatically expressed.

That said, Hawksmoor's work at All Souls was beyond fantastical. Two purely decorative towers overlook the college quadrangle, echoes of those he designed for the west front of Westminster Abbey. His Codrington Library window on the left is again a mixture, gothic outside but a Venetian window inside. Meanwhile the square's south side is formed by the flank of St Mary's Church, the old meeting place of the university congregation. Its tower offers a view over the square below.

At the south-west angle facing St Mary's is a final gem, the east window of Brasenose Chapel. Here a tall gothic frame is enclosed by a rich baroque surround, the 1660s designer clearly bemused by the enveloping stylistic indecision. Oxford could never quite make up its mind, which is perhaps appropriate for a great university.

SEVEN SISTERS
From Cuckmere Haven

The Cuckmere is a river descending from the South Downs to a tree-less flood plain across which it meanders to the last undeveloped river mouth on England's south coast, Cuckmere Haven. For the painter Eric Ravilious these meanders were scenery as art, a composition of humps and bends natural and yet hinting at abstraction. When the river reaches the haven, it does so amid the most glorious parade of chalk cliffs in Europe. I have to admit that this entry is a two-views-in-one experience.

The haven is now a 700-acre reserve, best approached from the Seven Sisters visitor centre, where the Cuckmere begins its looping path to the sea. This was once an ideal inlet for smuggling, the practice ending only when the Victorians cut a canal along the side of the valley. This left the meanders to be fed by sluices and thus less likely to erode, but also less likely to respond to natural forces. The basin is now unhedged grassland intermingled with tidal estuary, a place of sheep and waders, orchids and marsh samphire. There are controversial plans to 're-wild' Cuckmere and leave river and estuary to resume their contention.

We reach the haven where it is overlooked by a row of coastguard cottages, set to guard against smugglers. Here the Cuckmere path is joined by the precipitous but exhilarating walk from Seaford, the alternative point of access. The view now runs the full extent of the Seven Sisters, undulating over ridges and dry valleys some four miles to Beachy Head. It is breathtaking.

Even on a dull day the cliffs are startlingly white, as if a sea monster had risen from the deep and taken a giant bite out of England's coast. The Seven Sisters embody, more than even Dover's cliffs,

Overleaf: Crustacean spectacular: Seven Sisters from Cuckmere Haven

Shakespeare's England as a 'precious stone set in a silver sea/ Which serves it in the office of a wall.' In the sun they form a curtain of dazzling chalk between the green of the downs and the blue of the sky. Composed of trillions of crustaceans, the chalk is so pure as to be edible, a (modest) chunk of Seven Sisters apparently aiding digestion.

The reason for this purity is that the Seven Sisters have been left to erode, the sea pushing them back by a full three feet a year. Rocks fall regularly into the sea below, churning the water into a milky froth. The images are ever changing. At one point the cliffs are a sequence of curtain falls, at another a row of architectural buttresses struggling to hold back the downs above. On one cliff is a single blemish, a teardrop of sandstone.

Already erosion has made the seven sisters eight, Haven Brow, Short Brow, Rough Brow, Brass Point, Flagstaff Point, Flat Hill, Baily's Hill and Went Hill Brow. The final promontory, the celebrated Beachy Head, is not officially a sister – nor has it to do with beaches, deriving its name from the French beau-chef or fine head. At 162m it is the highest chalk precipice in England. A lighthouse guards its summit while another is out of sight at its base. Like Clifton suspension bridge, Beachy Head is associated with suicides or 'jumpers'. These are so frequent – at times one a month – that the area now has a night-time patrol led by local chaplains.

The cliff walk is dangerous. The edge is rough, crumbling and unguarded, the chalky soil slithery when wet. Since the topmost covering of earth is just a few inches thick, it can support no large flora. Chalkland is thus the preserve of small-rooted species in their hundreds, with rarities beyond the familiar campions, trefoils and vetches thriving in this windy, salty, splendid, untrammelled place.

THE SOLENT

From Hurst Spit towards the Needles

The Isle of Wight forms a giant breakwater protecting the Solent lagoon. This lagoon in turn guards the approach to the military port of Portsmouth and the commercial port of Southampton, jointly crucial to England's naval supremacy from Saxon times to the twentieth century. To millions of returning Britons, the sight of the Needles lighthouse brought tears to the eyes, welcoming them to home and hearth.

As early as the sixteenth century Henry VIII saw the importance of defending Portsmouth from attack down the Solent. He built a series of castles along the shore, of which the most prominent was on Hurst Spit, stretching almost a mile into the lagoon and narrowing it by a full half. The spit offered clear lines of fire in all directions, with views up and down the Solent, in particular covering the entry to Southampton Water. The castle was later used to imprison Jesuits, and held Charles I in 1648 on his way from Carisbrooke to his trial and execution.

Nothing was done to update Hurst until the Napoleonic era, when large batteries were built to house fixed guns. These were extended by Palmerston in the mid-nineteenth century, and in the twentieth century even larger guns were installed. These have never fired in anger, but Hurst is a museum of coastal defence.

The castle is reached either by a walk along the spit or by ferry from the shore village of Keyhaven. From here the scene is of a calm expanse of water across which pleasure boats glide and cruise ships move in stately progress. Only on bank holidays and during Cowes week is the water churned into life by speedboats and racing yachts.

Across the Solent lies the mass of the Isle of Wight, geological relic of the ancient 'third Down', a chalk belt stretching from Purbeck in Dorset under the sea to the Needles. These rocks were

Henrician line of fire: the 'broken teeth' from Hurst battlements

caused by a chalk stratum so 'crumpled' as to stand vertical, stretching a forlorn hand across the water to its Dorset relatives. The original needle was a fourth stack, demolished by the sea in 1764 and now leaving an uncomfortable gap. Its stump can sometimes be seen at low tide.

From the Needles the view ranges eastwards along the island coast from Yarmouth, whose tiny castle complemented that of Hurst. Invisible behind a promontory is the port of Cowes and the symbol of the Isle's Victorian decorum, Queen Victoria's home at Osborne. A constant procession of ferries floats back and forth out of Cowes Roads like miniature wedding cakes.

The shore at the base of Hurst spit is formed by the edge of the New Forest, originally conserved as a royal hunting ground and to supply wood to the navy at Portsmouth. It is blemished only by a chalet park on the salt marsh outside Milford, product of planning laws that permit 'temporary' development even when it is known to be permanent. But its days may be numbered. A notice sternly informs visitors that erosion is so rapid that the whole coast may soon be under water. It will be returned to its other inhabitants, an active colony of terns, plovers and lapwings.

STOWE
The Gardens

Why the Buckinghamshire hills became home to English radicalism, I do not know. They bred Quakers, John Milton, William Penn and the Temple dynasty at Stowe. The Temples were for Parliament against Charles I, supported Cromwell and helped drive James II from office at the Glorious Revolution. As prominent Whigs, they backed Walpole against the Tories and sponsored the first William Pitt. At one point they owned 50,000 acres of the county.

Sir Richard Temple inherited Stowe in 1697 at the age of twenty-one. In a career of frenzied building he turned the house and grounds into a centre of aesthetic taste and political power. The finest architects and landscape designers were summoned, Vanbrugh, Gibbs, Kent, Bridgeman and the young Capability Brown. The last refashioned the former seventeenth-century avenues and parterres and gradually replaced them with an Arcadian landscape.

Such men saw landscape as a metaphor for life. Nature was not a proxy for art but its raw material, to be dug, banked, channelled and planted, to become a stage set for myths of the classical world. Pope wrote his instructions for the new landscape with Stowe in mind:

To build, to plant, whatever you intend,
To rear the Column, or the Arch to bend,
To swell the Terras, or to sink the Grot;

In all, let Nature never be forgot.
But treat the Goddess like a modest fair,
Nor over-dress, nor leave her wholly bare;
Let not each beauty ev'ry where be spy'd,
Where half the skill is decently to hide.
He gains all points who pleasingly confounds
Surprises, varies, and conceals the Bounds.

When Temple died as Lord Cobham in 1749 his successors re-newed the building frenzy. Robert Adam arrived in 1771 to build a new south front, creating surely the most magnificent classical facade in England. By now Stowe had over 400 rooms while its grounds were dotted with fifty temples, pavilions and follies.

The predictable ruin to the family ensued under the second Duke of Buckingham and Chandos. The last great dinner was at-tended by Queen Victoria in 1845, with the bailiffs waiting outside for the guests to depart before forcing an entry. The duke, dubbed 'England's greatest debtor', fled abroad. In 1848 the house saw 'the sale of the century'. Yet somehow the building itself survived, now serving as a public school and with its grounds owned and opened by the National Trust.

The grounds are the view. The mile-and-a-half drive from the town of Buckingham was intended for show, culminating in an avenue of trees forming an arboreal guard of honour, rising and fall-ing across the contours until we can hardly wait for the anticipated climax. This takes the form of a Corinthian arch beyond which, still half a mile distant across a valley, rises Adam's south front of the palace itself. I once saw a low mist separate foreground from dis-tance, leaving Stowe floating on a cloud. It was indeed the paradise palace.

We approach the estate to the right of this initial coup de théâtre, through the visitor entrance and down the Bell Gate path to the lake. There we cross the Palladian bridge and regain the central axis on the sweeping lawn up to the south front of the house. This

Stowe's Corinthian climax, with Adam in the distance

honours the maxim of the eighteenth-century landscapists, that we should never approach a destination directly from the point where we originally see it.

Halfway up the lawn is the place to pause. To the south behind us is the now distant arch, with Vanbrugh's pavilions beyond the lake in the middle distance. To the north ahead rises the great house. On either side we can appreciate the inner symbolism of Kent's original garden, with its landscape depiction of good and evil.

To the left is the Path of Vice, to the right the Path of Virtue, messages clothed in antiquarian allusion and inevitably obscure to those not versed in the classics. The Path of Vice leads the eye to the Rotondo, containing a statue of Venus, which in turn looks down to the eleven-acre lake and a Palladian temple. Round this lake we are asked to imagine lascivious scenes: of Dido chased by Aeneas, of Bacchic revels and orgies by Cleopatra, Nero and Vespasian. The murals in the temples were considered so lewd as to be later erased.

The Path of Virtue is uplifting in every sense. It leads east to the Elysian Fields and the Grecian valley, with temples to liberty, concord, victory, pastoral poetry and a gallery of 'English worthies'. In its midst is a gothic temple, which Cobham regarded as the epitome of Christian piety amid all this pagan classicism. He wrote above its door, 'I Thank God I am not a Roman'.

The grounds of Stowe have undergone many changes, recently with a major restoration by the National Trust. Roughly thirty of the fifty garden structures survive. How to bring the landscape's meaning to life for a modern audience is more difficult. Its ideological force has gone, that of classical Greek and Roman cultures as a metaphor for contemporary politics. It needs a genius of reinterpretation. But the beauty of the place can at least speak for itself.

WHITE HORSE HILL
Towards the Vale of the White Horse

There is a gentle rolling quality to the Berkshire chalklands, unlike the rampant angularity of the North and South Down escarpments. The curves are more enfolding, the slopes more wooded and the landscape depredation of deep ploughing more pervasive. Yet they can still be wild and, above the Vale of the White Horse, mysterious.

This is the land of the Ridgeway, a path now officially eighty-seven miles from Wiltshire into East Anglia but believed to have linked the Dorset coast to the Wash in prehistoric times. The downs over which it passed were heavily populated, evidenced by earthworks, barrows, tumuli and hill forts on every prominence. To walk it is to sense the presence of a vanished England, of a people and a culture which, unlike the early Egyptians or Greeks, remains frustratingly unknown. The Ridgeway was used by travellers and drovers into the nineteenth century, keeping them and their flocks clear of enclosed settlements and the mud of valley roads. It was largely replaced by the network of toll highways.

The White Horse itself is best appreciated from a distance across the vale, but it and the vale can be seen at an angle along the escarpment of the downs from near the Dragon Hill car park above Uffington. The work has been variously attributed to King Arthur, Hengist and Horsa, King Alfred and others, but is now dated as much older, possibly to 1700 BC. It is thus among the earliest of the landscape 'engravings' found on the chalk hills of England.

The carving is 374 feet from nose to tail and extraordinarily

Mysterious pre-history: The Vale of the White Horse *by Eric Ravilious, c. 1939*

beautiful. The horse is depicted galloping, elongated and strangely modernist, an outline of unconnected lines, as if the artist were aware of the post-Impressionism of Matisse or Picasso. Admirers have been legion. Celia Fiennes, the indefatigable early-eighteenth century traveller, remarked on its 'perfect proportion'. G. K. Chesterton wrote that,

> Before the gods that made the gods
> Had seen their sunrise pass,
> The White Horse of the White Horse Vale
> Was cut out of the grass.

The chalk markings were cleaned by local people with celebrations paid for by the lord of the manor. A 1720s account reports that 'the neighbouring parish have a custom once a year, at or near midsummer, to go round it in order to keep the Horse in shape and colour, and after the work is over they end the day in feasting and merriment'. Other reports are that this took place only every seven years. The celebrations included sports and cheese rolling on the hill and often degenerated into days of riotous drinking.

Immediately below the horse is the remarkable geological feature of The Manger, so distinctive it has been thought man-made. It is a dry valley probably formed by the chalk freezing and thawing at the time of the last ice age. Sections of the chalk, thawing at a differential rate, would become unstable and 'sludge' downhill, as with the Devil's Kneading Trough on the North Downs. One of its sides has remarkable ridges or 'chutes', probably made by avalanches of ice tearing at the earth beneath.

Round the horse is what must have been a prehistoric metropolis. Below it stands the extensive platform of Dragon Hill, its top certainly shaped by man and dating from the fifth century BC, apparently with a ceremonial purpose. The patch of white chalk on its summit, where no grass grows, is said to have been caused by the blood of the dragon slain here by St George. Some even held that the white horse itself was that dragon. This at least suggests that some symbolic significance may have attached to the horse.

Above the hill are the earthworks of Uffington Castle, one of a row of Iron Age earth forts along the downs, possibly reused by Britons against Saxons and Saxons against Danes. Alfred's defeat of the Dane, Guthrum, in AD 878 took place at neighbouring Edington in Wiltshire. The fort, dating from the eighth century BC is unusual among such structures both in its remarkable size, a rough pentagon of walls embracing some eight acres, but also in the fact that archaeologists have found little sign of any buildings inside.

The ploughing of these uplands during and after the Second World War ended millennia of continuous grazing and turned the land into unhedged prairie. Only a few protected areas remained as natural chalk meadow. White Horse hill is one such, boasting its chalkland ration of vetches, scabious and orchid. Other forms of modernity press on all sides. The view north up the vale features wind turbines, waving for attention, while to the east can be glimpsed the steaming cooling towers of Didcot power station, now to be decommissioned. Will they, I wonder, be removed?

WINDSOR GREAT PARK
The Castle from Snow Hill

A long avenue sweeps down from Snow Hill across Windsor park before climbing to the walls of Windsor Castle. The vista is so long and the contour so varied it could be many miles, or just a few hundred yards. In some light, the castle is surreal, a silver mirage, a shimmering fantasy. As we walk towards it, we seem to come no closer.

The avenue, known as the Long Walk, is a green sward of 2.6 miles flanked by an honour guard of trees, its climax more suited to Versailles, Potsdam or the hunting lodge of a Russian prince. It was created by the most genially megalomaniac of kings, Charles II. But its authoritarian impact is softened by the enveloping acres of the Thames valley. Indeed in dry weather the Long Walk looks as if it has been driven across a wide savannah, dotted randomly with trees. The deer could be impala, and elephant and giraffe would not seem out of place.

The Great Park is part of the Norman royal forest of Windsor, one of six 'parks' making up the 4,800 acres that survive from that forest on the western outskirts of London. Like many of Charles's schemes it never saw the palaces, belvederes and drives of the continental residences he had known in exile. Modest houses were built in the park for various members of the royal family, but many have been demolished or converted. Today's lodges, rangers' houses and a small estate village are mostly Victorian or Edwardian. Windsor is no Versailles, more a quiet country estate, one of many reasons why England saw no revolution against its monarchy after the seventeenth century.

Snow Hill is reached from either the Ranger's or Cranbourne gates, busy with horses and bike riders. As the track rises the vista suddenly opens out north towards Windsor. We expect to see all west London before us, yet miraculously we see almost nothing but trees. The hill is crowned by a massive statue by Richard Westmacott of George III on horseback, known as the Copper Horse though made of bronze. The king is depicted in the habit of Marcus Aurelius with a laurel crown and the inscription, by his son George IV, as 'best of fathers'. Given their poor relations, this seems ironic.

The statue was erected posthumously in 1824, by when the grotesquely obese George had retired almost entirely to Windsor. Perhaps the statue was a penance. It has the king riding not down the Long Walk but across the hill at right angles to it, his horse perched precariously on a rugged pile of rocks.

The Long Walk itself has been through many changes. Originally of elms, it was replanted with oak but, when these did not prosper, a comprehensive renewal in the 1930s saw the introduction of two parallel rows of horse chestnut and London plane. These are now mature and form a magnificent arboreal colonnade.

To the left of the Long Walk is an even longer avenue, that of Queen Anne's Ride, though without the same view. To the right is Windsor Home Park with Frogmore House, the Royal Mausoleum and Home Farm running down to the bank of the Thames. This is the site of Old Windsor, home of the Saxon kings. Away in the distance is Heathrow airport, mercifully near invisible.

Harmoniously confused: the Long Walk at Windsor

The eye is drawn to the castle. Though it appears as if drive and facade are meant to complement each other, the castle is met at a slight angle and the facade is part medieval, part seventeenth-century and part Victorian. William the Conqueror's original keep rises to the left. From a distance the castle is low and almost domestic, resting along a rise in the land rather than towering over it. To the left is the jumble of roofs of Windsor, with beyond the pinnacles of Eton College Chapel across the river.

All else is ancient parkland, a precious survival on London's outskirts. Windsor is a retreat in which English monarchs have taken particular delight. Charles II came here to dream his magnificence, Anne to hunt, George III to find solace in his madness and George IV in debauchery. Windsor soothed Victoria's melancholy and is said to be the present Queen's favourite residence. In its honour Pope penned some of his happiest lines:

Here hills and vales, the woodland and the plain,
Here earth and water, seem to strive again;
Not chaos-like together crush'd and bruis'd,
But as the world, harmoniously confus'd:
Where order in variety we see,
And where, tho' all things differ, all agree.

Harmoniously confus'd. I can think of no better phrase to describe the English landscape.

EAST ANGLIA

Cambridge: The Backs   149

Flatford Mill   151

Holkham: From the obelisk   155

Lavenham: From the Swan   157

Sheringham: From The Turn   160

Snape Marshes: From the Maltings   163

CAMBRIDGE
The Backs

The view from the River Cam to the lawn of King's College is the essence of English picturesque. It has foreground, middle ground and background, asymmetry but balance. Though the eye is drawn to King's Chapel, each building has a style and personality of its own. As with Oxford's Radcliffe Square, there was no overall design. The composition just formed itself over time, a harmony of walls, grass, river, bridges and drifting punts. Even the cows in the meadow opposite seem arranged by some rustic fine-art commission.

The area round the Cam behind the university was once agricultural and very much the 'back' of what was in the Middle Ages an academic community formed of small residential colleges – much as it is today. The Backs still has a private air, and this is enhanced by collegiate exclusivity, meaning that visitors cannot walk along the river and take in the view as a whole. Each college charges a fee for access to its own grounds, with no crossing to neighbours. In addition, the view from across the Cam is obscured by trees. This all adds a touch of frustration to the delight of the place.

My preferred view is across the lawn from King's Bridge. The lawn itself was to be the site of the college founded by the hapless Henry VI in 1441 but never finished. He cleared part of the old town and began only the chapel. It is said that in dry weather the ghosts of medieval buildings can be seen marked out on the grass.

Seen from the bridge, the left-hand, north side of the lawn running down to the river is entirely filled by the palatial rear of Clare College, designed in the 1640s. The river facade is a flourish of baroque overlooking the water, a touch of Venice. Clare Bridge, which must be reached through the college, has a charming hump back that dips slightly in the middle, as if losing the will to proceed. It was a feature much admired by Henry James.

The 'inland' side of the lawn comprises the gothic King's Chapel and the classical Gibbs Building. The former is dominant, a wall of glass and tracery in what Osbert Lancaster called 'look-no-hands' Perpendicular. It is a triumph of medieval engineering as much as architecture. The contrasting Gibbs Building next door, unusually named after its architect, was begun in 1723, severely Palladian in cold Portland stone on a rusticated base. The juxtaposition with the chapel is subject of many a Cambridge essay: gothic versus classical, vertical versus horizontal, extrovert versus introvert.

The lawn's south side is Victorian, deferential to its surroundings. But here it is the river that grabs the eye. From King's Bridge it disappears into thick foliage, its punters like ferrymen crossing the Styx. In the distance we can glimpse the wooden 'mathematical

Asymmetrical equilibrium: the Backs from King's Bridge

bridge' of Queens' College. Supposedly designed by Isaac Newton, its triangular members were allegedly secured without nails. This is a myth. The bridge was built, with nails, twenty-two years after Newton's death and has often been reconstructed, with visible bolts.

A more miraculous survival is the meadow on the far bank of the river, where unkempt cows graze under trees that render the Backs barely visible from this viewpoint in summer. But at least, with the river in a dip, we can catch sight of punters seeming to pole their way through the branches before a splendid architectural tableau.

FLATFORD MILL

The play of light on water, lime wash on wall, a framing of grand trees and a distant vista of fields, these are the familiar components of an English landscape. All are present at Flatford, setting of one of John Constable's most popular works, *The Hay Wain*. Constable was born in 1776, son of a corn merchant and owner of Flatford Mill. He trained for the corn business and did not take up painting as a profession until his mid-twenties. Even then he commuted between London in winter and Flatford in summer. 'I should paint my own places best,' he later wrote. 'Painting is but another word for feeling.'

Of Constable's many depictions of Flatford the most evocative is this, of a horse with a wagon taking water in a mill pond. The scene is specific. It shows Willy Lott's cottage on the left under an elm. The meadows of Dedham Vale are visible past the elms over the river. The painting expressed the artist's fascination with 'the sound of water escaping from mill dams, willows, old rotten planks, slimy posts and brickwork'.

The view has been preserved insofar as that is possible and is

Nature struggles for order: Willy Lott's house at Flatford

recognisable today. The elm has gone, but is replaced by sycamore, yew and willow. The mill pond remains, thick with algae, rushes and ducks. Willy Lott's house, so often depicted by Constable, still has the same gables, slopes and wings, the same light and shade. The

chief loss is the distant view across the vale. What gave depth and perspective to Constable's composition is now enclosed by shrubbery and trees.

This raises the question of whether the scene should return more closely to the artist's specific inspiration. Few might quarrel with art reflecting nature, but coaxing nature back to art might seem

Constable's The Hay Wain, *1821*

fastidious. Horse-drawn vehicles are no longer used for farming. An immovable flood embankment has partly obscured the backdrop. Nor is Constable's social mission still so relevant, filling his paintings with human activity, hard work and changeable weather as a metaphor for his turbulent times. Today's countryside is not as raw as his was.

Yet it is tempting, in this instance, to seek as far as possible to reinstate a scene so close to the artist's vision. The mill pond is nearly the same. The old towpath may be higher, but much of the former view could be restored with some careful pruning. We might even put a hay wain in the pond – as they have done at Snape's marshes. Either way, the scene is of an East Anglian idyll. Across the pond is the red-brick mill house of Constable's father, with the workaday elegance of Georgian industrial buildings. Hollyhocks and roses tumble round its walls. Students at the nature studies centre languish on the bank. An artist paints.

HOLKHAM
From the obelisk

I stood at Holkham's obelisk and looked out over the park towards the sea, across one of the most crafted 'natural' countrysides in England. The far horizon was hazily lined with coastal pines, punctuated by a distant monument. Views east and west were closed by thickly planted woods. The land in the middle distance fell away at my feet, a grassy savannah dotted with trees and groves. Deer drifted across it like clouds forming and dissolving in a breeze, interrupted by a gentle game of cricket. In the centre of it all lay Holkham, the quintessential English palace in a landscape. It was a scene of the most exquisite beauty.

Corpulent, cultured and liberal-minded, its creator Thomas Coke was also rich. Born in 1697 into the family of Elizabeth I's chief justice, Sir Edward Coke, he inherited his estate as a child and then spent six years from the age of fifteen on a grand tour of France, Germany and Italy. Such an exile at so crucial a stage in a young man's career could have been disastrous, but Coke came home schooled in all the arts, especially architecture. Though he lost a fortune in the South Sea bubble of 1720, he had another to spare.

In Italy Coke had met the Palladian circle of Lord Burlington and his protégé, William Kent. They rejected the baroque Toryism of Hawksmoor and Vanbrugh in favour of the sedate neoclassicism of the Veneto villas, regarding them as Whig and innovative. The exterior of Holkham was Coke's own work, aided by Kent and his assistant, Matthew Brettingham. The house comprises three symmetrical pavilions lying sleek along the contour.

In fashioning the surrounding landscape, Kent seems to have been in charge. The house was to be approached along a two-mile drive behind the obelisk with the house suddenly appearing over the crest of the hill, as at the contemporary Stowe, where

Kent also worked. He designed a layout of walks radiating from the obelisk, still in the formal style of the seventeenth century. Traces of his plan can still be seen from the air. A pond was positioned in front of the house and an Italian garden laid round it.

This work was left unfinished on Coke's death in 1759, without a direct heir and near to bankruptcy. Holkham was supremely fortunate in passing the estate to his nephew, 'Coke of Norfolk', an agricultural innovator, social reformer and ally of Charles James Fox. This Coke was a true radical, an enthusiast for American independence and the French Revolution. Under his aegis Holkham came to exemplify the transformation of the English landscape over the eighteenth and nineteenth centuries. The sandy semi-barren heathland of Norfolk was ploughed and deep marl soil brought to the surface. Wheat and oats were planted and productivity quintupled. The Holkham estate expanded to 3,500 acres, planted with two million trees.

While Coke's farms were being enclosed and 'improved',

Holkham Hall as 'naturalised' in the eighteenth century

Humphry Repton and others set about replacing Kent's formalism in the park adjacent to the house itself. The pond basin was filled in and a large lake repositioned to the north-west of the house. Fences and hedges were moved and trees planted in clumps of artful naturalism. The house was left as if it had been set in the park at random, with grass up to its walls. A print of Holkham of circa 1800 shows it a place of studied irregularity, with sheep grazing a curving path down the slope from the obelisk.

For the Victorians this was informality too far. In part to protect family privacy – Coke had insisted the public be allowed to wander at will – formal parterres were introduced round the house, and a service wing was added to the east, disturbing the symmetry. Terraces were created and fountains installed. The long approach drive from the south was abandoned and a shorter access route was created from the coast road through a new estate village to the north.

This is the Holkham we see today. The track from the obelisk still curves gently to the left. The house sits grand on its pedestal, crowded with visitors as the first Coke would have wished. His descendants are still in occupation. Holkham is Italy for sure, but Italy at ease with English countryside.

LAVENHAM
From the Swan

There is nothing in Suffolk, said Pevsner, 'to compare with the timber-framed houses of Lavenham'. He might have said nothing in England. Lavenham's pre-industrial houses are not the usual 'historic buildings' dinosaurs surviving incongruous in a later townscape under the guardianship of the state. They are everywhere, as in the ancient towns of France and Italy.

The town centre dates mostly from the late Middle Ages, built on the profits of Suffolk's medieval cloth trade. Its survival largely intact is due to the arrival of competing Dutch weavers in Colchester in the late sixteenth century and the abrupt eclipse of Lavenham's business. Nothing took the place of cloth apart from local agriculture.

The most remarkable group of buildings is round the old market square, overlooked by the sixteenth-century clothiers' guildhall. The problem here is that the square doubles as a town car park. This obscures its layout and ground floors, and is as intrusive as if a modern industrial building had been sited in its centre. While the square's facades might interest an archaeologist, as a view it is of interest chiefly to car fanatics. There have to be other sites found for car parks in historic towns.

A hundred yards downhill is the Swan inn at the junction of the High Street, Church Street and Water Street. Though this has cars, they are at least in motion and often absent. The streets curve, almost spin, away from the viewer in all directions, uphill and downhill. It has both perspective and contour. The facades offer not just a variety of periods but the promise of more variety round each bend. I stood for half an hour taking notes, with passers-by wondering what intrigued me. Was I a planner proposing some horror? Was Lavenham not fine as it was?

From outside the Swan, Church Street climbs steeply out of town towards the invisible magnificence of Lavenham's parish church, apotheosis of East Anglian 'wool-gothic'. On the right is a double-fronted Georgian house with a Venetian window, gazing down like a stern prefect over the disorderly facades around it. Here Tudor jostles with seventeenth century, flat roofs with gables, lime wash with black-and-white. Some houses have East Anglian pargeting, reliefs carved in wet plaster. Every few yards trees and flowers burst through a gap.

In the opposite direction, the High Street climbs also uphill

The wealth of wool: the High Street, Lavenham

and again with each house almost perversely different in style. The Swan itself is said to date back to the fourteenth century and incorporates the medieval wool hall. The row opposite culminates in what is now the Crooked Gallery. Dating from 1395 and describing itself as 'vertically challenged', its pink plastered gable tips forward over the street. From here on, medieval, seventeenth-century and early Georgian facades play in counterpoint.

The view by the side of the Swan is down Water Street. This is more uniformly medieval, built over the path of a culvert used for washing cloth. The houses are half- and full-timbered, depending on whether the wood frame rises from the ground or from a brick ground floor. Some facades are black and white, others lime-washed cream, pink or ochre. Again the perspective curves downhill into the distance, surely the longest medieval town view in England.

SHERINGHAM
From The Turn

In 1811 Abbot Upcher, young squire of Sheringham, took the eminent landscape designer Humphry Repton on a tour of his new estate by the sea. Recently married, rich, artistic and liberal, Upcher had recently bought Sheringham and was full of enthusiasm for its potential. 'What scenes of rational yet heartfelt pleasure do we not anticipate in the lovely Sheringham,' he wrote exultantly.

Repton was some forty years his senior and a shrewd man of business. He saw his chance. Sheringham, he replied, had 'more natural beauty and local advantages than any place I have ever seen. It is my most favourite and darling child.' He told Upcher of his wish 'to unite comfort and convenience with the degree of elegance which the place would justify'. He cautiously added that such enthusiasm might lead 'yourself and me into plans most extravagant – were prudence and economy out of the question'.

The following year Repton sent Upcher a 'Red Book' for Sheringham, proposing to turn what was then an expanse of seaside dunes and scrub into a cultured landscape. The task was not easy. East Anglia was sparing in the contours Repton loved, while its coastal ridges of sand and clay were perpetually assaulted by the sea. But sandy hills, once open and barren, were now being stabilised by trees, and Norfolk agriculture prospered under the encouragement of the Cokes of Holkham.

Upcher established an easy bond with Repton, not unrelated to the former's wealth. The Red Book was among Repton's most elaborate, complete with sketches, plans, poems and ideas on architecture, geography, economics and social reform. It has copperplate text and painted illustrations, with flaps indicating present and proposed views. Upcher was overjoyed, recording, 'I am like the possessor of some gem of inestimable beauty . . . you have presented me with the key and I now perceive with astonishment all its hitherto latent beauties bursting on my raptured sight.' He was a most satisfied customer.

Upcher and Repton viewed landscape as having a social as well as aesthetic purpose. England at the time was afflicted by inflation and unemployment as the French wars came to an end. The Upchers were explicit in their sense of duty, distributing alms and food to the village, schooling their servants and allowing local people to forage for wood in the estate. There was to be a day a month when they could visit for their recreation.

Repton thus offered 'a humanising as well as animating beauty', not just grazing meadows but arable fields in which labourers could be given employment. He even quoted a poem by Payne Knight attacking owners of 'everlasting green' estates where,

. . . Not one moving object must appear
Except the owner's bullocks, sheep or deer.

As if his landscape were all made to eat
And yet he shudders at a crop of wheat.

The new house was proposed in the villa style of John Nash, nestling under the ridge of Oak Wood, facing south and thus shielded
from the coast. The Upchers had wanted a view over the sea, but
Repton argued that this was not the Bay of Naples and 'we must
consider how it may appear in winter'. The house was to be less
than a mile from Sheringham village, but Repton proposed a longer
approach from the south along an inland ridge.

This approach holds the key to our view. It wound round the
back of the hill both to ease the slope downhill and to delay the sight
of the house until a final coup de théâtre. Repton had a picturesque
horror of right angles. What he called The Turn required cutting

The Turn at Sheringham, from Repton's original 'Red Book', 1816

into the hill, so the house 'would burst at once on the sight like some enchanted palace of a fairy tale'. His illustration of this feature included not just his clients viewing the scene from their carriage, but a stout labourer wielding a pick by the road.

The Turn remains as he designed it, offering a view of the house across the sweep of a small valley. From here the lodge and farm are visible on the lane to Sheringham. Low ridges crowned with conifers close the distance. The sea offers a glistening backdrop on either side of Oak Wood knoll. It is the perfect Reptonian vista.

The chief change has been to the Upper Approach before the Turn. This now passes through a dense twenty-acre jungle, composed of some sixty-five species of rhododendron and azalea, with Scots pine, sycamore and sweet chestnut overhead. The invasive *Rhododendron ponticum* poses a constant challenge to the estate staff.

Repton and Upcher were both to die with the project uncompleted, but it was continued loyally by Upcher's descendants, eventually passing to the National Trust after the Second World War. I sense a desperate fragility to Sheringham. The ever-eroding sea presses on the dunes beyond its hill while regiments of wind turbines line up immediately offshore. I cannot quite believe this place is for ever.

SNAPE MARSHES
From the Maltings

We leave Snape Maltings in a concert interval and stroll away from the crowd out along paths through the marshes. The echo of the music recedes and a different sound takes over, that of the whispering reed beds of the Alde. As the eye searches the gloaming, the reeds come to life in the mist or the breeze, until a distant bell calls us back to the hall. It is a place of sensory enchantment.

Great views need contour, and this has always posed a challenge to lovers of East Anglia. As Graham Swift says in *Waterland*, it is a landscape 'which of all landscapes most approximates to nothing'. East Anglians asked to nominate their favourite local view always refer to sky and clouds, to stillness and atmosphere. Photographers rely on man-made things, on church towers and boat masts. These places evince few gasps of delight, rather the slow awareness of nature as it possesses the senses. Such is the estuary of the Alde.

Snape was a small port at the navigable limit of the river, much used by smugglers for whom the maze of creeks offered easy hiding places. The port was acquired in the 1840s by the Garrett family and made the base of a successful malting business. Barley shipped to London from overseas was landed from sea barges at the quay-side. It was converted to malt for beer by steeping in water to germinate the grain and then dried slowly by being spread on a large floor before being kiln dried. The business expanded into the twentieth century and the last warehouse was built as recently as 1952. Within a decade, technology moved on and Snape malting came to an end.

Benjamin Britten had by then established a music festival at Aldeburgh on the neighbouring coast. He saw that the wide drying floors of the maltings might convert into a concert hall and acquired them for this purpose. On the opening night, in 1969, the building dramatically caught fire, even burning Britten's beloved piano. All was rebuilt and the Aldeburgh festival in June is now a fixture of the music calendar. What was an extensive industrial complex has become a centre for music performance and education.

The view from the maltings to the sea is consoling. It is of reeds penetrated by creeks, seeping up and down in the tide. The ground on either side is only a little higher. On the left bank is Black Heath Wood, across which runs the 'sailor's walk' six miles to the sea. The

The music of the reeds: the Alde at Snape

shingle bar of Aldeburgh lies directly ahead along the coast, and the village church of Iken lies to the right, its tower the only visible landmark. Distant trees form an undulating silhouette on the horizon. During floods and high tides these marshes become open water.

The Alde wetlands are closely protected. The reed beds and freshwater marshes of the serpentine river form part of the Suffolk Coast National Nature Reserve, a place of walkers and bird watchers. On a good day, redshank, snipe and lapwing are in evidence, along with kingfishers, marsh harriers and reed warblers. At dusk barn owls hunt for voles. Otters are now repopulating the banks. The curlew, inspiration of Britten's oratorio, *Curlew River*, can be heard echoing across the marshes.

The concert hall authorities have populated the scene with modern sculptures, including work by Barbara Hepworth, and a plaster horse and cart in the reeds. Art here intrudes uncomfortably on nature.

WEST MIDLANDS

———

Bibury: Arlington Row 169
Broadway Tower: Towards the Severn Vale 171
Chipping Campden: High Street 174
Clee Hills: From Titterstone Clee 177
Clyro Hill: Towards the Wye valley 179
Hawkstone: From the Hill Monument 181
Ironbridge Gorge: From the Rotunda 184
The Long Mynd: Towards Church Stretton 188
Ludlow: From Whitcliffe Common 191
The Malverns: From British Camp 193
Peckforton: Towards Beeston 197
The Stiperstones: From Manstone Rock 199
Symonds Yat: From Symonds Yat Rock 202
Tyndale Monument: Towards the Severn estuary 206

CHESHIRE

Chester

Peckforton

STAFFORDSHIRE

Hawkstone

SHROPSHIRE

Stafford

Shrewsbury

Ironbridge Gorge

The Stiperstones

The Long Mynd

Birmingham

WARWICKSHIRE

Titterstone Clee Hill

Ludlow

Warwick

WORCESTERSHIRE

HEREFORDSHIRE

The Malverns

Worcester

Chipping Campden

Hereford

Clyro Hill

Broadway Tower

Symonds Yat

Gloucester

Bibury

GLOUCESTERSHIRE

Tyndale Monument

BIBURY

Arlington Row

If scenery could be worn out by photography, Arlington Row would be no more. The village of Bibury is Cotswold charm. Already by the eighteenth century Alexander Pope was remarking on its 'pleasing prospect', extraordinary in an age more attracted to landscape than villages. William Morris dubbed it unequivocally 'the most beautiful village in England'. The church boasts Saxon origins, the fulling mill is medieval and the manor Tudor. The trout farm was founded in 1902 to restock local rivers. But nothing is more celebrated than Arlington Row, overlooking the water meadow of the River Coln. It joins Bibury to the neighbouring hamlet of Arlington along a lane called Awkward Hill.

That said, there is something odd about Arlington Row. Why should anyone have built an isolated terrace running up a hill by a swamp, and away from the centre of a village mostly composed of individual cottages? The answer is that the row belonged to the mill and was not residential but commercial. It was built circa 1380 as warehouses for storing wool, which was dried on racks in the meadow below, hence known as Rack Isle.

The buildings were probably not converted into cottages until the late seventeenth century, when the roofs were tiled and gabled windows inserted. The group was celebrated for its charm but severely run-down, until it caught the eye of the American car tycoon Henry Ford. He decided to buy it and ship it across the Atlantic. Americans had a higher regard for English architecture than the English. The group was saved at the last minute in 1929 by the Royal Society

Meticulous wilderness at Arlington Row

of Arts, which restored it and passed it to the National Trust.

The familiar view of the row is from across Rack Isle, its grey stone walls and steep roofs ranged against a backdrop of green, like Flemish nuns in caped hats. Each is slightly different, some with dormers, some with gables. The stone roof tiles are carefully graded, heightening the steepness of the slope. The left-hand cottage still looks like a store house; later and larger houses are further uphill. From above, the row looks quite different, its roofs and chimneys crowded together and forming an almost urban composition, comparable with Castle Combe or Shaftesbury's Gold Hill.

Rack Isle opposite is surrounded by the River Coln, a nature reserve whose wildness is meticulously controlled by the National Trust. Curbing the mink and protecting water voles are currently the chief concerns. Frogs are abundant, otters are passing visitors and kingfishers dart overhead. Swans and mallards are present to excess. The island is occasionally grazed by Belted Galloway cattle, to keep it in some form of order.

The cottages are lived in by local people, but are under siege from coach parties and others whom these cramped Cotswold lanes can ill-accommodate. Arlington Row became exceptionally popular with Japanese sightseers following a publicised visit by their emperor. But 'off-peak' all is at peace.

BROADWAY TOWER

Towards the Severn Vale

Broadway Tower ranks with Dunkery Beacon and Gummer's How as a grand old man among English views. The tower stands at over 300m, crowning the Cotswold escarpment above the village of Broadway and boasting a visual radius of sixty miles over sixteen counties. Immediately north the limestone fold runs out of steam in the Vale of Evesham and England's spine is 'broken', until it resumes beyond Birmingham in the harder rock of the Staffordshire peak.

The tower is no simple lookout, but an inhabited folly with rooms on each floor. It was built in 1798 by the Earl of Coventry, to be seen from his new house, built for him by Capability Brown at Croome Court twelve miles away. As such it formed the finishing touch to one of Brown's boldest compositions. It was reputedly a signal point to indicate when his lordship had left his neighbouring house at Spring Hill, so staff at Croome could ready the beds.

Designed by James Wyatt, the stone tower is in the style called 'Gothick' by some, Saxon by Wyatt but, more appropriately, neo-Norman. The plan is hexagonal with three corner turrets. It is adorned with gargoyles and Regency windows with balconies, all most decorative.

After the earl's death the tower was sold to a Victorian book-collector, Sir Thomas Phillipps, whose impressive ambition was to own a copy of every book in the world. He amassed 60,000 manuscripts and published regular bibliographies from his press in the tower. A visitor described Broadway as 'a lighthouse signalling to the friends of letters that a hospitable roof exists under which all pilgrims are made welcome'.

The tower later passed to the Pre-Raphaelites, who would commune there with nature in some discomfort. William Morris's daughter recalled suffering cold baths on the roof, at least 'when the wind did not blow the soap away'. It was used as a lookout for enemy planes in the Second World War and reportedly has a Cold War nuclear bunker somewhere underneath it. The property was offered in 1949 to the National Trust, and was refused. It is now run as a private country park open to the public.

Inside, an excellent toposcope boxes the compass: south along the Cotswold escarpment from Birdlip to Cleeve Hill, then across

Fulcrum of England: Severn Vale from Broadway Tower

the Severn Vale to the Forest of Dean and the Malverns and then west to the Clee Hills and the Wrekin. It pans north to the Vale of Evesham, with Cannock Chase, Birmingham, Stratford and Warwick allegedly visible beyond. To the east lies the Cotswold plateau towards Chipping Norton and Stow on the Wold. Though most of this is a distant haze, the Broadway view has a magnificent openness. This is the fulcrum of middle England.

The location offers little foreground. The escarpment slopes down to the roofs of Broadway, offering a fine walk in summer across meadows heavy with wild flowers. Fields are dotted with cows, sheep and deer grazing amid dry-stone walls. Hawks hover overhead. As Housman wrote of neighbouring Bredon, here lovers would lie,

> And see the coloured counties
> And hear the larks so high
> About us in the sky.

CHIPPING CAMPDEN
High Street

Chipping Campden is a place charmed by rich, creamy limestone. Its walls dance by the light of the dying day. Its memorials recall times of great wealth. This was a leading town of the age of wool. From the fourteenth to the sixteenth centuries fleeces cut from the backs of its sheep were exported throughout Europe. From these western uplands, wool was harvested, treated, graded, baled and shipped to the east coast, and on to the markets of Flanders and France.

Confidence restored: the covered market at Chipping Campden

Wool dominated the medieval English economy as oil now dominates the Persian Gulf. It was the stuff of trade and banking. The symbol of the Royal Exchange in London was a sheep with a golden fleece. The Lord Chancellor sits on the Woolsack in parliament, to remind him of the nation's wealth. Twelve men of Chipping Campden rose to be lord mayor of London.

To the historian G. M. Trevelyan, Chipping Campden had no equal for beauty. To Pevsner, the high street is 'one of the best pieces of townscape in England'. It runs gently uphill from Sheep Street past the old town hall and market – chipping or cheaping means market – towards the mound on which sits the town's magnificent church.

The local economy began a long decline with the erosion of England's cloth monopoly in the sixteenth century, but it retained its status as a mercantile town into the eighteenth century. There was no greater symbol of this than the arrival in the early 1600s of the City merchant Sir Baptist Hicks. A classic 'second homer', he bought the manor of Campden, built himself a house next to the church and was made a viscount. The mansion has vanished but its banqueting house and gatehouse survive. Hicks built an almshouse, a grammar school and the market, a model of local philanthropy.

Other wealthy families followed, rebuilding houses along most of the High Street. Though each house is distinct they are joined in an unbroken terrace on each side of the street, forming a remarkably elegant composition. In 1902 when the town was extremely poor, the architect C. R. Ashbee arrived with fellow workers from the London Arts and Crafts movement. Ashbee was a charismatic figure, left-wing and emotional. He encouraged his friends to decamp, some of them reluctantly, from the capital to this supposed rural idyll. To most it seemed no less poor than the East End to which he had previously led them.

Ashbee's stay was short lived, but others remained and put down roots, linked with the Sapperton group round Ernest Gimson. Norman Jewson became a sensitive restorer of medieval buildings

and F. L. Griggs a brilliant etcher. They rescued one local building after another, their efforts coinciding with a wider growth of
interest in English vernacular building. This was reflected in the
founding of the National Trust in 1895 and *Country Life* magazine
in 1897. Griggs's engravings of Cotswold scenes have a mystery and
depth reminiscent of his hero, Samuel Palmer. His design, based on
Jewson's Owlpen Manor, is still the masthead of *Country Life*.

Chipping Campden's High Street is best viewed from Hicks's
covered market of 1627, looking up towards the church tower past a
whitebeam tree. The houses are of a creamy local limestone, spark-
ling in the sunlight. Walls are offset by grey-brown roof tiles and
white woodwork, fronted by foxgloves, hydrangeas and a skirt of
lawn.

The oldest house, on the left, is the fourteenth-century home
of the Grevel family. Opposite stands Woolstaplers' Hall of a similar date, where Ashbee himself took up residence. Other houses
are mostly seventeenth and eighteenth century, each with its own
name: Seymour, Westcote, London, the Gables. The handsome
Bedfont House on the right side of the street, of circa 1740, has a
richly pilastered baroque front, and would do credit to a London
square. Even a sudden splash of white stucco does not seem out of
place.

Peering off centre over the roofs is the church of St James. Its
Tudor tower, modelled on Gloucester Cathedral, has elegant strap-
work rising its full height to crowning pinnacles. In the churchyard
are twelve apostle lime trees. Within lie the memorials of the families of its prime, with Hicks most splendid off all.

Chipping Campden, poor when Ashbee and his friends arrived,
is again prosperous. Its population is representative of the new
rural economy: a mixture of creative entrepreneurs, commuters,
weekenders and the retired. The surroundings are carefully protected. While this makes few concessions to the old agriculture,
these Cotswold towns have recovered their former confidence.

CLEE HILLS
From Titterstone Clee

The Shropshire hills were, for me, the discovery of this book. I knew them only from afar, passing them on trips to Wales yet never exploring them. Most unusual was their remarkable upland terrain, wild heathland more familiar in the south-west on Exmoor and Dartmoor. Some had the rounded shapes of the old red sandstone Marches, others were sharp ridged with igneous obtrusions and rocky tors. Each seemed to have its own character.

To the poet A. E. Housman, these hills filled the western horizon from his childhood home at Bromsgrove in Worcestershire. He wrote about them so often that he considered himself a Shropshire man, and the hills became the inspiration for his poetic creation, *A Shropshire Lad*:

> Far behind, a fading crest,
> Low in the forsaken west,
> Sank the high-reared head of Clee.

The Clees lie between Corvedale and the Severn, south of Wenlock Edge. They comprise Brown Clee and Titterstone Clee (533m), the latter the more dramatic and easily accessible. The customary viewpoint is from a car park on the A4117 at Cleehill opposite the Kremlin inn, so-called for there being no obstacle, it is said, between it and Moscow. Wilder is the view from the top of Titterstone Clee, up a side road signed to Bitterley. The character and vegetation change abruptly above 400m. Fields and copses give way to open heath, covered in bracken and little managed. Roads narrow into cul-de-sacs. A damp mist often descends.

Near the summit the landscape becomes eerie, a place of quarried hillside, stark walls, inclines and unroofed warehouses. Titterstone

Titterstone Clee: the 'blue remembered hills'

was long populated by Iron Age forts and then excavated for its basalt, here known as black-stone, for road surfacing. The quarrying yields a string of mining hamlets, much like those round the Stiperstones and out of character with the surrounding lowlands. The road ends inside quarry ruins, which in a dying light can seem like the Baths of Caracalla or the relic of a giant prison. This has all the menace once ascribed to the Welsh marches. Buzzards and kestrels hover in the wind.

The view belies this setting. It looks west over the Teme valley towards Ludlow. On a clear day its church and castle stand out beneath Whitcliffe Common and the Clun Forest beyond. To the north lies the Long Mynd and, in the far distance, the heights of Snowdonia. To the south are the Welsh mountains and Brecon Beacons. Fertile valley bottoms contrast with bare hilltops.

From the car park a track curls up towards an air-traffic control beacon and meteorological station, commanding the entire Severn valley and the approach to Birmingham. Might satellites one day replace it and let us reach the summit? From this side of Titterstone there is a wide view eastwards over the Severn Vale. This is the true land of Housman's imagined youth and of his verse elegiac and tragic. It was of Clee that Housman penned his best-known lines:

Into my heart, an air that kills
From yon far country blows:
What are those blue remembered hills,
What spires, what farms are those?

That is the land of lost content,
I see it shining plain,
The happy highways where I went
And cannot come again.

CLYRO HILL
Towards the Wye valley

Walkers on Offa's Dyke and festival-goers at Hay know well the mound of Hay Bluff and the surrounding Black Mountains. Much of this is in Wales and outside my scope, but behind Hay the hills above Clyro are in England and offer a view back down the broad Wye valley towards Hereford. It forms an enchanted basin, through which winds this loveliest of rivers with a castle on its bank. We are here in England's most soothing county, Herefordshire.

Offa's Dyke was never a fortification or barrier. It was more a boundary between the Mercian kingdom of Offa and the Welsh principality of Powys. Constructed in the mid-eighth century, it marked the limit of the Anglo-Saxon incursion, where lowland Saxons met upland Britons and decided, or were forced, to call a halt. Offa ruled

The 'kingdom' of Hay at the head of the Wye Valley

more of England than anyone before Alfred, his power extending south to London and north to the borders of Northumbria.

From the fields and lanes above Clyro we see the Wye basin below, with Hay Castle nestling in the bottom, its sandstone walls, part Norman, part Jacobean, standing sentinel over the southern Marches. An eccentric entrepreneur, Richard Booth, turned it into a 'book town' in the 1970s and, in 1977, even declared it an independent statelet, with its own house of lords and himself as 'king'. The Hay book festival followed and the town now receives some half a million visitors a year, testament to the continuing appeal of the printed word.

Behind we can sense the dark rolling uplands of Wales as the Wye disappears over the border. On a dark day with storms pouring down from the Brecon Beacons it is easy to understand the Saxons deciding they had invaded far enough and calling a halt. Why push on when the view behind them must have seemed so blissful?

That view is across a valley patchwork of post-enclosure fields with straight edges, apparently saved from more recent hedge removal by being mostly devoted to fruit. The price is the plastic poly-tunnel, though few seem to spoil the view from here. To the right we can make out the defile of the Golden Valley, home to the River Dore.

This landscape is desperately vulnerable. Like so much of England, it could be transformed by a switch in grant, a shift in food price or a change in planning law. Already there is a plan for a row of wind turbines along the Golden Valley ridge. This country, beyond the protection of any national park, seems to be under perpetual siege. The kerbs are planted with protest placards, the halls alive with campaign meetings, the future uncertain.

HAWKSTONE
From the Hill Monument

England's finest 'created' landscapes have two prerequisites: un-usual geology and a fortune to consume. Hawkstone Park is laid out on an extrusion of red sandstone heaved up over the Shropshire plain south of Whitchurch. The fortune was that of the Hill family, Shropshire grandees from the sixteenth century to the end of the nineteenth. Grandest was Sir Richard Hill, 'the Great Hill', army paymaster and diplomat to William of Orange. His father admired his ability to make money, but worried, 'God send that he gets it honestly'. Hill's occupation was known as his 'lucrative arithmetick'.

Hill had inherited the Hawkstone estate from a forebear, the

Tudor mayor of London, Sir Rowland Hill. On his Shropshire estate he planned terraces and viewpoints, but was too busy ever to visit them. It was left to his nephew, another Rowland, to create what must be the most bizarre landscape fantasy in England. The crags were festooned with the paraphernalia of the Romantic imagination, a grotto, a cave, a Swiss bridge, a hermitage, urns, towers and monuments.

The park was widely celebrated. The 'four hills' of Hawkstone were declared by a visitor in 1748 to be 'more frequent and wild than at Studley Royal and the prospect more extensive and various'. Dr Johnson referred to 'striking scenes and terrifick grandeur . . . the awfulness of its shades, the horrors of its precipices, the verdure of its hollows and the loftiness of its rocks'. A cliff is still named the Awful Precipice after this quotation. The Victorians imported exotic conifers and rhododendron, against which today's gardeners fight a ceaseless battle.

The estate fell into ruin with the family's bankruptcy in 1894, eventually passing to the Roman Catholic Redemptorist sect as a seminary. In 1990 the estate was bought by the Barclay brothers and restored as a private park, now open to the public. The house is a hotel. Sales of land for farming and golf have diminished the scale of the original park, but it remains one of the most impressive, if least known, landscapes in the Midlands.

Choosing the best view of and from Hawkstone is not easy. A circular walk of some two miles includes a series of carefully staged vistas, usually involving a glimpse down a rocky gulley, along a cliff or out over the Severn Vale. That from the Swiss Bridge is the most dramatic. But the widest panorama is from the top of the Hill monument at the south end of the park. This is a short walk from the entrance through a wood of gnarled beeches, set amid an ornamental grove of pines and monkey-puzzle trees.

The monument commemorates the founder of the Hill dynasty,

Dr Johnson's 'terrifick grandeur': the precipice at Hawkstone

the Tudor Sir Rowland, first Protestant lord mayor of London. It was erected in 1795 'as an observatory and to feast the eye by presenting to it a luxurious and extensive prospect'. This was of twelve counties, 'or as some assert 15'. The monument was restored in 1992 and its viewing platform needs a head for heights.

From here is a 360-degree panorama of the northern Marches, with the ridge of the Hawkstone crags in the foreground. The house can be seen peeping over the contour to the east, with the Cotswolds in the distance. The view north is of the Peckforton Hills looming over the Cheshire plain, with a hint of Merseyside beyond.

To the west rise the Welsh hills, with Breidden prominent on the upper Severn. South-west are Hawkstone's sister prominences, the Stiperstones, the Long Mynd, the Wrekin and the Clees, serried rows of humps and ridges, like so many sandcastles hit by the tide.

IRONBRIDGE GORGE
From the Rotunda

Ironbridge is an odd place. The gorge is supposedly the cradle of England's industrial revolution, a place of coal and iron, fires and furnaces, titans of capitalism and slaves to labour. It was here that the Georgian writer Arthur Young could contrast the 'beautiful sheets of hanging wood' with the valley bottom, where 'the noise of the forges and mills and all their vast machinery, the flame bursting from the furnaces . . . are altogether horribly sublime'. Today it seems a cross between an arboretum and a Dickensian movie set. It has no fire in its belly and certainly no dirt.

In 1709 Abraham Darby took over the derelict ironworks of Coalbrookdale, lying in a gorge where the River Severn cuts a gap between Wenlock Edge and the Wrekin. Iron had been mined here for half a century, but Darby could see the value of local low-sulphur coal for iron furnaces, a fast-flowing stream for power and access to the Severn for transport. He so improved his casting technology that, by the mid-eighteenth century, his works were producing everything from pots to railways and even pig iron for steel.

In 1779 Abraham Darby III decided to advertise the versatility of his iron by building a bridge made of the material over the gorge, linking Coalbrookdale to Benthall on the road to Bridgnorth. It was to be the first iron bridge to be built anywhere. The project soon overran its £3,000 budget and left Darby in debt for the rest of his life.

The design was a replica of what would have been built had it been of wood. This led to too much weight and stress, thus losing the virtue of iron's inherent strength. When Thomas Telford built another bridge ten years later upstream at Buildwas, he used only half as much iron for a larger span. But if Darby's bridge was ponderous and lost money, it served its purpose, being celebrated worldwide.

To assist its promotion, in 1782 Darby's fellow ironmaster, Richard Reynolds, laid out a recreational walk onto the promontory that juts out between the main Severn gorge and the tributary of Coalbrookdale. It would offer his workers a smoke-free promenade and views over the surrounding hills. It was an attempt to appease anti-industry critics such as Anna Seward, whose contemporary poem 'Colebrook Dale' lamented the pollution of the air and the river by 'thick, sulphureous smoke that doth stain thy glassy waters'.

Reynolds's walk begins opposite the White Horse pub at the top of Lincoln Hill. The path leads through thick woods with views down into Coalbrookdale, where an iron foundry is still in operation, assembling Aga and Rayburn stoves. The old Darby factories can be seen among the warehouses, with the Darby family houses beyond. The residential neighbourhood under the hill was hopefully named Paradise.

The path ends in a belvedere on the site of Reynolds's vanished Rotunda. The view of the gorge, especially in winter when the

trees relent, is sweeping. The gorge was created relatively recently, some 15,000 years ago in the last ice age, when a frozen lake to the north began melting and the Severn made its way south underneath it, cutting down through layers of coal, lime and ore as it did so and thus supplying the essential resources for an industrial revolution.

The iron bridge is to the left, splendidly leaping the gorge. Next to it are the red and mauve brick houses of Ironbridge village, with tall chimneys and jumbled courtyards. Round the corner downstream are the ruins of the Blist Hill blast furnaces, workshops,

Ironbridge Gorge, relic of the 'horribly sublime'

inclined planes and canals, part of what is now a fascinating display of industrial archaeology.

Upstream from the Rotunda is a remarkable sight, the cooling towers of the Ironbridge power station, peering round the corner of the gorge like giants in Lilliput. Erected between the wars, they were carefully sited to be hidden behind the hill. Red was even mixed into the cement to reflect the surrounding sandstone. Beyond is a glimpse of the upper Severn valley.

Given the effort put into preserving Ironbridge, it is surprising the Rotunda has not been rebuilt and its belvedere restored. It appears in contemporary prints with Georgian ladies enjoying uninterrupted views of the horrors and marvels below. The place is now a neglected muddy patch and the view largely obscured by trees. This is one of the worst cases of 'view vandalism' I know. Small wonder that when I asked for directions in the pub, no one knew what I was talking about.

THE LONG MYND
Towards Church Stretton

This is not soft, gentle Shropshire. The Long Mynd has a character far from the fertile Severn Vale, as if deep into Wales or on the heights of Exmoor. Heather clings to peat. Treeless heathland stretches for miles, broken only by dry combes, known here as batches or hollows. While the adjacent Stiperstones can be likened to a shark, restlessly patrolling the Welsh border, the Long Mynd is a beached whale, its surface blistered and scarred by time.

Most of what can be seen from the top of the Long Mynd is Long Mynd. The view from its summit, Pole Bank, is of heath in all directions and not much else. I prefer to drop down into its most distinctive feature, one of the flanking combes. The most impressive is the precipitous Burway, leading from Boiling Well into Church Stretton valley. Halfway down is a rocky outcrop on the right. From here we can appreciate the bulk of the Long Mynd behind and see ahead the elegant fingers of its outliers stretching towards the Severn. The contours here are supremely dramatic, with a clear boundary between green valley bottoms and brown-blue heath above.

At our feet lies the geologically celebrated Church Stretton fault, running deep into Wales. It is an example of Precambrian rock thrust upwards through later sedimentary layers. Paleontologist Richard Fortey sees it as a metaphor for the nation's collective sub-conscious, the old rock emerging from 'a more deeply hidden history, yet one upon which everything else is built'.

To the left lies the deep cleft of Carding Mill Valley, site of an old mill and now a small resort. The visitor centre displays fossilised raindrops somehow preserved from a primordial storm. Across the fault is the first of the fingers pointing out into the plain, the long hump of Caer Caradoc. This is followed by Hope Bowdler Hill and Ragleth Hill. Further south can be seen the long sweep of Wenlock Edge, its slope clothed in a strip of continuous woodland. To the north-east stands the cone of the Wrekin.

Long Mynd's 'deeply hidden history'

Lord of the Marches: Ludlow and the Clees from Whitcliffe Common

This is a landscape of constant visual delight. The west flank of
the Severn Vale is completely different from the Cotswold east, the
tough sandstone more resistant to weathering than the soft limestone. Its contrasting scenery of wayward contours and difficult
byways has long rendered it less populated. Still today it is relatively
free of visitors.

LUDLOW
From Whitcliffe Common

When I was a boy the old sandstone town of Ludlow was the last 'staging post' on the family drive to Wales. It was a place of teas, ice creams and bad jokes. When my mother was taken ill en route,

Ludlow became 'laid-low'. My father would pun the poet's Petra, calling it 'rose red city half as old as Teme', after its adjacent river.

The ancient capital of the Welsh Marches sits proud on its rocky promontory at the junction of the Teme and the Corve. Its castle and church tower rise above a long market square. Lanes lead down to the encircling river on a Norman bastide grid. Ludlow is Durham in miniature.

The March was the name given to the Welsh border country at the time of Domesday. Here the Norman king, William Rufus, erected the largest line of forts in England. Conquest, treaty and settlement gradually pacified the southern part of Wales, but constant rebellion left Wales proper, or Pura Walia, unsuppressed in the north. Ludlow matched Chepstow in the south and Chester in the north as Marcher fortresses.

The lords of the March enjoyed quasi-regal powers, to enable them to act immediately in the event of trouble from the Welsh. They could build castles, raise armies and levy taxes. Following the defeat of Llywelyn by Edward I in 1282, all Wales came under the king's rule, with the royal heir as titular prince. In 1472 Edward IV set up a Council of the March at Ludlow and the town became administrative capital of all Wales.

By then the town was rich on wool. Its great civic church of St Laurence was built on the profits of the palmers' guild, whose superb medieval window survives to record pilgrimages to Jerusalem. Town houses were acquired or built by courtiers, lawyers and merchants. The town's status did not survive the centralising government of William and Mary. The Council of the March was abolished in 1689 and the castle leased to the earls of Powis. It duly became a 'romantic ruin', remaining as such in their ownership to this day.

The best view is from the slope of Whitcliffe Common to the west, with the castle directly across the river and the town beyond. The name Ludlow derives from the Saxon for loud water and the Teme is here a tumbling rapid. From this point the castle rises red and angry over the rocks. Its walls run from the original hall and solar on the left, across the inner and outer baileys to the circular Mortimer's Tower on the right. In summer this is mostly obscured by trees.

The castle glacis down to the river was laid out by the Countess of Powis in 1771 with ornamental walks and views of the river and the country beyond, reached from Whitcliffe by Dinham Bridge. A painting by the Regency landscapist William Marlow shows townspeople promenading this early urban park. To the right of the castle was, and still is, the red-brick Dinham House, residence of the Knight family, ironmasters of neighbouring Coalbrookdale.

Above are spread the roofs of the town. The church, with what Pevsner called its 'arrogant tower', still dominates the horizon, a glorious Perpendicular beacon looking out over the Teme valley. The Clee Hills form the backdrop, shielding the valley from the great Severn Vale beyond. This is all a surprisingly private England. On a moonlit night the view of Ludlow from Whitcliffe Common recalls El Greco's of Toledo, piled up on its hillside.

THE MALVERNS
From British Camp

The Malverns stand guard over the Wye and the Severn valleys as a barbican against wild Wales. Their many summits offer panoramas of England, alive with hope at dawn, restful with consolation at dusk. Nostalgic Englishmen in India were said to regard these hills as the England of which they dreamed when longing for home. They created the up-country resort of Simla as a Worcestershire facsimile.

Overleaf: Evening consolation: British Camp and Severn Vale

The Malvern ridge is remarkable for its ruggedness, one of the volcanic outcrops that break through the sandstone and interrupt the Severn Vale from Cheshire to Chepstow. The Malvern quarries are museums of granite, gneiss, schist and dolerite. Deep underground, the rock retains and filters rain, yielding the famous Malvern water, bottled long before Perrier. Far above, each prominence along the ridge has its name: North Hill, Jubilee Hill, Worcestershire Beacon, Perseverance Hill, Midsummer Hill. These were the uplands from which the Malverns' composer laureate, Edward Elgar, drew inspiration for music as redolent of them as Britten's was of Suffolk.

My preferred viewpoint is British Camp on Herefordshire Hill. It is lower than the others, showing them in close relief. The camp is Iron Age, surrounded by steep concentric defences. Legend claims it as scene of Caractacus's final stand against the Romans in the first century AD. An excellent study of the heathland flora by Keith Barnett lists, month-by-month, the presence of orchid, harebell, yarrow, self-heal and, a new one to me, pellitory of the wall. The Malverns are one of the few places outside the south east where, we are told, nightingales are still heard.

The view from the camp was called by the seventeenth-century diarist John Evelyn 'one of the godliest vistas in England'. It looks out across the Severn Vale to the promontory of Bredon Hill. In between lies a rich agricultural basin where, miraculously, little of the building sprawl that disfigures the lower Severn is visible. Under the hill at our feet is the tower of Little Malvern priory, with the ornamental trees of the adjacent court running up the slope.

To the south the mood changes. Here is the dark outline of the Forest of Dean with the hills of Monmouthshire beyond. Round to the west the character of the landscape becomes more undulating. The Eastnor estate gives precedence to woods over fields, to the needs of country sports over traditional agriculture. Its castle sits proud by its lake, with the spacious woods of Coneygree and Frith to its right. Far beyond, the Wye stretches towards Wales and the Brecon Beacons.

The Malverns have suffered for their popularity. They have been assaulted by builders, quarried and tunnelled. A minor road has been built along the west side of the ridge and three roads cut across it. The village of Colwall Stone encroaches up the western slopes. All this was supposedly under the protection of a group of conservators (early planners) formed by statute in 1884 specifically to stop such development. They have not always succeeded.

For all that the Anglo-Indians were right. This is the England of that most English of sounds, the ghostly theme of Elgar's cello concerto. He said on his deathbed, 'If you ever hear someone on the Malvern Hills, whistling that tune, don't be alarmed. It's only me.'

PECKFORTON
Towards Beeston

The twin castles of Peckforton and Beeston rise above the Cheshire plain like mounted knights rearing and wheeling before battle. They occupy an outcrop of the long Marches ridge, whose red stone colours churches, houses and fields in these parts. The outcrop is now so coated with trees that I searched for an hour for a clear view of the castles in line, finding one only on an unmarked track directly above Peckforton itself.

The castles are chiefly the creation of a man described by the historian Mark Girouard as 'one of those tremendous, rock-hewn Victorians who seem built on a larger scale than ordinary men'. Lord Tollemache was born John Halliday in 1805. To his surprise he inherited the Suffolk and Cheshire estates of his maternal grandmother on condition he adopted her name. Thus renamed, Tollemache went on to have twelve children and expand his Cheshire property to 29,000 acres, becoming the local MP and High Sheriff.

Tollemache was eccentric and progressive. He took great pride in building fifty farmhouses and boasted that he rehoused all his tenants, believing every one should own 'three acres and a cow'. Gladstone called him 'the best estate manager in England'. But he suffered from forebodings of revolution and built himself, on a bluff at Peckforton, the last deliberately 'fortified' mansion in England. Designed in 1844 by the medievalist Anthony Salvin, it was admired by the gothic revivalist architect George Gilbert Scott as 'the largest and most carefully and learnedly executed Gothic mansion of the present', and 'the very height of masquerading'.

The Tollemaches left Peckforton in 1939. The castle passed through various hands and was used by TV programme makers as an appropriately grim setting for both *Dr Who* and *Robin Hood*.

Peckforton and Beeston: Ludwig of Bavaria meets Crac des Chevaliers

Now a hotel, it was damaged in 2011 by an arsonist, a bridegroom who excused himself as being 'under intense strain'. The restored castle is complete with dry moat, gatehouse, great hall, chapel, grand staircase and service wings. Birds of prey are kept in the courtyard.

Not content with his own castle, Tollemache restored another, the ruins of Beeston a mile away on the neighbouring crag, ideally sited to enhance his view from Peckforton. It was Ludwig of Bavaria meets Crac des Chevaliers. Beeston had been built in 1225 by Ranulf, Earl of Chester, on his return from a crusade and was modelled on forts he had seen in the Levant. It comprised inner and outer baileys, with two powerful drum towers flanking the gate.

Beyond Beeston the view north from Peckforton is over the Cheshire plain, once rich dairy country supplying the booming towns of Lancashire. Fields are divided by rectangular hedges, with ash trees rising at regular intervals along their length, punctuated by an occasional black-and-white timbered farmhouse. To the west lies more turbulent scenery, the valley of the Dee with the Clwydian hills and Snowdonia beyond. We can just make out Chester with the adjacent white sheds of the Airbus works at Broughton. Over its shoulder is Merseyside with the smoking chimneys of Ellesmere Port. A beacon on the horizon is the tower of Liverpool Cathedral. This is industrial England at its most discreet.

THE STIPERSTONES

From Manstone Rock

———

Sometimes weather is all. I stood on Manstone Rock one August day and watched pandemonium break out round me. Howling south-westerlies were sending shafts of sunlight followed by thick curtains of rain across the Welsh border, as if on a search-and-destroy mission against invading English. Far below lay the Berwyns, the Vale of Montgomery and the humps and bumps of the Shropshire hills. The weather changed them by the minute, from brilliant greens and yellows to thunderous black, from calm pastures to raging Alps. The pagans were right. The Marcher hills are occupied by dark spirits.

The Stiperstones are among England's least visited viewpoints. They are an outcrop of quartzite some five miles long, with the Dartmoor-like feature of rocky tors along their ridge and with fields of rocks spilling down their sides. The highest tor, Manstone Rock, is 536m, easily reached from the nature reserve road. Fractured by the freezing and thawing of the ice age, these tors yield lifelike profiles of men, dogs and monkeys. Their tumbled boulders buried in thick heather give every step the potential to twist an ankle.

The scenery contrasts with the Malverns to the south. Here the Severn Vale is at a distance and the Welsh hills close to. This is a landscape of high moors, dark combes and isolated farms. It was once much mined for lead. The place names describe the landscape, Bridges, Gravels, White Grit, The Bog and Black Marsh, as if people in these parts did not expect to stay long. The rocks above were considered a haunt of the Devil, the northernmost tor being named the Devil's Chair.

The view on either side of the ridge is steep, down into the river valleys of the East and West Onny. The east is wild and open, fields unfenced and sheep few and far between. The west side is also steep, but intimate with verdant slopes and scattered mining hamlets, Shropshire at its most secret.

The chief spectacle is west into Wales. The border darts up and down these valleys, apparently at random. The bulging folds of the Marches yield Corndon Hill, Heath Mynd and the Clun Forest. Most dramatic, if the sun is right, is the glimpse due west into the Vale of Montgomery, where the Severn appears to have turned 180 degrees

Stiperstones: sculpted rock on heather carpet

on the way from its source in the Cambrian Mountains. The tumbling uplands suddenly part to reveal a soft, fertile valley, the upper Wye lost in the northern Marches. It must have been this sight that first enticed the Norman Montgomerys (from Calvados in France) to venture deep into Powys – and danger.

The Stiperstones are covered in heather, ling and gorse that fights an annual war with the bracken. It is also home to a colony of wild holly. Local whinberry pie is much prized. Grouse, ravens and stonechats rise from the heather and swoop round the stones. Can this really be gentle Shropshire?

SYMONDS YAT

From Symonds Yat Rock

In 1770 the writer William Gilpin took a boat on the River Wye in the company of the poet Thomas Gray in search of what Gilpin called 'nameless beauty'. Twelve years later he wrote his *Observations on the River Wye*, launching the concept of the 'picturesque' and of the Wye as its embodiment. It was the first English travel guide. This was tourism not of the created aristocratic landscapes of William Kent and Capability Brown but of the ordinary countryside, bequeathed by nature to everyone.

The book became a lasting best-seller. The closure of Europe to tourism during the revolutionary wars led thousands to use the Lake District and the Wye as substitutes for the Alps. By the turn of the century a dozen boats a day were leaving Ross-on-Wye, passing Goodrich Castle and navigating the Symonds Yat rapids to Monmouth and Chepstow. Some even had Gilpin drawing boards installed, so tourists could sketch their 'picturesques' as they went.

The yat, or gate, is the entrance to a deep gorge where the Wye plunges through the Forest of Dean. The land was owned in the seventeenth century by a local sheriff, Robert Symonds, but was let to a series of iron smelters, who turned the rapids into a miniature Coalbrookdale. The surrounding forest offered ore, wood for charcoal and plentiful water power. The smelting works produced nails and other metal goods, while the rapids were re-engineered to enable barges to carry produce downstream. The slag was dumped in the river and now forms an island.

The Victorians brought a different prosperity by colonising the gorge for tourists, lining it with hotels, villas and cottages. The rapids have since been restored and are devoted to canoeing. The river continues downstream through the gorge on a six-mile run through the woods to Monmouth. This section has few accessible viewpoints.

The one prominent lookout is from Symonds Yat Rock, reached from the A4136 through Christchurch. The rock juts out over the wide loop of the Wye, with the gorge on one side and the Wye meander on the other. The lookout has been discreetly terraced and decked by the Forestry Commission and the RSPB. The view on the gorse side is steeply down through thick forest in the ravine. The trees are mostly beech, forming a seemingly impenetrable mass of green. On the river bank is a quaint clutter of Victorian tourist facilities. Peregrine falcons ride the thermals in the foreground, attended by the clicking of cameras.

The view on the valley side is gloriously different. We see the Wye meander in a sweeping horseshoe as if weaving this way and that to find a way to the sea. The river snakes back past Goodrich church and castle, round Howle Hill to the barely visible Ross-on-Wye. Beyond, the Wye plain opens out into a vista of meadows and hedges, backed by the distant hills of the Welsh Marches. This to Gilpin was 'the landscape of the sublime', and it still is.

Overleaf: 'The landscape of the sublime': the Wye meanders

TYNDALE MONUMENT
Towards the Severn estuary

As Broadway Tower covers the northern Cotswold view over the Severn Vale, so Tyndale covers the southern view. It looks towards the Severn bridges and ranges across the Cotswolds, the Severn estuary and the Forest of Dean. The lookout tower demands a steep climb through woods from the village of North Nibley. The hills are here fragmented and detached from the main escarpment and orientation is needed from the toposcope in the meadow.

The tower commemorates the first complete translation of the Bible from Hebrew and Greek by William Tyndale, a native of Nibley (Wycliffe's earlier version was partial and translated from Latin). A brilliant but cantankerous scholar, he was one of the harbingers of the English Reformation. He promised a critic of his labour that he would 'defy the Pope, and all his laws; and, if God spares my life, ere many years I will cause the boy that driveth the plow to know more of the Scriptures than thou dost!' He eventually fled charges of heresy in England in 1525 to work in Germany, where he was executed in 1536, just four years before Henry VIII licensed his work for reading in churches.

In 1863 local citizens decided to build a memorial to their favourite son on the hill above his birthplace, designed by the eccentric neo-goth, S. S. Teulon. The monument is over a hundred feet high, in the form of a Romanesque obelisk with a pyramid cap and cross. A copy of Tyndale's Bible was once displayed in its viewing gallery, though no more. The tower is open, with a slot for a contribution and narrow steps to the top.

The view benefits from being partly enfolded in two jutting shoulders of the Cotswolds, the main escarpment being above Wotton to the east. Also to the east, and obscuring the view of the main Cotswold ridge, is a hill on which stands the Iron Age fort of

Brackenbury Ditches largely hidden among trees. West, the great River Severn is visible as a strip of silver/grey light. The two motorway bridges can be seen to the south, twelve miles distant, with on their left the Lansdowne ridge above Bath. The backdrop is formed by the Forest of Dean and the Welsh mountains beyond.

Upstream lies Oldbury nuclear power station, opened in 1967, with near it the dark outline of Berkeley Castle, begun in 1067, a year after the conquest. It was the scene of the brutal murder of Edward II, his agonised cries heard across the Vale of Berkeley, or so his champions claimed after his death. The nuclear power station is no more and should be returned to pasture. The castle is still going strong.

In the foreground to the north lies Stinchcombe Hill, with beneath it a romantic early-Victorian park. Its creator, the Reverend

The Severn bridges seen across the Vale of Berkeley

David Edwards, is reputed to have designed it with secret corners for trysts with his gypsy girlfriend. The wall doorways were supposedly built too narrow for his obese wife to pass. If so, she must have been truly vast.

At our feet is Tyndale's village of North Nibley, lapped by a tidal wave of trees descending from above. It is a lesson in English village evolution. A cluster of cottages round the church slowly grew outwards with Victorian additions, until it had plugged into it a twentieth-century housing estate. In the process it lost all intimacy and visual coherence, a sprawl without a focus, a village perhaps in the mind of its residents but not in the eye of the beholder.

EAST MIDLANDS

———

Chatsworth: From the Derwent Valley 211
Dovedale: From Thorpe Cloud 214
Kinder Scout: From White Brow Hill 216
Mam Tor: To Stanage Edge 219
The Roaches: Towards Leek 222

Kinder Scout
Mam Tor
Chatsworth

The Roaches

Dovedale

DERBYSHIRE

Derby

NOTTINGHAMSHIRE

Nottingham

LINCOLNSHIRE

Lincoln

LEICESTERSHIRE

Leicester

Oakham

RUTLAND

NORTHAMPTONSHIRE

Northampton

CHATSWORTH
From the Derwent Valley

—

'The eye was instantly caught by Pemberley House, situated on the opposite side of the valley, into which the road wound with some abruptness . . . a large, handsome, stone building standing well on rising ground, and backed by a ridge of high woody hills.' So wrote Jane Austen, giving Elizabeth Bennet's account of Darcy's stately mansion in *Pride and Prejudice*. She continued, 'In front, a stream of some natural importance was swelled into one greater, but without any artificial appearance. Its banks were neither formal, nor falsely adorned.'

This can only be a view of Chatsworth. The passage is known to have been written when Austen was staying in neighbouring Bakewell. The setting was perfect for Darcy's character, half disdainful, half assured. Chatsworth does not float in the sky like Castle Howard, or roar defiance at the world, like Blenheim. For all its wealth and beauty, it seems at peace with nature and Derbyshire in one. Most remarkable, it is built of millstone grit, so often the harshest and blackest of stone, yet here displayed in what might be the golden tones of Bath.

Chatsworth has long been the seat of the Cavendishes, a local family that married Bess of Hardwick in the sixteenth century and went on to become the grandest of grandees, dukes of Devonshire, Whig, liberal, mildly progressive. The house seems at first conspicuously retiring, set off-centre at the side of its valley, glowing beneath a wooded hanger on the hill above. There is no grand avenue, obelisk or belvedere to lead the eye to the house. Chatsworth borrows

'Neither formal nor falsely adorned', Chatsworth in the eighteenth century

privacy from its surroundings. Only at night does the view from across the Derwent burst into magnificence, indeed literally electrified by the Chatsworth floodlights. Then the house becomes a golden palace in a darkened gallery.

The first duke's architect after the Restoration was William Talman, such that the present south and east facades were influenced by the Franco-Dutch taste of the time. Twelve even bays with no central feature gaze down the valley, crowned only with a parapet. The west facade has a small pediment and was apparently designed by the duke himself. A long basement pedestal allows for the fall of the land.

The original gardens were laid out in the seventeenth-century style, with promenades, parterres, ponds and a long cascade down the hill. A baroque temple crowned its summit. Trees were planted in formal squares. The result depicted in a Kip and Knyff print of the early eighteenth century is like a Persian carpet laid across a flat Dutch polder. Then in 1755 Capability Brown arrived from Stowe to work his naturalistic magic. Promenades became curving hill walks. Parterres became lawns. Tens of thousands of trees were planted, many from America. A portrayal by William Marlow at the end of the century shows Chatsworth as if returned to the Derbyshire countryside.

The Regency brought another change. In 1826 the twenty-three-year-old Joseph Paxton, who had been working at the Horticultural Society's garden in Kew, resumed where Brown had stopped. His diary describes his first day:

> I arrived at half-past four o'clock in the morning . . . As no person was to be seen at that early hour, I got over the greenhouse gate by the old covered way, explored the pleasure grounds and looked round the outside of the house. I then went down to the kitchen gardens, scaled the outside wall and saw the whole of the place, setting the men to work there at six o'clock; then returned to Chatsworth and got Thomas Weldon to play me the water works and afterwards went to breakfast with poor dear Mrs Gregory and her niece. The latter fell in love with me and I with her, and thus completed my first morning's work at Chatsworth before nine o'clock.

Such energy led to giant rockeries, arboretums, pinetums, azalea dells and ravines. Paxton built the largest glasshouse in the world (now demolished), the highest gravity-fed fountain and an extravagant lily house, model for his later pavilion at the Great Exhibition in Kensington. He refashioned the hamlet of Edensor on the opposite side of the valley as a model estate village.

When Queen Victoria visited Chatsworth in 1842 she wrote in her diary that Paxton's works were 'the most stupendous and extraordinary creation imaginable'. He became rich and was knighted by the queen, a paragon of Victorian upward social mobility. The duke called him 'the least obtrusive of servants . . . and a friend if ever man had one'. Paxton made Chatsworth a wonder of England.

The view today is much as Brown and Paxton left it. The glass-house has gone, and a Victorian wing been added with a prominent tower to the north of the house. Later dukes have contributed to the margins, with a kitchen garden, a sensory garden, a sculpture garden, a cottage garden and a maze. But what we see from the distance is a respectful marriage of architecture, landscape and nature.

The house has been open to the public every day since the coming of the railway, with instructions from the duke that 'even the humblest' be shown everything. Already by 1844, 80,000 visitors were arriving each year, a figure that is now close to a million. They come to see not just a great garden and great house, but one of the finest private collections of paintings in the country. Though owned by a trust, it remains the Devonshire family seat, testament to the English genius for social continuity.

DOVEDALE
From Thorpe Cloud

Where lies England's north–south divide? For some southerners it is Potters Bar, for some it is the Trent, while a true Northumbrian puts it at the Tyne. My north starts where the rocks age and the contours tighten north of a line from Stafford to Derby. It starts with the noble Peak District.

'The Peak' was the first of England's national parks, declared in a burst of post-war welfarism in 1951. It has become the most visited such public space in the world after Japan's Mount Fuji. The gent-ler southern half is known as the white or low peak, a landscape of rounded limestone hills and dales, its economy once dependent on rich deposits of coal. Yet these hills have many moods, as they flex their muscles in preparation for the great Pennine heights ahead.

If the Peak needed a gateway it would be through the dark gorge of Dovedale. The mouth of the gorge, round which visitors swarm in their thousands on all but the wettest days, is overlooked by two hills, Bunster Hill and the cone-shaped Thorpe Cloud. The latter rises over the confluence of the Dove and the Lin Dove streams. Dove is from the Anglo-Saxon *dubo*, or dark, while cloud is a corruption of Old English *clud* or hill.

Thorpe Cloud's cone is the geological relic of a reef knoll, or pile of underwater coral once buried in the surrounding limestone. The climb to its summit takes just twenty minutes from the main dale car park, but is enough to take us clear of the crowds on the valley trail. From the top is a view both up the gorge and out from the mouth over the lower Dove valley. To the north the Peak District begins in earnest with the Manifold valley.

The rocks overlooking the gorge take many sculpted forms, with names such as Jacob's Ladder, the Twelve Apostles and Lover's Leap. The last relates to a girl who, on hearing her lover had been killed in the Napoleonic wars, hurled herself from its heights. She

Gateway to the Peak: Bunster from Thorpe Cloud

was saved by her skirts catching on branches as she fell, and duly discovered that he had not been killed after all. Another version has a girl throwing herself off after being jilted by her lover. She landed unhurt in a bush, walked home and lived happy, and single, ever after. Such tales attach to most English 'leaps'.

Over the river below are stepping stones, inserted for visitors by the Victorians. They now fight a running battle with health-and-safety officialdom, terrified someone might slip into two feet of water. A different battle is fought with erosion. Walkers understandably claim untrammelled access to nature, but in such numbers that nature is increasingly pleading for relief. How future generations will handle Dovedale is a mystery, unless it has timed tickets as in a blockbuster exhibition.

The view out of the dale to the south reinforces the sense of this being a north–south border. The Dove valley stretches a softer, more subtle landscape towards the rolling hills of Cannock Chase. In the middle distance lies Ilam Hall and village with, in the foreground, the hotel named after the Staffordshire author, Izaak Walton, whose *Compleat Angler* of 1653 did much to bring crowds to these limestone trout streams. I rarely plead for more trees, but some are surely needed to hide this hotel from view.

KINDER SCOUT
From White Brow Hill

Kinder Scout is the high gritstone plateau that forms the summit of the Dark (or High) Peak. Its long escarpment overlooking Cheshire and Lancashire long stood as a tantalising magnet for millions living and working in the cramped towns and cities of the industrial north-west. The Dark Peak foothills were a mere bus ride away for most people, offering those with little or no open space the promise of exercise and clear air. By the end of the Great War, the Dark Peak was a challenge to the radical mood of the day. While the ancient drovers' tracks had customarily been open to wayfarers, a crisis came in 1932 when a group of ramblers sought access to the moors for recreation. This brought them into conflict with landowners wanting to keep the moors for grouse-shooting.

On 24 April 1932, some 400 ramblers set out from Hayfield, three miles west of Kinder, under the auspices of the British Workers Sports Federation, intent on a mass trespass. They assembled at the Bowden Bridge quarry, climbed to Kinder reservoir and struck uphill to White Brow. Here they fought a brief skirmish with the Duke of Devonshire's estate gamekeepers and pressed on, joining another group of trespassers who had walked over Kinder from Edale to the east. On their descent, half a dozen of the Lancashire ramblers were arrested and jailed, predictably winning publicity and sympathy for their cause.

The trespass spread, with thousands subsequently gathering at Winnats Pass under Mam Tor, and in the south at Leith Hill in

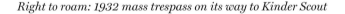

Right to roam: 1932 mass trespass on its way to Kinder Scout

Surrey. Most landowners avoided confrontation by turning a blind eye. The result was an ineffective Access to Mountains act of 1939, but more crucially the setting up of national parks after 1950. Continued pressure achieved little for half a century, until the 2000 'right to roam' act gave public access, where designated, to moors, heaths and coast.

In 2002, on the seventieth anniversary of the Kinder Scout trespass, a more liberal Duke of Devonshire summoned a rally to the quarry at Bowden and publicly apologised for the 'great wrong' done by his grandfather. A plaque at Bowden Bridge car park commemorates this generous act. The Ordnance Survey now firmly marks Kinder Scout an 'access area'.

The classic Kinder Scout view is from the summit of the ridge at Kinder Downfall, a hundred-foot waterfall with the longest drop in the Peak. It is impressive only in spate, when a swirling wind sometimes funnels up from below and sends the water not down but up, in an impressive spume. Those familiar with the Peak may feel that upward driving rain is no novelty in these parts.

Kinder plateau towards Cheshire plain

The moor plateau is blasted by wind and often bare even of a dressing of peat or soil. Mark Richards in his survey of walks in the High Peak deplores its image as 'bleak, boggy, boring moorland, redeemed but briefly from eternal damnation by King Downfall'. I fear the geology is against him. Millstone grit (or gritstone) is an unyielding rock that seems to feed off soot and rain, moisture turning it from grey-brown or russet to coal black. Small wonder grit has lent its name to north country machismo.

Since Kinder Downfall is well beyond my half-hour climb limit, I choose the viewpoint from White Brow Hill below. This has other advantages. From here we can sense the majesty of the great bowl of Kinder reservoir, while the Kinder ridge towers menacingly overhead. These slopes feel still inhabited by the ghosts of the trespass, as if the mountain itself wished to forbid access. They are a store of ancient peat, to conservationists more precious and 'rarer than rain forest'. They contest these uplands with the grouse and the meadow pipit. The most audible bird, the curlew, has a sad cry.

To the west is a sweeping view across the north coast of Wales to the Cheshire-Lancashire plain, with Manchester and Liverpool in the distance. Once these cities would have been enveloped in thick clouds of pollution. That is no more, which is some progress.

MAM TOR

To Stanage Edge

Which view: from Mam Tor to Stanage Edge or from Stanage Edge to Mam Tor? The Peak District has the finest views in England outside the Lake District, with a drama that seems to benefit from wild fluctuations in weather. I have stood on Mam Tor and watched heavy snow clouds spilling blizzards down Edale from Kinder, while a warm sun to the east was illuminating the Hope valley towards Stanage. Equally I have stood on Stanage Edge and watched a shaft of sunlight move over that same valley, turning the prominent Hope cement works into a ghostly white galleon, tossing on a sea of rain. This country has no need of blue sky. In the Dark Peak, fine weather is for the feeble.

Of the two prospects, that from Mam Tor has my vote. It forms the southern end of the 'great ridge' walk between the Hope and Edale valleys. Its name means mother mountain, so called for the instability of its gritstone on layers of shale. They form unhappy

bedfellows, slithering off each other and leading to frequent land-slips, creating heaps of debris round its base. When Daniel Defoe was writing up his travel notes during the 1720s, Mam Tor was known as the shivering mountain.

Most of the eastern flank, facing Hope, is now a dramatic land-slide scar above a field of debris, its so-called backscarp a full 70m high. In 1979 the main road up from the valley, built in the 1800s, had to be closed, its pavement found to be six feet thick from

'Shivering mountain': Mam Tor looking over Hope to Stanage Edge

constant past attempts to secure it. It remains closed and only the steep Winnats Pass offers access to Mam Tor from the south. The ground underneath is a warren of limestone caves, including the celebrated Blue John cavern. Its multicoloured, crystalline stone has been prized since Roman times.

The summit of Mam Tor is easily reached from a car park. The view back over the Hope valley begins with the great landslip scoop. On all its sides are signs of Bronze and Iron Age settlements, in irregular mounds and ramparts. The caves beneath have yielded copious human and animal remains. Far below, the road snakes down Winnats Pass to Castleton, Hope and Hathersage, with Stanage Edge surging up onto the skyline in the distance.

North over Edale the view is quite different, a majestic sweep of bare mountain and fertile lowland. The Edale valley seems isolated beneath the harsh and towering Kinder plateau, like some private kingdom in the Himalaya. It was from here that the 1932 marchers set out to meet their co-campaigners from Manchester in the great Kinder Scout trespass. I am told that on a clear day the towers of central Manchester are visible.

To the south of Mam Tor is a landscape of softer hills towards Staffordshire and the Low Peak, a patchwork of light green fields and dark forests. Kinder suddenly seems far away.

THE ROACHES
Towards Leek

The Roaches lie across the Staffordshire landscape like the jagged back of a giant dinosaur. They are a coarse ridge of hard red sandstone grit, standing high above the Tittesworth valley north of Leek. In winter snow the ridge can look Alpine. Its slabs of rock offer ideal practice routes for climbers but for walkers they can be lethal, unsignposted and dangerous when wet. The scramble along the Roaches is considered the best in the Peak District.

The ridge extends for three miles at a height of some 500m, from the detached southern cone of Hen Cloud (steep hill in Anglo-Saxon) to Roaches End at the north end, where it descends to the eerie chasm of Lud's Church and Hanging Rock. The climb from the valley road takes half an hour, rising from lush meadows to peaty moorland, in places stripped to bare rock by the wind.

A path leads along the rear of the ridge, but to get a good view we must strike up onto the actual rock face, the easiest path being from the south. The chief view is of the rocks themselves, their name taken from the French for rocks, *roches*, and dubbed the Five Clouds. They are composed of a gigantic tilted slab of stone, formed into a jumble of triangles set on edge. With the sun on them at dawn

Staffordshire Alps: the Roaches towards Tittesworth

or dusk, the sandstone glows a deep, magnificent red. The rocks are undercut and rounded into natural sculptures by wind and rain. I detected a whale, a lion's head and a devil's chair.

Climbers give each of the ascents a different name, the Valkyrie, the Sloth, the Mangler and Saul's Crack. Each climb seems to have queues waiting to scale them. On a busy day the rocks echo with the clink of equipment and the shouts of instructors. A British Council for Mountaineering hut sits in a spacious pine wood on the slopes below. It is named after Don Whillans, a mountaineer who, with Joe Brown, did much to popularise rock climbing on the Roaches and elsewhere.

The finest view from the Roaches is south-west over the Churnet valley to the Tittesworth reservoir, built in the 1960s. Beyond it lies the town of Leek with its prominent steeple. This is fertile country, stretching out towards the Cheshire plain with the uplands of Wales and Snowdonia in the distance. To the north is the higher land of the Peak District.

Eastwards behind the ridge the landscape is quite different, a barren moor of heather and moss, interspersed with pools. Sheep wander past derelict cottages. The Roaches are one of England's strangest places, one minute almost a playground, another a mysterious and frightening moonscape, reminiscent of Australia's Ayers Rock.

That may be why a local zoo released a group of Bennett's wallabies here in the 1930s. The creatures are unobtrusive. Sightings continued infrequently, but none has been confirmed since 2009. Two yaks released at the same time died in the 1950s. The rocks are a more successful habitat for nesting peregrines.

YORKSHIRE

Bempton Cliffs   227
Gordale Scar   231
Hebden Bridge: From Fairfield   233
Ribblehead: Towards the Viaduct   235
Richmond: The Market Place   239
Rievaulx: From the Terrace   241
Roseberry Topping: Towards Teesside   244
Saltaire: From Shipley   246
Swaledale: From the dale head   249
Whitby Harbour: From West Cliff   252

Swaledale

Richmond

Roseberry Topping

Whitby Harbour

Rievaulx

NORTH YORKSHIRE

Ribblehead

Bempton Cliffs

Gordale Scar

York

EAST RIDING OF YORKSHIRE

Saltaire

Leeds

Kingston upon Hull

WEST YORKSHIRE

Hebden Bridge

SOUTH YORKSHIRE

Sheffield

BEMPTON CLIFFS

Even the most ardent Yorkshireman would not claim the East Riding as blessed with England's most beautiful coast. Despite patronage by David Hockney, the Yorkshire Wolds are a lost corner of England, a place of modestly rolling hills and sparsely populated valleys. The towns seem poor and the seaside resorts of Scarborough and Bridlington have seen better times. But where the wolds meet the sea they do so with a great roar of chalk.

The road from Hunmanby to Flamborough was, on my visit, deserted. Flamborough Head is 'cul-de-sac' England, a place through which no one passes to anywhere else. It is Philip Larkin's land, where 'removed lives' are clarified by loneliness and 'silence stands like heat'. A sign leads to the RSPB reserve of Bempton Cliffs, from where there is a short walk to the cliff edge, 130m above the sea.

East Riding chalk is less white than that of England's south coast, being vividly layered in horizontal sheets, as if sediments of mud had mixed with the crustaceans on the sea floor. In places these layers are heaved and twisted, as at Lulworth in Dorset. Everywhere they are indented by erosion, creating deep gulleys, caves and passages, best appreciated from the sea (on the *Yorkshire Belle* out of Bridlington). This is a living, moving shoreline, with which the sea seems in perpetual combat.

The chief attraction of Bempton, indeed of much of England's north-east coast, is ornithological. The RSPB has helpfully located decks at strategic points along the cliff edge, overlooking rocks and

Overleaf: Wild Bempton's great roar of chalk

inlets with such names as Noon Nook, Scale Nap and Nettle Trip. They offer a clear view down to the sea and its caves. One cliff ends in a sculpted arch, except that the chalk is so angular as to look more like a woman in a skirt with one leg in the sea. Locals known as 'climmers' used to descend these cliffs on ropes to collect much-prized guillemot eggs, dozens at a time, until banned in the 1950s.

Birds swarm over these cliffs in what is the busiest nature reserve in England, with 200,000 birds arriving each summer. They crowd the cliffs with their nests and fill the air with a curtain of shimmering white. Fulmars, guillemots, kittiwakes, razorbills and puffins are in a perpetual state of wheeling, calling and swooping over the waves.

Bempton claims to be the only mainland nesting sites for gannets, most athletic of seabirds and usually preferring rocks at sea. Fieldfares and redwings come down from Russia to winter on the shore. When I was there great excitement attended the arrival of a pair of short-eared owls. The bare fields above are alive with hares. Stoats and weasels reportedly inhabit the cliff tops.

The view south is towards Flamborough Head, scene of a confused and inconclusive battle during the American War of Independence in 1779. An 'American navy' roaming the North Sea engaged a British convoy. The ships were French under French captains, but were commanded by an American, John Paul Jones, who was later idolised by Americans as a naval hero.

The view culminates short of Flamborough at North Cliff, roughly half the height of Bempton and thus creating the optical illusion of seeming further away. The lack of trees or any human settlement gives this coast a noble wildness. Humans seem intruders. It is a place for birds.

GORDALE SCAR

As the Pennine Way reaches the end of its Yorkshire stretch, it descends into the Malham valley. After a hundred miles of gritstone plateau, the change down to the softer limestone is abrupt, but the upland does not give up without a fight. At Malham Cove, a cliff of bare white rock looks out from a giant amphitheatre over the valley. Below is the picture village of Malham, from which a lane leads a mile to the east. A footpath then crosses a meadow and, so it seems,

Enveloping gloom: A View of Gordale Scar *by James Ward, c. 1812–14*

runs into the side of a cliff. A small notice offers not a map or explanation, but reproduces a painting in Tate Britain, James Ward's *Gordale Scar*. This is tourist information with class.

Ward's painting is often dismissed as a romantic exaggeration. I have to disagree. It seems accurate enough, and is confirmed by other paintings, notably by Turner. The scar is awesome, a narrow ravine 100m high, the apparent wreck of a glacial dry valley. Its floor is littered with debris, while through it flows the Gordale Beck, cascading from the plateau above and on to Malham and the River Aire, attractively lined with watercress.

As we progress into the gorge, the cliffs open and the shadows lengthen until the gloom is all-enveloping. The rock striations change from white to red to grey. Vast limestone shapes start out of the darkness. Round the final bend a waterfall appears in the depths of the scar, usually peppered with walkers trying to scramble up to the cliff top, a venture possible though difficult. Peregrines nest above.

Ward's painting, with its blackened flanks and stormy clouds, was first exhibited in London in 1815 and made Gordale a celebrity venue. It surely inspired Wordsworth's sonnet, 'Gordale', of 1818:

> . . . let thy feet repair
> To Gordale-chasm, terrific as the lair
> Where the young lions couch; for so, by leave
> Of the propitious hour, thou may'st perceive
> The local Deity, with oozy hair
> And mineral crown, beside his jagged urn
> Recumbent.

I am sure there is oozy hair among the students and trippers who now crowd the spot, but the only deity is Gordale itself. This is nature at its most theatrical.

HEBDEN BRIDGE
From Fairfield

The Calder is one of Yorkshire's neglected valleys. Like the Colne and the Aire it was ignored as scenic no-man's-land between the Peak and the Pennine national parks, considered insufficiently beautiful to merit protection. As a result planners and developers have visited a terrible fate on Calderdale.

That said, the dale's capital of Halifax is distinguished, while Hebden Bridge, higher up the valley, is the most intact surviving Yorkshire mill town. Cloth was initially spun from local wool in farmhouses on the moor. In the 1850s, manufacture moved to the valley floor, where fast-flowing water powered ever larger mills. Hebden Bridge shifted from making cloth to making clothes, notably corduroy and fustian, supposedly strong enough to resist molten metal spilled from a forge. It was dubbed 'trouser town'. A canal arrived, and later a railway.

With plentiful building stone, workers lived comparatively well, many in a distinctive type of hillside house known as a 'top and bottom', with legally unique 'flying freeholds'. These were buildings of four storeys containing two homes, the bottom two floors accessed from the front below, the top two from the hill behind. Arranged in terraces, these houses dominate the appearance of the town, almost all built in the 1880s and 1890s. Prosperity lasted barely a century.

The swift decline of the clothing industry and the lack of alternative activity so far up the dale meant much of the old town was preserved, and this has helped it back to life. Mills, outhouses, tenements and stables have proved ideal conversions for the service industries of today. As at Saltaire, the spinning and weaving floors attract users that find modern buildings characterless.

Hebden's stately terraces may make it the Bath of the north, but as a town it is hard to see. A deep valley site and the convex slopes

Mill town in embryo: Hebden Bridge from Fairfield *by John Holland, 1869*

of the surrounding hills make it near impossible to get a clear view from a distance. The two local vantage points, Hardcastle Crags and Stoodley Pike, have fine views out over the moors. It was here that a local boy named Ted Hughes promenaded his American wife Sylvia Plath, who wrote plaintively, 'The horizons ring me like faggots,/ Tilted and disparate, and always unstable', or as her husband put it, '*Wuthering Heights*, withering into perspective'. But even they could not get a good view of Hebden Bridge.

The best prospect is from the walk back from Stoodley, a favourite Hebden recreation. As the path approaches the town, a side road climbs up over the canal towards Fairfield, yielding a view across the three arms of the town, along the Calder and Hebden streams. In the foreground is the railway and old canal, with its leisure barges and mooring posts, the surviving mill chimneys still prominent. From here Hebden is impressive, tiers of pale stone 'top and bottoms' curving away towards the wooded hillsides. Each terrace bends round the contour, with those above Birchcliffe particularly eager to escape into the woods.

Hughes supposedly signed Hebden's epitaph in his 'Crown Point Pensioners':

Old faces, old roots
Indigenous memories
Flat caps, polished knobs
On favoured sticks.

Hughes was wrong. The town's conservation has bred a lively cultural life and its mild bohemianism even has a book to its credit, by the sociologist Paul Barker. This was one of a hundred cloth-based mill towns in the north. Most have seen their buildings demolished and their heritage gone. By retaining the physical legacy of its past, Hebden has given itself a chance of a future.

RIBBLEHEAD
Towards the Viaduct

The Blea Moor road west out of Wensleydale crosses the watershed of the great Pennine spine. Its open wilderness is bare of the normal features of a temperate landscape. There are few fields, trees, hedges, woods. Even sheep are sparse. This is England's gritstone cap. Poverty guarded it from change or exploitation, other than by the hardiest drovers and miners. The eye lights only on an abandoned lead mine or a buzzard wheeling overhead.

To the south of Blea Moor rises Pen-y-ghent (694m), across whose summit a masochistic path maker has led the Pennine Way. The hill appears so dominant that visitors in the early nineteenth century thought it the highest mountain in England (even guessing it at over 5,000 feet). Its stepped appearance and flat top are the result of layers of gritstone round which softer rock has eroded.

Overleaf: Stately Ribblehead, Ingleborough in the distance

Soon the road becomes an old Roman road and reveals Whernside (736m) and Ingleborough (723m), the others of the 'three peaks' with Pen-y-ghent. They are on the far side of Ribbledale overlooking the Lune valley into Lancashire. Their limestone interiors are riddled with cave systems, some attractively lit for visitors. The three peaks are a venue for numerous walks, runs and cyclo-crosses, the customary challenge being to climb all of them in a day.

Just as the bleakness is overwhelming, an apparition comes into view below Ingleborough. It is the Ribblehead viaduct on the loneliest stretch of railway in England, the Settle-to-Carlisle line. If we are lucky, we might see a train snaking across it with, if luckier still, a plume of white smoke from a steam engine.

Completed in 1876, the viaduct was a massive undertaking, employing over 2,000 navvies, of whom a hundred died and were buried in the local church. It is of twenty-four arches, 400 yards long and has a curve that enables passengers to view it from train windows. The viaduct is beautiful, fusing visually with the contours of the surrounding hills. It became an immediate tourist attraction and a house near the adjacent station was built specifically 'for the accommodation of visitors to the romantic and secluded part of the district'. Ingleborough's caves were an added appeal.

In the 1980s an outcry greeted the proposed closure of what was then a little-used line. As a member of the British Rail board at the time, I remember walking the viaduct while examining the cost of its repair, expense being the chief argument for closure. Estimates had been made by the engineers of a prohibitive £6 million. This was challenged by a quote of £250,000 from a Yorkshire contractor and another from a local builder, who told me all it needed was a wheelbarrow of tarmac to last another hundred years, which he would do 'for a couple of thou'. Closure was rescinded and the line saved in 1989.

I am often asked why, if old viaducts and bridges can be said to add to a landscape, later intruders such as wind turbines and power stations should detract from it. The answer lies partly in materials.

Ribblehead viaduct was built from the stone on which it sits, like the walls of fields and farms. Also now it is in place, its survival alone gives it status. Waving, white turbines are far more prominently sited, drawing the eye from every point of a vista. There is no comparison.

RICHMOND
The Market Place

Richmond is one of England's least known historic towns. Its medieval plan dictates a tight cluster of Georgian and early Victorian streets, with a Norman castle high on a bluff over the River Swale. Its suburbs still comprise woods and fields. Everything about Richmond pleases the eye.

The town was granted by William the Conqueror to a Breton, Alan the Red, in 1071. Alan needed a serious fortress to defend himself from the fury alike of the Scots and the expropriated Saxon earls. The territory became one of the largest Norman domains in the north, its earldom later inherited by Henry VII, who used its name for his new palace by the Thames in Surrey. He was not alone. Richmond is reputedly the most copied name of any English town, there being at least fifty-seven round the world.

Richmond is best viewed from the north-west side of its polygonal market place. From here the Norman keep can just be seen looming over the roofs to the right, as if keeping watch on the Saxon merchants below. The cobbled market place is charmingly asymmetrical, with facades seeming to spin away from Holy Trinity church, located on an island of small buildings in the middle. Here it competes with an extraordinary market cross. It was erected in 1771 and has a stupa-like obelisk, as if Mammon were eager to rival

Richmond Market in the 1920s: God and Mammon in contention

adjacent God. The effect is enhanced by contours enticing the eye through from the many outlets. Some lead down to the river, others up onto the adjacent hill. Nothing seems calculated or predictable, everything a surprise. Richmond is a supreme evocation of the English talent for townscape informality. There is hardly a straight line in the place.

Richmond's most ardent champion, the architectural historian Alec Clifton-Taylor, noted the variety of its building materials. Most of the houses are faced in limestone and sandstone from the adjacent dales, though some have walls of rounded cobble stones swept down the Swale. Some houses are composed of a flint-like stone known as chert. Few buildings are of brick, and few are rendered. The variety is sufficient to give each facade individuality while culminating in an overall harmony.

The market place is rich in decorative windows, doorcases and old shopfronts. The Georgian town hall graces the south side with, next to it, the market hall. Opposite is the handsome King's Head hotel. Every corner invites further exploration: down The Bar to the town wall, down The Green to Carr of York's bridge, along Finkle Street to the handsome Newbiggin, and by Fryers Yard to the lovely Georgian Theatre Royal. But please, free it of parked cars, and not just on market days.

RIEVAULX
From the Terrace

Rievaulx was founded in 1132 in a burst of monastic patronage under Henry I. The then abbot of the order's French headquarters at Citeaux was an Englishman, Stephen Harding. Cistercians were ascetic and dedicated to charity, deliberately putting monasteries far from political and other distractions. Rievaulx was duly described as 'a place of horror and dreary solitude'.

That said, nothing was stinted. Citeaux sent masons from France, bringing with them 'early English' gothic architecture, replacing the round-arched Romanesque with pointed arches. Rievaulx had some of the earliest lancet windows in England. The abbey was a success, growing to 350 monks in its first decade and 640 at its peak. For all its proclaimed asceticism, the residential quarters, certainly those of the abbot, were among the most sumptuous in northern Europe.

All this is now a ghostly memory. The monasteries are gone. In her *History of England*, Jane Austen remarked of Henry VIII that he dissolved the monasteries only to make ruins 'of infinite use to the landscape of England'. Rievaulx is certainly that. It sits on the banks of the Rye, from which it takes its name, as the river passes through a steep, wooded defile in the moor. While the best view of the ruins is from the valley floor, it was the prospect over them down the valley that appealed to the Georgians. They should be set 'picturesque', overwhelmed by nature swelling up behind them as a backdrop. If this was a place of horror, it was what the Romantics called a sublime horror.

The owner of the embracing Helmsley estate, Thomas Duncombe of Duncombe Park, decided in 1758 to lay out a serpentine terrace to capture this scene. His guests would drive out after dinner to admire vistas carefully crafted to be seen through the trees. These trees have since swamped the terrace, but the National Trust ensures that thirteen views are kept open. These are almost too artful, with glimpses of ruins, fields and the valley, located as if with a photograph in mind. The woods are mostly oak but have ash, lime and other species to give an appearance of wildness. Spring finds them awash in bluebells and wild garlic.

At one end of the main promenade is a Doric temple, at the other a banqueting house in the form of an Ionic one. The latter

Sumptuous solitude: the ruins from the terrace walk

is extraordinary, its ceilings decorated to designs from the Palazzo Farnese in Rome, copying Annibale Carracci and Guido Reni. While the mon-astic buildings have been merely stabilised in their ruined state, 'as found', the classical temples have been grant-aided for their splendid restoration. Conservation is a strangely biased ideology.

ROSEBERRY TOPPING
Towards Teesside

Roseberry Topping is a cone at which someone has taken a swipe, a topping without a top. It is Yorkshire's modest Matterhorn. A mound of red sandstone 320m high, its shape had long made it distinctive, visible from across the Vale of York as far as the Pennine dales. Then in 1912 a geological mishap occurred. Either some subterranean earthquake or centuries of mining led the peak to collapse, leaving a raw wound of cliffs and rocks tumbling round its summit.

Access to Roseberry Topping is easiest from near Great Ayton on the A173. A track leads to a pleasant oak wood through which steps reach open ground to the summit. A detour from the Cleveland Way joins halfway up. It was this climb that the young Captain Cook took from his home in Great Ayton and from which, it is said, he was inspired to global exploration. Various Cook monuments are dotted about the district.

The summit offers views over Teesside, the Vale of York and most of the North York Moors. The best is towards Teesside with, on a clear day, the Cheviots on the far horizon. In the middle distance lies the industrial belt of Thornaby, Stockton, Middlesbrough and

Roseberry Topping from Gribdale gate

Redcar. Despite the closure of the steelworks, this remains a centre of industry, notably chemicals. By day cooling towers emit plumes of sanitised white steam, by night the oil refineries send up dramatic flares. Once it might have been a scene from hell. Today the valley is a cluster of towers, chimneys, factories and wind turbines. All this is seen over a landscape of strange serenity.

At the foot of Roseberry, farms, fields and woods are arranged with decorum. Beyond Great Ayton are traces of pre-enclosure strip fields. Round to the north-east lies the North Sea, with Hartlepool, Tees Bay and the horizon that stirred young Cook's imagination. Round again are the cliffs of the Cleveland Hills overlooking Saltburn. The market town of Guisborough lies in the middle distance.

To the west runs the Cleveland escarpment. On my visit, late one autumn day, it was bathed in sunset, falling low over the dales far to the west. This was Yorkshire, a land that never disappoints, at its most dramatic and unexpected.

SALTAIRE

From Shipley

Champions of the Yorkshire landscape came too late for Airedale. Like the Calder and the Colne, its post-industrial planners showed little interest in rehabilitating old buildings or in the careful siting of new ones. Warehouses and housing estates colonised green fields while dereliction crept along the old valley bottoms. The atmospheric pollution of the nineteenth century was replaced by the visual pollution of the twenty-first.

All was not lost. An unassuming small park at the junction of Carr Lane and Wrose Road above Shipley offers a view of two of the most splendid monuments to England's industrial past, the great Bradford mills of Manningham and Saltaire. Below runs the Bradford Beck. On the far side of the valley, housing gives way to the farmers struggling for existence on the Yorkshire uplands. Their

Saltaire with Manningham Mills and Bradford in the distance

farms, many dating back to Viking days, are the heroes of this countryside, surviving over the centuries as industries, indeed whole populations, come and go in the dales beneath.

To the left are the northern outskirts of Bradford, a prospect of roofs and trees crowned by an extraordinary Italianate palace. Manningham Mills, also called Lister Mills, was owned by the Cunliffe-Lister family and was the largest mill complex in England. The present building was rebuilt in 1873 after a fire, and produced silk, velvet and worsted. At its peak it employed 11,000 people and remained in business until 1992. Saved from demolition, the building reopened in 2004, converted into a mix of apartments and work-spaces after the pattern of Dean Clough mill in Halifax. Four thousand people now work there.

Seen from Shipley, Manningham Mills rises over the trees of Lister Park, looking down over Bradford city centre, still blighted by the council's reckless demolition of much of it in the 1970s in the vain hope of redevelopment. Bradford has been saved by the Indian sub-continent, now comprising a third of the city's population. There seem more minarets than mill chimneys.

The view to the right leads up the Aire valley, with the Leeds and Liverpool canal along its bottom and Shipley Glen on its slopes. Here lie the comfortable houses of Bradford's one-time plutocracy. It was once said that more Rolls-Royces could be counted on the Ilkley road out of Bradford than anywhere in England: hence Eliot's reference in *The Waste Land* to those 'on whom assurance sits/ As a silk hat on a Bradford millionaire'. Eliot knew such tycoons when working at Lloyd's bank in the City.

Dominating this right-hand view is Sir Titus Salt's mill and model village. Salt was a giant of Victorian commerce. Son of a local wool stapler, he rose to become Bradford's chief mill-owner and mayor. Shocked at the town's pollution, he bought land three miles away in the Aire valley and erected a large Italianate mill of red sandstone, opening it on his fiftieth birthday in 1853. He named it after himself and the Aire river. Round it he laid out a model village, with generous stone terrace houses, chapels, bathhouses, schools, clinics and almshouses. There was no pub.

Salt's mill remained working until 1986, specialising like Manningham in the finest cloth, notably angora and alpaca. After its closure a rescue campaign led to its designation in 2001 as a world heritage site. The mill buildings are now mostly reoccupied, their massive stone floors adaptable to any use. The attics are so vast they could double as motor racing circuits. As in Hebden Bridge, we can only reflect on how few of what zoologists would call these 'charismatic megaspecies' of architectural history survive. The cloth industry of the Middle Ages left us magnificent churches and we respect them. The Victorian cloth industry left equally magnificent memorials, and we destroy them.

SWALEDALE
From the dale head

———

Swaledale, with its offshoot of Arkengarthdale, is the most intimate of the valleys running east from the Pennine watershed. The settlement of these dales predates history, when early humans cleared them of trees and occupied the valley bottoms. Here the place names are mostly Saxon. Later the invading Vikings settled higher up the fellsides, with place names correspondingly Norse, ending in -by, -thwaite and -garth.

Swaledale's narrowness renders the contrast of fell and dale, side and bottom, easiest to 'read'. Swale in Saxon suggests windy, cold and bleak. The soil is thin and, since the demise of lead mining in the nineteenth century, the area is devoted chiefly to sheep and tourists. Most distinctive are its fields with barns, a surreal pattern of shapes with seemingly no rhyme or reason.

This field pattern can be appreciated from anywhere along its length, mostly clearly from Reeth, Gunnerside and Muker in the upper dale. I prefer the view from the dale head, where a splendid amphitheatre overlooks the village of Thwaite. From here we look down the valley but also north and south over the high fells, purple with heather in autumn.

Gritstone geometry at Swaledale head

The valley floor walls are made of tough gritstone and cannot have been easy to erect. They are formed into every shape known to geometry, a Rorschach test for landscape historians, of triangles, rhomboids, lozenges, semicircles, even enclosures one within another. The pattern must reflect ancient landholdings but of what nature is a mystery. Higher up the valley sides, the walling becomes more rectangular and this may be due to later enclosures of open strip fields. Or it may suggest an earlier difference between Saxon and Viking areas of occupation.

Most of the fields contain handsome free-standing barns, often two-storey and with stone roofs. Though such barns occur elsewhere in the dales, nowhere do they so dominate the personality of the landscape as in Swaledale. They were used, and some still are, for storing hay and sheltering sheep in winter.

Swaledale is largely unwooded, with trees confined to the winding course of the river, where ash, sycamore and alder offer a colourful guard of honour in autumn. Summer's colours are of meadow buttercup, wood cranesbill and pignut, a flora that peters out as the valley head is approached. Also found is the poignant 'melancholy thistle', its solitary flower once used to cure sadness.

On all sides of the dale head are traces of mining, the valley sides scarred from the explosives used to reveal lead-bearing ore. The remains of workshops, chimneys, inclines and trails are everywhere, the detritus contrasting with the immaculate pastures below. The landscape features speak the language of the mines, as in bands, shake holes, seats, sides, gills and edges. All are slowly sinking back into the moorland ecology.

North from Swaledale head we look across to the high moor of Kisdon. The road south leads onto the gritstone cap and Hawes, the names of the fells evoking the scenery. Here is Buttertubs, Lovely Seat, Shunner Fell and Grimy Gutter Hags. Onwards and upwards we go, to the widest, wildest expanse of upland England, the Pennines.

WHITBY HARBOUR
From West Cliff

I looked across the harbour to the East Cliff, in hope or fear, I don't know which, of seeing Lucy . . . There on our favourite seat, the silver light of the moon struck a half-reclining figure, snowy-white . . . but it seemed to me as though something dark stood behind the seat where the white figure shone, and bent over it. What it was, whether man or beast, I could not tell.

I have no idea if the citizens of Whitby thank or curse Bram Stoker. It was here the Irish writer, holidaying in 1890, found inspiration for his great work of gothic horror, *Dracula*. He had heard of a Russian ship recently wrecked on the coast, and fused this with the legend of the Devil coming ashore in the form of a great black dog. It was in Whitby library that Stoker researched information about the count's Transylvanian roots, and it was in the headland churchyard that he felt the Devil's presence. The novel has cast a shadow over the old port, though it is not above hosting a Bram Stoker film festival with a website dripping blood.

The view of the church high on the cliff overlooking the quayside was a favourite of Victorian artists, notably the painter of moist nocturnal scenes, John Atkinson Grimshaw. But the best prospect is that described by Stoker, from the West Cliff across the mouth of the harbour to the church and abbey on the opposite headland. The cliff itself boasts the statue of Captain Cook, who served his naval apprenticeship in Whitby on coastal colliers. He built all four of his ships here, including the *Endeavour* in which he 'discovered' Australia and New Zealand. Next to his statue is a whalebone arch, recalling days when whaling was the other prime Whitby industry. The view out to sea is of waves crashing against the curving breakwater that protects the harbour entrance.

Bram Stoker's inspiration: Whitby Abbey, church and harbour

Across the harbour is the headland of Whitby Abbey, its windows silhouetted against the sky, magnificent in a low winter sun. Founded in the seventh century and dedicated to St Hilda, the abbey was venue for the synod of 664, at which English Christianity opted for the Roman rather than Ionan rite. Whitby thus ensured that England looked south to the cultures of continental Europe rather than north to Scandinavia, a pivotal moment.

[253]

The ruin is of a later, gothic abbey, and is less a place of horror than of departed grandeur. Round about it are the remains of monastic buildings and of the Restoration mansion of the Cholmley family, built in 1672 in place of the dissolved abbey. Its patio garden has been restored and turned into a visitor centre.

To the left stands the site of Stoker's vision, Whitby's parish church of St Mary. It is set in a graveyard of the blackest and gloomiest headstones, many of men lost at sea. A contrast is offered by the church's jolly Georgian interior, built like a ship's quarter-deck, probably by naval carpenters. The box pews are crammed into every corner, some so exclusive they are reached by private external staircases. Next to the three-decker pulpit is an ear trumpet for a rector's deaf wife. The church is reached from the harbour up a flight of 199 steps.

The port below is spread along the waterfront, its houses described by Stoker as 'all red-roofed and seeming piled up one over the other'. With the fishing fleet below and the marina inland, it presents a charming image of a busy coastal fishing port. Even the quayside lamps are as in Grimshaw's paintings. Long may the fish hold out.

THE NORTH WEST

Borrowdale: From Castle Crag 257

Buttermere 261

Castlerigg: Stone Circle 264

Derwentwater: From Friar's Crag 266

Gummer's How: A Cumbrian panorama 268

Langdale: From the Blea Tarn road 271

Ullswater: From Gowbarrow Hill 274

Wasdale Head: From Wastwater 278

Wrynose and Hardknott: From Cockley Beck 280

Hartside Pass: Towards the Eden valley 282

High Cup Nick: Above Dufton 285

Liverpool: The Three Graces 287

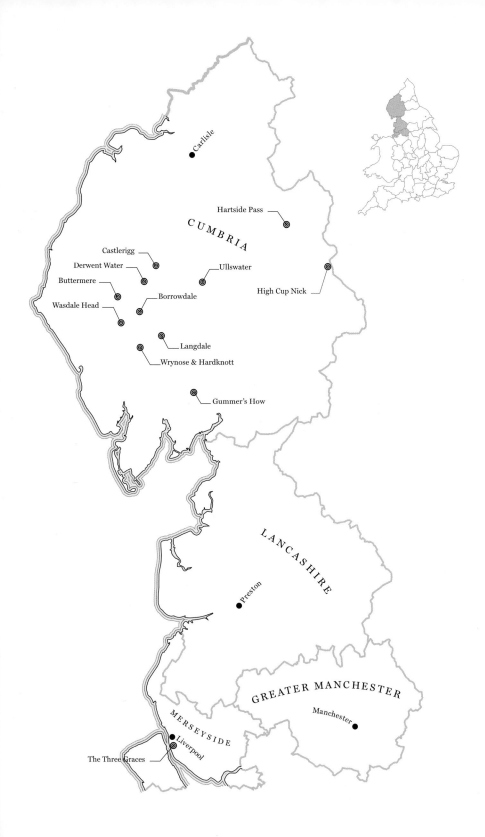

Carlisle

Hartside Pass

CUMBRIA

Castlerigg

Derwent Water   Ullswater

Buttermere   High Cup Nick

Wasdale Head   Borrowdale

Langdale

Wrynose & Hardknott

Gummer's How

LANCASHIRE

Preston

GREATER MANCHESTER

Manchester

MERSEYSIDE

Liverpool

The Three Graces

BORROWDALE

From Castle Crag

The glacial sweep of the Derwent from the heights of Scafell into a secluded basin and out through the 'Jaws of Borrowdale' is the definitive Cumbrian landscape. When bathed in sun, Borrowdale can seem a secret paradise, a Voltairean El Dorado. But it is seldom a place for sunbathing. The dale has the heaviest rainfall in England and is better known for swirling mists, sheeting storms, icy drizzle and just the occasional, exhilarating, shaft of sunlight dashing here and there to illuminate its peaks. It is like a dark gallery in which masterpieces are lit by a random spotlight, one at a time.

Early travellers professed terror at Borrowdale's wild beauty. The poet Thomas Gray, visiting in 1769, found Derwentwater 'lap'd in Elysium', but the Jaws of Borrowdale 'a turbulent chaos . . . rolled in confusion'. He was scared even of the road. The eighteenth-century Newcastle composer Charles Avison recalled the dale as 'Beauty lying in the lap of Horrour'. These were followed by the Welsh traveller Thomas Pennant, who contrasted Skiddaw, rising 'over the country like a generous lord', while the fells of Borrowdale 'frown on it like a hardened tyrant'.

Towering over the exit from the dale towards Derwentwater stands Castle Crag, a block of igneous rock hurled from the Scafell eruption 400 million years ago. It and its fellow crag King's How stand over 'the Jaws' like two sentries set to keep outsiders at bay. Somehow they survived the scouring of later glaciers and became the

Overleaf: Wainright's 'finest square mile': Borrowdale towards Scafell

focus of almost every painting of this part of the Lakes. Castle Crag stretches my half-hour accessibility rule, but is not a hard climb. The path to King's How is shorter and has the famous Bowder Stone at its foot, but the view is less impressive.

The view from the crag looking north towards Derwentwater shows the river prettily snaking its way down to the village of Grange. To the left rises the Catbells ridge, while Keswick at the far end of the lake is dominated by the massive presence of Skiddaw. On a clear winter day, with blue sky and snow on the distant hills, we might be in Switzerland.

The opposite view, into the dale itself, was dubbed by Cumbria's topographer laureate, Alfred Wainwright, 'the finest square mile in the Lake District'. It is enclosed by the rear slopes of the Scafell horseshoe, with the back of Great Gable dominant. These are the flanks of England's Vesuvius, the volcanic hub of the Lake District round which the dales radiate as spokes. Running up its side is the combe of Stonethwaite with the Eagle Crag outcrop. Golden eagles once occupied the valley but were wiped out by farmers for stealing lambs. Their successors are the less rapacious falcons and buzzards.

In the centre of the basin lies the village of Rosthwaite, attended by a glacial moraine. Green fields spread round it like water lapping the edges of the fells. To its right the lip of the basin becomes Honister Pass, with the old mining hamlets of Seatoller and Seathwaite rising above it. This is officially England's wettest spot, with an annual average of 124 inches of rain. Its screes host small sessile oaks and are rich in moisture-loving lichens and mosses.

Above Seathwaite stand three of the 'four fraternal' yews, some 1,500 years old, celebrated by Wordsworth as

Joined in one solemn and capacious grove,
Huge trunks! And each particular trunk a growth
Of intertwisted fibres serpentine.

They serve as sentinels of the place, at the drenching, throbbing, thrilling heart of the Lake District, source of its volcanic birth and champion among its views.

BUTTERMERE

As the pilgrimage from Windermere to Keswick became ever more popular, adventurous souls penetrated beyond. They travelled the track into Borrowdale and then north over Honister to Buttermere. Here was their hearts' content, a wild pass, a mountain range and a wild lake 'almost savage, the waters . . . deep and sullen', wrote Coleridge.

Nor was that all. Here, in innocent isolation, lived a maiden of beauty beyond compare. In 1792 an early Lakeland eulogist, Joseph Budworth, circulated an account of a visit to the valley, in the course of which he encountered the daughter of Buttermere's innkeeper, a girl named Mary Robinson. He was rapturous: 'Her hair was thick and long . . . her face was a fine oval with full eyes and lips as red as vermilion; her cheeks had more of the lily than the rose.' Few guide-books are written thus today.

A stampede ensued. Buttermere was under siege as Romantics starved of romance descended on the inn, hoping for a glimpse of the poor girl, for a chance to sketch her, or for more. She had never left the valley and was eventually carried off by a fraudster and big-amist, who ended up hanged for his pains. The story ended hap-pily when she remarried a local farmer and featured in a novel by Melvyn Bragg, *The Maid of Buttermere*.

The lake is said to take its name from an eleventh-century Viking, Jarl Buthar, who sustained resistance to the Normans from this Lakeland fastness. Buttermere's bluebells are particularly fine because, it is said, they grow from land soaked in the blood of Normans.

The ideal view of the lake is from above the church on the Newlands road, a short walk to the right onto Buttermere Moss. From here we look down to the water and across to the peak of Fleetwith Pike and the Honister Pass. Over it stands the mass of Haystacks, called by Wainwright 'a shaggy terrier amongst hounds'. Behind Haystacks lies the secret valley of Ennerdale, accessible only on foot and now being 're-wilded' with indigenous species.

The row of Scots pines at the left end of the lake, known as the Sentinels, must be the most photographed trees in England. Each stands separate along the shoreline, with a personality of its own. The favourite picture is of the trees reflected in the still water of the lake and thus capable of being read upside down, cause of confusion to jigsaw puzzlers down the ages.

To the right is the village of Buttermere and Mary Robinson's inn, where the lake ends in a flat strip of meadow before resuming as Crummock Water. Buttermere is sparsely visited and far from the crowds of Keswick and Windermere. It looks rather to the north, to Cockermouth and the coast. Even the trees seem to bend in that direction.

This was the lake of which Wainwright was patron saint. A Blackburn man who became borough treasurer of Kendal, he devoted his leisure to eulogising the 214 fells of the Lake District, going on to describe his marathon 'coast-to-coast' walk. He died in 1991, his ashes scattered by his wife over a tarn on Haystacks, 'where the water gently laps the gravelly shore and the heather blooms and Pillar and Gable keep unfailing watch'. Wainwright wrote that 'if you, dear reader, should get a bit of grit in your boot as you are crossing Haystacks in the years to come, please treat it with respect. It might be me.'

Lakeland in repose: Buttermere's 'sentinels' beneath Haystacks

CASTLERIGG
Stone Circle

As sacred landscapes go, this must be closest to the gods. Far above Derwentwater in the shadow of Skiddaw, Castlerigg circle dates from the end of the Stone Age, some 3,000 years BC. It is impossible to stand in this place and think its builders blind to its beauty. They must have sensed the genius of the place, though how they read it or expressed it in these stones is a mystery.

The circle is reached by a side road near the A5271/A591 junction, east of Keswick. Thirty-three of an estimated forty-two original stones remain upright, all roughly five feet in height and some weighing over ten tons. The circle has no defensive features and its

purpose must have been astronomical or religious. There is a gap, apparently for an entrance to the circle, and a square grouping of stones, as for a sanctuary, inside the rim. This is a spot of strange intensity, where the whole Lake District seems to gather in one composite view, to be honoured in a ring of stone.

The views from the circle are sweeping in all directions. To the west is the expanse of Derwentwater with Catbells rising above it. The jumble of peaks, especially in silhouette, is like the saw-tooth back of a dragon asleep on the bank of the water. To the north-west beyond Keswick lies lovely Bassenthwaite, unfairly neglected among lakes. The chief spectacle from Castlerigg is north, where the twin humps of Skiddaw and Blencathra gaze down over the pass to Ullswater.

Castlerigg circle with Catbells in the distance

Castlerigg's mysteries have fascinated not just archaeologists but also poets. Keats referred to the scene in *Hyperion*:

> Scarce images of life, one here one there,
> Lay vast and edgeways; like a dismal cirque,
> Of Druid stones, upon a forlorn moor.

Coleridge was more uplifted. To him 'the mountains stand one behind the other, in orderly array, as if . . . attentive to the assembly of white-vested wizards'. I prefer lines written by the orienteer Martin Bagness in 2009, inscribed on an adjacent meadow wall. The poet calls out to the silent stones,

> 'Who were you?'
> And the echoes in the stones
> Just sigh, as if too wise to break the spell
> With answers.

This place is at its finest at dusk as the fells darken and the shadows of the stones lengthen on the grass, turning Castlerigg into a true Cumbrian Stonehenge.

DERWENTWATER

From Friar's Crag

All views of Derwentwater are rewarding: from Castle Crag and Castlerigg, from much-pictured Ashness Bridge on the Watendlath road and from the adjacent Surprise View overlooking the water. But the view from Friar's Crag on the Keswick shore is most justly celebrated of all.

This was where the five-year-old John Ruskin, brought by his nurse, experienced his first precocious memory: the view through a gnarled tree root which overwhelmed him with 'intense joy mingled with awe'. He became the Lakes' champion, building himself a house at Brantwood on Coniston, with a panorama of the waters visible from his study. After Ruskin's death, Canon Hardwicke Rawnsley, co-founder of the National Trust, set a memorial to him on this spot. Nearby is one to Rawnsley himself.

Friar's Crag is a modest promontory, a rock by the water half a mile out of Keswick beyond the landing stage. A wooded glade gives

'A place too beautiful to live': Derwentwater from Keswick

onto a natural belvedere adorned with pine trees. All Derwentwater can be seen from this point. It is classic Gilpin 'picturesque', of pine branches framing an expanse of still water, dotted with islands and with a mountain backdrop.

The many islands in Derwentwater are the result of its shallowness, from silt washed down from Borrowdale. St Herbert's Island was the site of the hermitage of St Herbert, who brought Christianity to these parts in 685 and was mentioned by Bede. His shrine became a place of pilgrimage, hence Friar's Crag. From this spot, in her illustration to *The Tale of Squirrel Nutkin*, Beatrix Potter had the squirrels paddling out to the island on rafts.

The one island still inhabited is Derwent Isle, once owned by Fountains Abbey and later acquired by an eccentric Regency entrepreneur, Joseph Pocklington. He used it as the focus of regattas and fake sea battles on the lake. 'Fleets' darted in and out of the bays to assault the fiercely defended island fort.

The view's calm perfection moved Coleridge to praise 'the majesty of its beauties and . . . the beauty of its majesty'. Ruskin declared Keswick 'a place too beautiful to live in'. Arthur Ransome's *Swallows and Amazons* was located in an amalgam of Derwentwater, Coniston and Windermere. He used Friar's Crag for his peak of Darien, from which the young adventurers kept lookout for pirates. It even led me as a boy briefly to crave a life at sea.

GUMMER'S HOW
A Cumbrian panorama

Short of climbing Scafell, the best overall view of the Lake District is to be found a short walk from the road above Fell Foot at the southern tip of Windermere. Gummer's How may be just 320m high, but it offers a panorama from Scafell and Helvellyn to the Pennine ridge, the Lancashire plain and Morecambe Bay. Windermere stretches itself lazily below.

Here the ancient kings of Cumbria might have viewed their domains, protected from Saxon raids by the Pennines and on guard against the Vikings from the sea. Wainwright subjects Gummer's How to a dismissive put-down, describing it as 'a fellwalk in miniature, a little beauty, with heather, a few rocks to scramble on, soft couches for repose, a classic view . . . just like the real thing'. It is none the worse for that.

From here we can read Cumbria's volcanic origins. Far to the west are the heights of Scafell where, 400 million years ago, an eruption blasted through the sedimentary rocks and sent granites, basalts and dolerites hurtling upwards and outwards. These created mountains reputedly as high as any in Europe. Millions of years later the ice came, crushing, scouring and eroding peaks and ridges to their present appearance. The glaciers scooped rock out of the valleys, leaving some blocked by moraines and others with dips that were later to form lakes.

Gummer's How itself is a lump of volcanic rock, hurled across Coniston and Windermere as if Scafell wanted to offer visitors a grandstand view of itself. Today it is hard to imagine the tempestuous extremes that might then have filled that view. Geology privileges us with a time-lapse picture of the Earth as it carved its way into the present.

The view starts to the east with the mighty Pennine ridge, backbone of England, stretching the length of the horizon. It rises to the north across the Eden valley and continues with the naked humps of Howgill and Orton Fells, the 'forgotten fells' east of the Lakes. To the south is the old royal hunting ground of the Forest of Bowland, with below it the valleys of the Kent and the Lune feeding into Morecambe Bay. Here the low plain and wide, fish-rich sands must have seemed enviably fertile to the hardy uplanders of the fells. On a clear day Blackpool Tower is visible.

Guarded by enthusiasm: Windermere to the Langdales

West lies the pendulous bosom of the Lake District drooping into the Irish Sea, the view sweeping from the coast at Ulverston north across the two great horseshoes of Scafell and the Langdales and round to Helvellyn. The peaks are idiosyncratic, some rounded, some conical, some craggy, some smooth, as if each were sculpted to order by nature. These are England's only true mountains, lonely and compelling. The tree line is mostly respected, its greenery foaming through the dales and leaving the hills bare above.

At our feet lies England's largest lake, the old lady of Windermere. It wends its crooked way north from Newby Bridge, swerving left at Belle Isle to reach Ambleside. Its shores are lined with Victorian and Edwardian mansions of the Lancashire rich, built before conservation put a halt to such development. Immediately below is

Storrs Hall, where Wordsworth and Southey in 1825 scandalised their radical friends by attending as 'bards of the lakes' a regatta staged by the Merseyside slave-trader John Bolton.

Today Windermere is dotted with peacefully drifting yachts, speedboats having been banned to protect its peace. But the summer crowds are so intense that it may yet become England's first 'rationed landscape', succumbing to some form of park-and-ride or park-and-sail. This popularity is often said to have 'spoiled' the Lakes. I believe it has done the opposite, by ensuring their preservation. They are as pristine as they are because of their champions, from Wordsworth and Coleridge to Ruskin and Potter and crowds of Victorian trippers, fell-walkers and climbers. It was their combined enthusiasm that brought the protection of National Trust ownership and national park status. This is everyone's England, to be protected in everyone's name.

LANGDALE
From the Blea Tarn road

The Great Langdale horseshoe, while less dramatic than Scafell, is visually more appealing. While the Scafell peaks are hard men of business, gathered in private conclave in the clouds, the Langdale peaks are an old boys' reunion. They stand on their ridge like a *Dad's Army* photograph, and with names to match: Blake Rigg, Sergeant Man, Pike o' Blisco, Harrison Stickle and Pavey Ark. The horseshoe offers an entertaining circuit of walks and scrambles, with easy drops to the valley below.

The first glimpse of Langdale for most visitors is from the upper end of Windermere, the first hint of real fell and a promise of heights to come. The dale rises from Ambleside, splitting into Little and

Great Langdale, the one soft and gentle, the other a grand glacial scoop, its excitement growing as we reach the dale head. The best view is from half-height, at the cattle grid on the narrow road over to Blea Tarn. Here we look down onto Great Langdale head, with its twin valleys of Oxendale and Mickleden.

These fells were places of prehistoric industry. Their stone was renowned for its ease of knapping, and for its smooth surface when polished, making it ideal for stone axes. Ancient quarries have been found high on the Pikes, as well as on Scafell and Glaramara. Their axes have been traced to sites across England. Langdale was the Sheffield of the Stone Age.

In the valley's bottom are fields of the smoothest green, rolled out along its length and curled up against the abrupt slope of the fells. They are divided by dry-stone walls of baffling geometry, reflecting lost water courses, pathways, parish boundaries or perhaps domestic disputes long out of mind. They dart this way and that like those of Yorkshire's Swaledale.

The walls are of Cumbria's most characteristic building material. Beck cobbles are hard stones smoothed by water abrasion to rounded shapes, exported as 'cobble stones' for city streets. Here they are piled on each other, mostly undressed but periodically strengthened by larger stones known as 'throughs'. The tops are sometimes laid vertically to produce a serrated edge, harder for sheep to climb.

The view into Langdale illustrates the conflicting demands of centuries of human occupation. For decades, Lakeland farmers have banked the rivers to prevent their fields from flooding after heavy rain. Water thus moves fast downstream and floods the lower land. In 2009 the town of Cockermouth was devastated as a result. Policy is now to retain water upstream by allowing water meadows to flood, strongly resisted by farmers. Two precarious livelihoods are thus in conflict. I have to side with the 're-wilders'. Langdale is a

'O let them be left': the peaks of Langdale head

superb glacial amphitheatre in which it is hard not to see mankind as an intrusion. Here Gerard Manley Hopkins applies:

What would the world be, once bereft
Of wet and of wildness? Let them be left,
O let them be left, wildness and wet;
Long live the weeds and the wilderness yet.

ULLSWATER
From Gowbarrow Hill

Ullswater is the aristocrat of the Lakes. It is second in size only to Windermere, aloof, photogenic and at ease with popularity. In shape it meanders from north to south, with three 'reaches' in an attenuated letter Z. To the north it is an ordinary English lake, but to the south it buries itself in the flanks of Helvellyn and takes on a more montane character.

Wainwright declared the waterside path from Sandwick to Patterdale as giving 'the finest view in the lakes' – though like Betjeman on churches, he was generous in his superlatives. Wordsworth's favourite view was from the water. In *The Prelude* he recorded stealing a boat at night and rowing out to see Helvellyn: 'Growing in stature, the grim shape/ Towered up between me and the stars.'

I prefer a view high enough to see the surrounding mountains but not too high as to diminish the lake. The Memorial Seat is located halfway up Gowbarrow Hill which, in turn, is mid-way along the lake. The seat is reached along the path to Yew Crag from Aira Force waterfall. An anonymous inscription simply records, 'A Thank Offering, Oct 1905'. I do not advise climbing an alleged path through Gowbarrow woods from the shore road. Wet boulders coated in moss make a lethal climbing surface. I finished with twisted ankles, bruised shins, torn clothes and a broken stick.

The view embraces almost all of Ullswater, with the viewer at the apex of the curve of the lake with Place Fell opposite. Below to the right, meadow-clad Aira Point juts into the water and next to it is Glencoyne Park, where Wordsworth was staying when he composed 'Daffodils'. Many a student hour has been spent seeking the definitive spot where he 'wandered lonely as a cloud'. Aira Point fits the bill, with the requisite

> host of golden daffodils;
> Beside the lake, beneath the trees . . .
>
> They stretched in never-ending line
> Along the margin of the bay.

Beyond Aira Point lies Glenridding, bustling gateway to Helvellyn towering above it. From Gowbarrow the peaks can here be confusing, especially as they are often dodging in and out of cloud. Their names include St Sunday Crag, Dollywaggon Pike and Nethermost Pike. Helvellyn may lack the harsh virility of Scafell Pike, but it is my finest walk in the Lake District. The traverse of Striding Edge is truly Alpine and the long summit promenade is a superb vantage point, even if on a bank holiday I once had to queue to proceed.

The higher we climb behind Memorial Seat the more extensive the spectacle, eventually including Skiddaw and Blencathra. The view north is along the lower reaches of Ullswater towards Pooley Bridge, the lake crowded with sails. Beyond, the land stretches towards Penrith where the Lake District comes to an abrupt end. Driving this road, I am left recalling with Wordsworth 'what wealth the show to me had brought'.

Overleaf: Where Wordsworth wandered lonely as a cloud:
Ullswater towards Helvellyn

WASDALE HEAD

From Wastwater

This is Lake District with machismo. It is country of towering peaks, impassable screes, climbing boots, anoraks and real ale. The horseshoe of Great Gable and Scafell Pike forms the highest range in England. At Wasdale Head, cars must park and only intrepid walkers continue. Whenever I have visited the climbers' pub, the Wasdale Head Inn, it has been crammed with damp and huddled masses, crouching over steaming bowls of soup, usually cursing the weather. Normal mortals seem out of place here, bystanders at a stern, masochistic ritual.

The road inland from the coast is a fitting prelude. Above Ravenglass it begins gently agricultural, climbing through villages and meadows, changing from lowland to upland only beyond Nether Wasdale. Suddenly Wastwater comes into view and we are in a different world. This cold, dramatic sheet of water is 80m deep, the deepest lake in England, dominated on its right-hand side by a 300m scree. As we go on towards Wasdale Head, the tempo rises until the full grandeur of the Scafell horseshoe unfolds.

The most celebrated view of Wasdale is from the lake shore, with rocks and bracken reflected in the water and Scafell in the distance. A more imposing prospect, but without the lake, is further up at Wasdale Head, with the peaks dramatically grouped against the sky. I would take Wasdale Head on a clear day and Wastwater on a cloudier one, when we must find solace in water for want of a mountain.

Wasdale Head is a settlement almost wholly devoted to hill walking and climbing. The dale claims England's deepest lake, highest mountain and smallest church, St Olaf's sitting alone in a field, its recent dedication reflecting the area's Norse past. (I rank it only the third smallest church.) The graveyard holds memorials to climbers who died on the heights above, many with the favoured inscription, 'I will lift up mine eyes unto the hills.'

In summer the surrounding fields leading up to the horseshoe can look like the start of the London marathon. Yet Wainwright warns that 'the ascent of Scafell Pike is the toughest proposition the "collector of summits" is called upon to attempt . . . There is no bigger trap for the unwary and uninformed walker than this.'

His forerunner Wordsworth agreed. He wrote in his guide that these summits were not for the timid. His sister Dorothy climbed Scafell in 1818 and reported graphically that they were totally bare, covered in rocks 'like skeletons, or bones of the earth not needed at the Creation . . . covered with never-dying lichens, which the clouds and dews . . . adorn with colours of vivid and exquisite beauty.'

The circuit of the horseshoe begins with the rounded breast of Yewbarrow to the left and runs clockwise to Great Gable and the

Lakeland machismo: Scafell horseshoe from Wastwater

rugged crags of Lingmell, Scafell Pike and Scafell. They may seem friendly in the dusty brown of a dry summer day, but rain turns them a menacing black. They acquire an added presence when wreathed in cloud, as the eye can imagine the peaks towering ever upwards. Scafell is most magnificent in snow, its verticality giving it a peculiar splendour. The horseshoe includes the classic rock ascents of Napes Needle, Pillar Rock and Scafell Crag.

The Wasdale valley floor is smooth, as if the glacier had only just departed, leaving behind a scattered litter of eroded boulders. These yield the rounded stones seen in most Lake District walls, stacked and mortared as their dimensions permit. The walls tend to be thick and coated in vegetation, ecosystems all of their own. Enclosed over the centuries, they are a desperate attempt to wrest a living from this harsh terrain. The hills are the preserve of Herdwick sheep, a breed possibly of Viking origin that knows its territory and can find its way home unaided by man or dog. When a Cumbrian farm is sold, its sheep remain behind.

WRYNOSE AND HARDKNOTT
From Cockley Beck

A single tarmac track rises west from Coniston through Little Langdale and climbs busily alongside Widdy Gill stream with Bow Fell to its right. The route surmounts Wrynose and then swoops down the open fellside to the head of Duddendale, reached at the hamlet of Cockley Beck. It then climbs again, precipitously, over Hardknott pass into Eskdale. The traverse is some fifteen miles of uninhabited moorland. So bare is the terrain that the road can be seen ahead for almost all its length, wrestling with the contours. It is mocked for much of the way by a parallel Roman road, now a track

Duddendale Head looking towards Hardknott pass

that is straight as an arrow. Over the final summit into Eskdale is Hardknott Roman fort, the loneliest site imaginable for such a base. The posting must have been the Roman equivalent of a Siberian power station.

These passes are not for the faint-hearted or the underpowered. At one-in-three, Hardknott vies with Rosedale in Yorkshire as the steepest public road in England. There are few passing places other than the open fell. On my last visit the way was blocked by a motor-cyclist who said he had fallen off his machine 'backwards'.

The best place to halt is above Cockley Beck, in the depression between the two passes. Here the valley of the Dudden can be seen running twenty-five miles south to Morecambe Bay. A luxuriant flow of green fields sweep down between the yellows, browns and mauves of the flanking slopes, a vivid Lakeland juxtaposition of fell and dale. The upland culminates in bare ridges, soft grey in summer, forbidding black in winter unless utterly transformed by snow.

The valley, sometimes called Dunnerdale, is among the loveliest of dales. The line of the river meanders into the distance through tree-clad banks. Falcons circle overhead and red squirrels nest in the woods. The chief town has the Norse name of Ulpha. Wordsworth walked this valley for years and composed his thirty-four 'Duddon' sonnets in its honour. They serve as his Lakeland epitaph:

All hail, ye mountains! hail, thou morning light!
Better to breathe at large on this clear height
Than toil in needless sleep from dream to dream . . .
For Duddon, long-loved Duddon, is my theme . . .

Child of the clouds! Remote from every taint
Of sordid industry . . .

Still glides the stream, and shall for ever glide.

HARTSIDE PASS
Towards the Eden valley

Of all the crossings of England's limestone spine, Hartside is the wildest. Whether approached from east or west, there is no doubting we are on a mighty divide. At 590m Hartside is the highest, most northerly and certainly the most deserted of the trans-Pennine routes. The watershed runs on one side to the River Eden and the Solway Firth, on the other to the South Tyne and the North Sea. This is raw country. Farms are non-existent and the occasional gamekeeper's cottage is painfully alone. One was recently declared England's remotest habitation.

The Lake District from the Pennine ridge

The road uphill from the Eden valley is precipitous, and its ever widening views are dramatic. Even more dramatic is the approach from the east across open moor from the attractive Pennine settlement of Alston. Alone in its wooded glade and often cut off in winter, the town's streets seem impossibly steep, but it clings to its narrow gauge railway, the highest in England.

The road out of town towards Hartside passes through drenched heather upland. It crosses the bleakest stretch of the Pennine Way, with the summit of Cross Fell, highest point in the Pennines at 893m, to the south. We then turn a corner and suddenly what looks to be the whole of north-west England and much of Scotland come into view. The point is marked by Hartside Top café, which might be a beleaguered refuge hut in the Antarctic.

This spot is buffeted by England's only named wind, the Helm. It races in from the North Sea until it meets Cross Fell, where it sweeps down the escarpment into the valley, generating the meteorological phenomenon of a föhn, or lee wave. In 1968 this achieved the highest wind speed recorded in England, 134 mph, destroying barns and crippling cows. The shriek of its passage has inspired many tall stories, and led to the fell being dubbed the 'fiend's fell'. Even the name 'cross' is said to refer to its temper. In my case it briskly removed a sheaf of notes from my frozen hand and sent them flying across the moor.

The view west to the Lake District is over one of the loveliest river valleys in England. Eden's towns and villages lie compact within their ancient boundaries, surrounded by woods and meadows. Throughout history this valley was the safe route to Scotland, contrasting with the bandit-ridden highways of Northumbria to the east.

The Hartside view is best seen when there is snow on the Lake District summits, allowing Skiddaw and Helvellyn to stand clear on the western horizon. To the north are the Solway Firth and the hills of Dumfries and Galloway. At our feet, the road snakes downhill across what seems like tundra, marked only by snow posts. There are reputedly fifty-seven bends on the way to the bottom, where lies the village of Langwathby. Its station was used as the set for the wartime film *Brief Encounter*, a fame now recalled in an eccentrically themed café and a respite from the wind.

HIGH CUP NICK
Above Dufton

I have walked the Pennine Way only in sections. Laid out as a national trail in 1965, it can be a perverse test of endurance. It takes bends where a straight line would do, it goes up and down where level country is to hand and it has an affection for bogs. Yet the path's 268 miles, from the Scottish border to Edale in Derbyshire, remain England's greatest walking challenge.

After braving the winds of Cross Fell, the way drops down into the Eden valley at the picture village of Dufton. Whether or not this is out of compassion for exhausted walkers I do not know, but the route does not stay down long. Soon we are back on the escarpment at Peeping Tom Hill. Even on a warmish November day, I encountered snow and icy wind on the way up, worsening dramatically above the 500m contour.

Round a bend just half an hour out of Dufton the track reaches the edge of the canyon of High Cup Nick. The Nick (as the name implies) cuts through an outcrop of the Whin Sill, the slab of volcanic dolerite and basalt rock thrust upwards through the limestone. The sill crosses northern England to Hadrian's Wall and Lindisfarne. Here it forms the rim of a 'cup' or gorge running dead straight down a U-shaped ravine and out into the Eden valley.

The edge of the sill juts out as a serrated ledge above and below which the softer rock has eroded. In places the Sill sticks up as stacks. The valley floor is littered with boulders while, on some of the sides, lines of lichen on the scree look like primeval hieroglyphs. The ravine is botanically barren, apart from scattered grasses, algae and lichen clinging to the rocks, though I am told tiny sub-Alpine flowers cover the ground in spring.

At its head, High Cup Nick leads onto the high fell. The stretch north over Great Dun and Little Dun to Cross Fell is the widest expanse of uninterrupted moorland in England. Across it the Helm wind blows almost incessantly, driving before it England's most penetrating rain, which is perhaps why I have found this one of the least known views in my collection. No one complains about 'overcrowded England' who has spent time on this stretch of the Pennine Way.

The ravine looking into the Eden Valley

LIVERPOOL
The Three Graces

England has few waterfront cities. Most of its ports were tucked safely up estuaries and rivers and many of these, such as Bristol, Hull and Chatham, are hardly ports any more. Liverpool was different. It was a late developer, growing on the back of the Atlantic trade in the eighteenth and early nineteenth centuries, mostly for slaves, cotton and coal. Seven miles of docks extended along the river, second only to London in size and forming one of the most gracious – and spacious – commercial harbours in the world.

Georgian warehouses rose along the waterfront in cliffs of red sandstone and brick. Behind them were lanes and courtyards crammed with ships' chandlers and suppliers. Uphill rose the palaces of trade and finance. Though bombed in the Second World War, Liverpool entered the second half of the twentieth century poised to be a jewel of Europe's industrial heritage.

In the mid-1960s Liverpool's municipal elders, facing the decline of the shipping industry, hired the communist architect Graeme Shankland to design them a socialist utopia on the Mersey, to be financed they knew not how. The plan involved demolishing most of the city centre and creating a landscape of motorways and tower blocks. While other cities in western Europe were realising the economic potential of regenerating historic centres, Liverpool sent in the bulldozers.

Some eighty per cent of the old docks area and hundreds of Georgian and Victorian buildings were wiped out. Many sites were to remain empty for decades. Much of central Liverpool became a ghost town, with a population reduced by the 1980s to just a few hundred thousand. Shankland later recanted, declaring that 'a country without a past has the emptiness of a barren continent, and a city without old buildings is like a man without a memory'.

By then the damage was done. In 2004 Liverpool was declared by UNESCO a World Heritage Site, but by 2012 new towers and slabs crowding the demolished north waterfront led to its reclassification as 'world heritage at risk', the only one in the developed world.

Yet Liverpool is still an exciting place. Nothing in travel equals the approach to a city by water. A distant ridge becomes a line of buildings, which separate and acquire volume as they come closer. With the heave of a ship's deck underfoot, they take on an added solidity.

Of nowhere is this more so than of Liverpool's Pier Head, where stand the palaces of commerce known as the Three Graces. The classic view is from Birkenhead on the far side of the Mersey, but better still is from the ferry, immortalised in Gerry Marsden's ballad, 'Ferry, Cross the Mersey' (cross here being a verb). In my youth the ferry, the Beatles and Marsden's Pacemakers, among others, gave

Liverpool's Edwardian prime: Three Graces and two cathedrals

Liverpool an extraordinary status as a centre of cultural invention. The ballad portrayed it as a city paved with gold, though it was still gripped by decades of depression.

The Three Graces were an evocation of what seemed a lost glory. Pevsner wrote that they 'represented the great Edwardian imperial optimism, and might as well stand in Durban or Hong Kong as in Liverpool'. Built before the First World War on the site of former docks, their sites were irregular and their designs both contrasting and imposing.

The Royal Liver insurance building (left of centre) was begun in 1908, faintly oriental and with cupolas and statues of golden (mythical) liver birds on top. Next to it (on the right) is the more restrained classicism of the Cunard building of 1914, with the ventilator tower of the Mersey tunnel behind it. Third is the Mersey Docks and Harbour Board headquarters, opened in 1903 in a splash of Wren revivalism, looking like a city hall (which in a sense it was). Each 'grace' sings a different tune, yet each is in harmony with the others.

All round them is cacophony. To the left is the development that so distressed UNESCO, looking like any modern downtown. In front of the Pier Head lies the white tent-roof of a new landing stage, destination for the hoped-for tourist boats. Then comes the white horizontal gash of the Liverpool Museum (far right), loitering gormlessly near the dignified ladies that tower over it.

To the right of the Three Graces is spread what survives of old Liverpool, notably the group of the Canning and Albert docks. Completed in 1846, they were the first iron-framed commercial structures in England and considered fire-proof. For half a century their efficiency and security made them a centre of high-value trade. Closed after the war, they became ruinous and vulnerable, their leisure potential realised only in the 1980s. Today they contain flats and the Tate Gallery's northern outpost, clean, red-faced and handsome.

Behind rises Georgian Liverpool, punctuated by the dramatic later towers of the Anglican and Catholic cathedrals. The first (right), by Giles Gilbert Scott, is one of the largest churches in England. Begun in 1904 at the same time as the Pier Head, it marks the final flowering of English gothic revival, as well as of Liverpool's ability to pay for it. The Catholic cathedral (left) was completed in 1962. This spiky lantern on the hilltop is the work of Sir Frederick Gibberd, superseding Lutyens' neoclassical design, which had been rejected as too costly.

I remember visiting Liverpool with a group of economists in the 1980s. We returned with the conclusion that a one-industry city that had lost its industry had no future and should be left to gently decline. Recent history shows how wrong experts can be. The view of Liverpool waterfront today, scarred as it may be, is not one of defeat.

THE NORTH EAST

Coquetdale: From Lordenshaws   293
The Cheviots: College Valley   296
Durham: From Framwellgate Bridge   298
Hadrian's Wall: From Steel Rigg   300
Lindisfarne: Towards Bamburgh   304
Newcastle: Grey Street   308

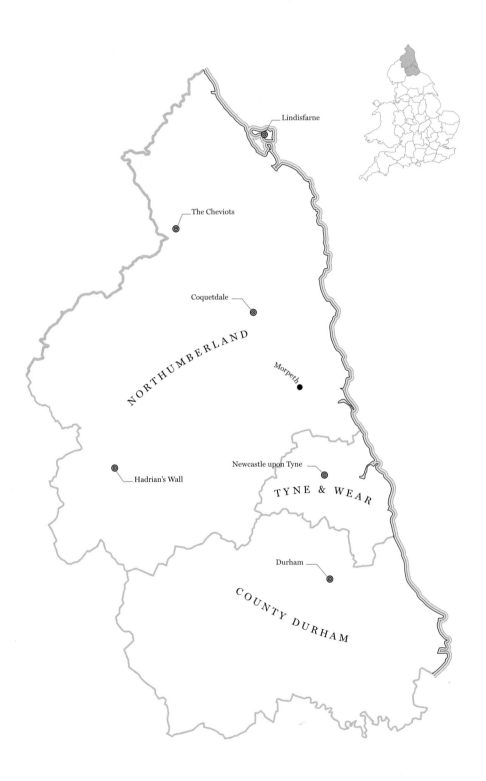

Lindisfarne

The Cheviots

Coquetdale

NORTHUMBERLAND

Morpeth

Newcastle upon Tyne

Hadrian's Wall

TYNE & WEAR

Durham

COUNTY DURHAM

COQUETDALE

From Lordenshaws

The Coquet rises in the Cheviots as they roll along the Scottish border. Descending, it encounters the Simonside Hills, forcing it to spread over a broad valley running south-east towards the sea at Warkworth. To the west lies the plateau of the Kielder Forest and Otterburn, part of the northern empire of the defence ministry. This Northumberland ranks among the least known beauties of England.

Tosson, the highest Simonside summit, offers a fine panorama of lower Coquetdale, but my favourite view is from the Lordenshaws outcrop, two miles south of Rothbury. Early one winter morning I scrambled the quarter mile from the road, cursing an unexpected blizzard that blew in on an east wind and suddenly obscured the Cheviots. It was redeemed only by a brilliant early sun over the coast at Blyth, silhouetting its chimneys and wind turbines against a red and yellow sky. The full drama then unfolded. Fronts poured in from the coast, depositing sheets of rain on Rothbury. Then a curtain to the north drew back and the full glory of the Cheviots came into view, bathed in sun.

Star of the show was the Coquet river, its water reflecting the light like a writhing snake. In quieter weather it offers a spacious meander, its shores abused by gravel extraction but its flanking trees and heather a palette of yellows and mauves in autumn. On the far bank the land rises to the heights of Alnwick, where stands the castle of the dukes of Northumberland. Beyond Rothbury, 'capital of Coquetdale', runs the steep ravine above which the Edwardian

arms magnate Lord Armstrong built his fantasy Tudor mansion, Cragside.

The Simonside Hills were celebrated as home of the Duergar, a tribe of Norse dwarves. Like will o' the wisps, they would come down from the heights at dark with torches and lead travellers astray into the upland bogs they inhabited. Lordenshaws is also home to the most extensive prehistoric archaeological remains in the north, as yet unexcavated. They form a wide enclosure of ditches and ramparts, covered with moorland grass, heather and bracken. Stone huts survive, as do plentiful lookout posts, cairns and standing stones. The settlement is believed to have been re-occupied by Romano-Britons after the Romans withdrew and their forts were abandoned.

Most remarkable are the cup-and-ring marks carved into the rock. They are Stone Age, long before the fort, and take the form of a hollowed indentation, surrounded by concentric rings. These marks baffle archaeologists, who offer the standard explanation that they must be religious. I like to see them as somewhere to steady a thermos flask in a Northumberland gale.

The view from Lordenshaws embraces the whole of the northern extremity of England, the triangle bounded by the North Sea, the Scottish border and Hadrian's Wall to the south. Behind us lies Upper Coquetdale and the Cheviots, a country little populated and mostly devoted to hill farming and forestry. To the west the rolling hills disappear into Scotland to become Dumfries and Galloway. To the east is the coastal plain, much of it still owned by the dukes of Northumberland.

When in 2004 the people of these parts were invited to join a north-east regional assembly, they voted firmly against. I feel here, as in Cornwall, that I am in an England apart from England, a place hankering after the ancient kings of Northumbria.

Stone Age mystery: cup-and-ring marks, with Coquetdale in the distance

THE CHEVIOTS
College Valley

The eastern slopes of the Cheviots to the north of Coquetdale are wild and mostly barren. They lack the scenic drama of the Pennines or the Lakes, their genial beauty dependent on the weather, on light varying with season, drawing colour and character from the changing vegetation.

This region was heavily populated in warmer, prehistoric times. Every hillside is corrugated with settlement mounds, their archaeology displaying signs of agriculture and mining. This was border country between the North Britons and the incoming Anglo-Saxons and as such was fiercely contested, with few of the agreements reached along similar boundaries in Wales and the south-west. A

College Valley from above Mounthooly hostel

culture of conflict gave rise to the 'border reivers', families of upland horsemen whose feuds kept the land in anarchy into the sixteenth century. Their vendettas and thievery were tolerated by both Scottish and English authorities as a cordon sanitaire between the two countries. Not until the Stuart settlement were they suppressed.

College Valley is the heart of reiver country, a long enclosed ravine running south from Kirknewton to its end high under the peak of Cheviot (815m). The area was acquired as part of the Hethpool estate by a shipping tycoon, Sir Arthur Sutherland, at the turn of the twentieth century. He imaginatively rebuilt the big house and cottages round the entry to the valley in the then fashionable Arts and Crafts style. The estate was bought by the Sir James Knott Trust in 1953, essentially for its conservation.

This trust is now replanting the slopes with native broadleaf trees and conserving the heather for grouse, the industry on which, with tourism, the local economy depends. It claims extensive sightings of red squirrels and otters, and there is a large and contentious population of feral goats. The sparse sheep wander the slopes more like established residents than profitable livestock.

A single road runs into the valley along College Burn, with a day permit for cars from the local estate office. After the Battle of Trafalgar the lower slopes were planted with oaks for the navy by the widow of Nelson's second in command, Admiral Collingwood. By the time of their maturity iron had replaced wood in shipbuilding and the trees remain as a memorial to Trafalgar.

A two-mile walk or drive from the entry gate leads to the best view of the valley, at the junction of the College and Lambden burns. Here, alone and forlorn, stands Cuddystone Hall, cuddy being local dialect for horse. The building was erected by the estate as a community centre for the few remaining residents. It sees occasional dances and secluded mountain weddings, with a church service once a year. Across the valley is the old schoolhouse, Southernknowe, in use from 1854 to 1968. It had one room and one teacher and was shared with a shepherd. It is now a holiday cottage.

Upstream the valley grows wilder, as do the names of the hills: Black Hag, Fleehope, Coldburn, Sinkside and Bellyside. The track leads to Mounthooly youth hostel, surely the most isolated in England, its conifer plantation about to be removed. In the distance lie the Scottish border and the infant Pennine Way. At least seven RAF planes are scattered over these hills, crashing on the Cheviots in bad weather during the war.

Downstream the land is flanked by rounded hills billowing their way down to the valley mouth, closed by two symmetrical breast-like hills. The valley floor is marked by the stream wandering between shingle banks. Its shore is thick with gorse that turns it into a river of foaming yellow in spring.

DURHAM
From Framwellgate Bridge

Durham's cathedral and castle form England's most dramatic architectural composition. Indeed, Pevsner considered only Avignon and Prague its equal in Europe. On a high rock over a tight loop in the River Wear, these two massive structures were built to assert Norman authority over a hostile north. The castle was ordered by William the Conqueror in 1069, just three years after Hastings. The cathedral was begun in 1093, its bishop created an earl and granted quasi-monarchical power over the 'palatinate'. He administered the law and could raise armies and wage war without awaiting authority from London.

Durham is a city of views. One is from the station platform, where the cathedral seems to float above the Wear ravine, brilliantly floodlit at night. Glimpses of the rock can be had from almost any point along the river, though in the city centre they are marred by half-hearted attempts to make new buildings fit in with old. Durham, like many a historic English city, should have taken lessons from France or Italy on this subtle art. But the best view is from immediately below the rock, from Framwellgate Bridge, with the castle and cathedral piled across the skyline and the river tumbling below.

The bridge was begun at the same time as the castle and rebuilt in the fifteenth century. It leads from North Street across to the 300-yard neck of the Durham isthmus at Silver Street. In 1657 John Duck, Durham's Dick Whittington, is said to have loitered here after coming to make his fortune as a butcher and being rejected by his guild. As he pondered his fate a raven dropped a golden sovereign at his feet. It was enough. By 1680 he was mayor of Durham and a knight of the realm.

Towering above the bridge is the castle's keep, now Durham

Durham Cathedral and Castle, *by Thomas Girtin, c. 1800*

University and surely the only one where students squat in Norman alcoves and gossip on Norman stairs. The wall here conceals the fourteenth-century great hall, much altered and reinforced over the years with service floors stepping below down the hillside.

To the right the cathedral rises over the over-abundant trees, with two west towers and the central crossing behind. Since the nave here is invisible, the west towers appear as mighty gateways to a detached keep. The crossing was rebuilt in the fifteenth century, while the west towers had fussy pinnacles and battlements added during the Regency, an incongruous touch of picturesque gothic on the robust Romanesque.

The river below forms a canyon of greenery through the heart of the city, with trees falling to the water's edge. I once watched a blue kingfisher skimming over the water, keeping company with a lone sculler, silent on a misty spring morning. It made me want to migrate north.

Over the bridge the houses along Silver Street climb to the market square. The slopes of their roofs reflect the contour. Red brick and white woodwork form a pleasing skirt to the dark stone of the castle above, remarkably unchanged from Girtin's painting of the scene.

HADRIAN'S WALL
From Steel Rigg

Hadrian's Wall was the outer limit of the Roman Empire. It marked not just a local border but the boundary of classical civilisation. Another wall was later built to its north, the Antonine, but this was abandoned as indefensible. Nor was the wall the usual wood-and-mud affair. The original structure, built in six years after Hadrian's visit in AD 122, was probably some twenty feet high, of stone and studded with eighty gates or forts. It was engineered to protect a communication line between the east and west coasts of England and thus had to be defensible on both sides. To the emperor Hadrian the wall was a gesture of imperial completeness, of vanity as much as conquest. It is one of the most impressive creations of the Roman Empire.

The most dramatic stretch of wall is from Steel Rigg three miles east to Housesteads. The view symbolically divides Roman order to the south from the uncivilised north, the upper Tyne valley from the moors and mountains of the Scots and Picts. The best vantage point is above Steel Rigg car park, where the wall can be seen snaking east along the escarpment of the Whin Sill ridge. This limestone outcrop, calcified as hard as granite, is part of a sill that extends for sixty miles across northern England, also encountered on the Pennines at High Cup Nick and at Lindisfarne.

The sill is here tilted into an escarpment on its north side, as if the rocks of England had been arranged by prehistory to keep the Scots at bay. When a dawn mist settles on the land on either side of the ridge, Hadrian's Wall can appear a magic causeway, running through thin air to a distant ocean.

That said, today's wall is not strictly Hadrian's. It is a nineteenth-century reconstruction by John Clayton, a Newcastle enthusiast who bought farms along its line specifically to save it. The original structure had all but vanished, its stone used to patch local houses and build roads. Clayton rebuilt the masonry usually to seven layers of stone, leaving open the question of why he did not rebuild completely. The sinuous line is impressive in its continuity, but as a wall it is hardly different from a grass-capped field wall in the West Country. If the Chinese could rebuild the Great Wall of China, we could surely do likewise for Hadrian.

From Steel Rigg, the route along the wall is steep and, on busy days, congested. This is where the two great pedestrian highways

Overleaf: An empire's outer limit: Hadrian's Wall at Steel Rigg

of the north, Hadrian's Wall Path and the Pennine Way, meet and march briefly in tandem. The path dips out of sight at Sycamore Gap, where stands the 'Kevin Costner tree', a sycamore featuring in the film about Robin Hood in which he starred. It then rises to Crag Lough and the ridge to Housesteads.

To the north beyond lies a plateau of deserted bog and moor stretching to the Kielder Forest and the Cheviots. The view south is friendlier. Fields, barns, roads and settlements have filled the Tyne valley since Roman times. The landscape is fertile, sparsely populated with small farms and widely fenced fields. In a fold two miles from the wall lies the Roman town of Vindolanda. It is emerging from excavation as England's most complete Roman settlement, its full extent yet to be revealed.

LINDISFARNE
Towards Bamburgh

The Northumbrian shore is as redolent of the Middle Ages as Hadrian's Wall is of the Romans. England's east coast does not often rival the west for spectacle. Short of cliff and contour, it suffers from the leaden seas and skies of the Saxon shore. It compensates in the works of man and the drama of their setting.

Holy Island lies offshore at the end of a long shingle causeway, one of a line of Northumbrian citadels from Berwick southwards to Bamburgh, Dunstanburgh and Warkworth to Newcastle. The island was home to one of the earliest and, for a time, most civilised centres of Christianity in northern Europe, the monastery at Lindisfarne. Founded in 635 by St Aidan, it was destroyed by the Danes and rebuilt by the Normans. The old priory museum displays reproductions of the Lindisfarne Gospels, still held in London as if hostage to Northumbria's good behaviour. One day they should go back.

The castle on the far tip of the island is everything a castle should be, lonely on a rock, vertical and imposing in outline, with a wild sea beyond. The rock is the final outcrop of the Whin Sill ridge, which we met at Hadrian's Wall. While the most popular view is from the coast, with the castle isolated across the sands, the best prospect is from the castle itself, south to Bamburgh on its own lonely outcrop. Offshore lie the Farne Islands.

Both castles are creations largely of the twentieth century when owners and architects could let their imaginations run free and before the law froze every ruin in time. Lindisfarne was originally built by Elizabeth I to guard the harbour of Holy Island from Scots armies. It fell into long ruin until rescued by the founder of *Country Life* magazine, Edward Hudson, in 1901. He commissioned Edwin Lutyens to reconstruct it as a summer home in medieval style, making as much use as possible of the surviving fabric. The reinstatement has yielded a dramatic profile.

Across the adjacent field is a walled enclosure protecting a small spring garden, designed for Hudson by Lutyens' friend and collaborator Gertrude Jekyll. Its flowers defy the elements on this windblasted coast. Below the castle on the shore, grey seals loll beneath the Piranesian ruins of an old lime kiln.

The view south, as along most of England's eastern shore, depends heavily on the weather. It is of an expanse of sea and sky, misty and moody on all but the brightest day. Bamburgh Castle was almost as heavily restored by its Edwardian owner as Lindisfarne. It looks impregnable above the surrounding dunes, gazing out to the Farnes, their visible features being an old pele tower and church on Inner Farne.

On the northernmost island is the Longstone lighthouse, where in 1838 the keeper's daughter, Grace Darling, helped her father

Overleaf: Eastern sea and sky: Lindisfarne with Bamburgh in the distance

rescue sailors from the rocks, duly joining the ranks of Victorian heroines. Today the islands are thick with puffins, guillemots, kittiwakes and terns. The terns can be savage, attacking visitors during the breeding season.

In the foreground is the small harbour of Holy Island, where the carcasses of upturned Northumberland boats, known as cobles, are converted into simple cottages. On the shore opposite stand two conical navigation beacons, built in the nineteenth century to guide sailors over these treacherous sands.

NEWCASTLE
Grey Street

In the years before the Second World War, Tyneside launched a quarter of the world's shipping tonnage. When decline took hold in the 1960s, the city could have frozen its dockyards and preserved the quays and back lanes leading down to them. It would have been a cultural-historical centre of European significance. Instead in the 1960s the local-government regime of T. Dan Smith subjected the city to an orgy of destruction. Two sides of stately Eldon Square were razed to the ground. The riverside was left to rot and warehouses demolished.

Yet fragments of Newcastle's great age survive. The Regency city was fortunate to have a developer and an architect, Richard Grainger and John Dobson, who imagined a city to rival Bath and Edinburgh. Grainger set up as a builder in 1816 and exploited the city's booming trade in coal and shipping. He explicitly sought grandeur for the town, and as a result was constantly at loggerheads with the corporation, which, he said, merely wanted the place like a 'coal hole'.

'Indelible surprise': mansions in Grey Street

In Dobson, Grainger found an architect worthy of his ambition. Dobson's layout of a new smart quarter running uphill from the docks was largely built by the 1830s and its core remains intact. It is best appreciated by walking from the Quayside up Dean Street and under the arch of a soaring railway bridge. The climb continues up Grey Street, emerging from Victorian darkness into Georgian light.

The street was laid out in the thirty years after 1821, when Newcastle's population more than doubled. Unlike Nash's formal quadrant at the bottom of Regent Street in London, which the Edwardians demolished, Grainger allowed his mansion facades to respect the hillside, rising and curving in satisfying rhythm. The intention, said a contemporary, was 'to impress the beholder with indelible surprise'. The mansions are a sequence of joined pavilions, like the grandest of terrace houses. They were occupied by the merchants, bankers and clubs of the new city, often with shops on the ground floor.

The prominent Theatre Royal at the top of the hill dates from 1837, when it opened appropriately with *The Merchant of Venice*. The interior is later, a masterpiece of the Victorian theatre designer, Frank Matcham, inserted after a fire in 1899. The theatre's tall portico has an oddly baroque pairing of columns, the two outer pairs closer than those in the middle.

Grey Street culminates in the domed Exchange Building. It faces the monument to Earl Grey, Northumbrian landowner and architect of the 1832 Great Reform Act. The effect of the dome is to lead the eye round the corner into the adjacent Grainger Street, which returns downhill. The building facades were coal-dust black when I first saw them. They have been cleaned to a dull limestone brown. I wonder how they would look if stuccoed a creamy white.

LONDON

———

Greenwich: From Blackheath 313

The City: From the Monument 318

Parliament Square: From the Abbey Sanctuary 322

From Primrose Hill 326

Richmond Hill: The Thames towards Twickenham 329

Waterloo Bridge: Towards the City of London 332

GREENWICH
From Blackheath

———

London does not lend itself to views. It lies in a basin of thick clay, across which the Thames winds in a succession of meanders. The metropolis is hard to see from a distance, the few vantage points being from greensand outcrops mostly in the suburbs. Most of these offer little beyond an undistinguished horizon and rarely much by way of foreground.

Not so Greenwich. Here the Thames runs against the hill of Blackheath and veers to the north. For centuries this point marked the entry to London from the sea and overland from Canterbury and Dover. Only as London's docks developed upstream on the north bank did Greenwich lose importance. Sailors acknowledged it as their landfall, and the red ball on the observatory still drops daily at 1.00 p.m., for setting maritime chronometers. But Greenwich, variously as royal palace, hospital, college and museum, has always seemed a town apart.

The most celebrated view is by Canaletto from across the Thames. It shows Wren's great palace with barges gliding before it over a sunlit river, a picture of regal serenity recognisable today. This view is now rivalled by that in the opposite direction, downhill from Greenwich Park. The palace remains in the foreground but as a gilded gateway to the new commercial London of Docklands rising in the distance. It is the one London view that can accurately be described as sensational and I give it precedence.

The vantage point is from the top of Greenwich Park, reached from Blackheath by the Royal Observatory. As we approach along

the avenue we wonder why the statue of General Wolfe at the end
has his back to us, apparently looking into space. At the last minute
we see the reason. The park falls suddenly away at our feet, a green-
sward flanked by trees and rolling steeply downhill with all the
eastern half of London beyond.

In the eighteenth century the poet William Gifford wrote of this
prospect of London from the South-East:

How pleasant from that dome-crowned hill
To view the varied scene below,
Woods, ships, and spires, and, lovelier still,
The encircling Thames' majestic flow!

Old London battles new: Greenwich with Canary Wharf beyond

Byron's Don Juan was less complimentary. He saw London as 'a huge dun cupola, like a foolscap crown/ on a fool's head'. To Turner and others, this was the definitive prospect of London from a distance.

That view has gone. There are no more ships and spires, while the Thames is only glimpsed between buildings, as if a moat to the new Docklands. But in the foreground is still the Queen's House, commissioned in 1616 for Anne of Denmark, wife to James I. The architect, Inigo Jones, had recently returned from Italy and proposed 'a curious device . . . according to rules, masculine and unaffected'. His clean, white rectangle was revolutionary in Jacobean England.

View of London from Greenwich, *JMW Turner, 1825*

It is simple and lovely, flanked by nineteenth-century colonnades drawing the eye to the later buildings of Greenwich Palace below.

This palace was begun by Charles II on his restoration, abandoned and then resumed in 1692 by Sir Christopher Wren under William and Mary. It was to be a naval hospital and monument to their generosity. Two domed and colonnaded wings run down the slope to the water's edge, framing the Queen's House from below and above. Their use evolved from naval hospital and then college to the present university and maritime museum.

From the park above, Wren's domes have lost their pre-eminence.

They must now fight against a backdrop of bruising skyscrapers in Canary Wharf. When this development was begun in the 1980s, I wondered if it could ever succeed. It was the office equivalent of an out-of-town shopping mall, an ersatz city-within-a-city, almost inaccessible on foot and with no sense of neighbourhood.

Canary Wharf initially went bankrupt, despite being freed of regulation and taxes and supplied with new road and rail links. Regularly portrayed as an icon of capitalism, it was the most heavily subsidised development in England. But modern Docklands is a commercial success, its skyscrapers shimmering in the sunlight as if newly imported from the Persian Gulf. A light railway snakes among their depths.

Sandwiched between Greenwich and Canary Wharf is the green mound of the Mudchute Park. It was created of spoil and ballast from the old docks and is now home to London's largest urban farm. This has yielded the remarkable telephoto shot of a llama standing on a hillock backed by a curtain wall of office blocks.

To the east we see relics of the grand projects – perhaps follies – that tend to litter the outskirts of bombastic world cities. On the Greenwich peninsula stands the carapace of the Millennium Dome, now the O2 entertainment arena, with its cable car to the north bank. Beyond are the ice-cream scoops of the Thames barrier. To the north up the Lee valley is the ghost of the 2012 Olympic Stadium and Anish Kapoor's Orbit at Stratford. Epping Forest crowns the horizon beyond.

To the west rise the towers of the City of London. The success of Canary Wharf drove the City Corporation into a frenzy of imitation, demolishing a swathe of eighteenth- and nineteenth-century districts north and east of its centre. Rather than copy Westminster and use historic streets as a template for renewal, the City copied Docklands. What might have been a planned corridor of growth east into Essex became two exclusive outcrops of wealth, glaring at each other across a valley of poverty. But they make a good view.

THE CITY
From the Monument

Since London lacks strong contours near its centre, views must be either of towers or seen by climbing them. But there are towers and towers. Those of Tuscany's San Gimignano carry the patina of age. Those of New York are clustered by zoning regulation, while those of Paris, Madrid and most European cities are banished from historic centres and planned on the outskirts.

London's skyline has evolved spasmodically. Over most of the metropolis towers have risen at random, wherever an enterprising developer has been able to cajole or con the authorities into indulging him. Views of St Paul's are occasionally protected by the City of London and this has guarded its aspect to the west. There was to be a cluster of towers in the east of the City along the Gracechurch Street–Bishopsgate axis. But rules have been so often breached that the policy is hardly noticeable. In regulating a horizon, one exception destroys a rule and London's horizon is a forest of exceptions.

Canary Wharf and Tower Bridge from the Monument

Panoramas of London are now offered from the tops of many tall buildings, including Centre Point, Tower Forty Two, the London Eye and, highest of all, Bermondsey's Shard. But from these heights London looks much like a map of roofs. I prefer to see its towers, like mountains in the Lake District, from 'half-way up'. My favourite therefore remains Wren's old vantage point, The Monument. What was once a lofty lookout is now like a tree platform in a jungle. Structures loom up on all sides, enlivened by the occasional kestrel and cars and buses streaming below.

The Monument was commissioned by the City of London in 1676 and built by Wren and his assistant, Robert Hooke, to commemorate the great fire of 1666. Its height, 202 feet, is also the distance between its base and the seat of the fire. It was placed in the most conspicuous spot, so that anyone crossing old London Bridge was greeted by the steeple of St Magnus Martyr and by this secular assertion of London's rebirth. The Monument has 311 steps and remains the tallest accessible stone column in the world. It was intended to double as a telescope and hollow tube for scientific experiments, James Boswell had a panic attack when climbing it. The flaming ball on top is described in Dickens's *Martin Chuzzlewit* as casting a shadow on the street below 'with every hair erect upon his golden head, as if the doings of the city frightened him'.

The top reveals a 360-degree panorama both up and down the Thames, offering a sometimes hilarious insight into London's planning failures. The attempt to retain some view of the Tower of London has left just the tips of its turrets visible. Tower Bridge remains clear, with the bulbous mayor's office lurking like a snail on the bank next to it. Beyond rise the towers of Canary Wharf and the heights of Blackheath. Upstream is moored the old cruiser HMS *Belfast*, looking splendidly incongruous. Due south on Lower Thames Street we fight to see St Magnus Martyr, Eliot's 'inexplicable splendour of Ionian white and gold'. It once dominated the entry to the City over old London Bridge, but is now dominated by commercial buildings.

To the south looms the shadow of the Shard. Located on the south bank, it was strongly opposed by the City as unbalancing its eastern cluster. It is sleek and huge, a 'vertical city' deferring to no concept of scale, visual context or social purpose. It was intended merely as a 'statement' of London's wealth, placed in what was a poor part of London when so large a structure would never have been tolerated north of the river. It is now an unavoidable feature of the London skyline, absent from none of my London views except Richmond.

The Thames bank westwards takes its cue from the Shard. A series of slabs and towers is expected to form a wall of glass running along the river past Westminster to Vauxhall. The river's wide loop north will thrust this wall up towards the West End, making its towers visible across west London. Even Moscow balked at skyscrapers so near its historic centre.

The City foreground of The Monument to the west remains a minor miracle. The roofline from here has been mostly protected as far as St Paul's and the cathedral still rides above it as Wren intended. The one lapse is Rem Koolhaas's Rothschild bank, whose box tower intrudes on the view, reminding the City that financial muscle still writes its own rules. A superb close-up of the St Paul's east front can be had from a viewing platform on top of One New Change at the end of Watling Street.

The view north is completely different. This has all the buzz of crude commercial architecture let rip. To the left of Bishopsgate are the towers that defied the cluster, those of Tower Forty Two, London Wall and the Barbican. To the right is a lowering cliff of glass, cast in the geometrical shapes fashionable at the turn of the twenty-first century and craving nicknames, the Gherkin, the Helter-Skelter, the Cheese-grater. An attempt was made to step their profiles down Gracechurch Street towards the river. This failed with the erection of the colossal Walkie-Talkie on Fenchurch Street. It does not taper but the opposite, leering outwards towards the river, its upper floors overhanging the lower ones to capitalise on higher rents. In the City money does not just talk, it screams.

The heavy footfall of these buildings not only crushes the older one – the once-dominant Lloyds building on Leadenhall Street now seems almost quaint – but leaves the medieval maze of alleyways, courts and churchyards close to obliteration. Those that remain are the one distinctive feature of London as an office capital, crammed with cafés and boutiques, not waving but drowning. I feel like a man aboard the last ship afloat amid a sea of icebergs, tossing life-rafts to those struggling in the water.

PARLIAMENT SQUARE
From the Abbey Sanctuary

Big Ben stands bold over Westminster Bridge where, since 1859, it has marked the nation's time and acted as its guardian angel. The tower presides with benign familiarity over the institutions and ceremonies of state. It introduces each day's television news and is the capital's most recognisable logo. As visual focus of the City of Westminster, it gathers up river, bridge and government quarter and commands their collective obedience to the gods of parliament.

Big Ben's immediate environs are curiously disjointed. Most nations create spacious citadels round the heart of government, a Capitol, a Red Square or a Rajpath. London has the village green of Parliament Square, set in a moat of swirling traffic. It contains not even a seat, and tourists photographing Big Ben must cram onto a narrow pavement. Yet the general concourse stands firm in public affection. It is a licensed venue for public demonstration and woe betide any authority that tries to change it.

The medieval city of Westminster developed a mile upstream of London as the capital's ecclesiastical, legal and administrative base.

The towers of Westminster from the Sanctuary

The abbey of St Peter, founded by Edward the Confessor, was the home of national ritual. The Royal Palace of Westminster was the seat of government, its 'courts' giving their name to institutions of monarchy and law alike. Public offices grew up haphazard in its purlieus. Only in 1868 did the Victorians clear Parliament Square of a warren of government buildings to give the neighbourhood some dignity and allow citizens free passage. The square saw the world's first traffic light.

As a result, it is hard today to get a single clear view of this national tableau without being knocked over by a bus or a scrum of tourists. The garden in front of the Supreme Court offers a good sight of Big Ben, but my best view is little known, from the 'Olympic gold' pillar box at the junction of Victoria Street and Tothill Street. It looks across the Abbey Sanctuary and fortuitously contrives to embrace Parliament Square, Big Ben, St Margaret's, Westminster Abbey and the Victoria Tower in one frame, with the London Eye and the Shard peering over the horizon. It is a quiverful of towers, an enjoyable hotch-potch of famous buildings floating on a stream of traffic.

The view slices neatly left and right. Left is Methodist Central Hall, started in 1905 with 'a million guineas from a million Methodists'. Its grandiose Edwardian baroque glares boldly across the road at the abbey of its old antagonist, the Church of England. Next to it on Storey's Gate is Powell and Moya's 1986 Queen Elizabeth II Conference Centre. A modernist building on a crucial site, its broken facade and layered elevation is not dominant and is wearing well. Beyond is the fussy neo-Elizabethan former Middlesex Guildhall, echo of the days when this was still a municipality in the old county of Middlesex. It now houses the Supreme Court.

Ahead across the square is Portcullis House, parliamentary offices designed in 1990 by Sir Michael Hopkins. Again Westminster has been well served by modern architecture. Its tapering pink stone pilasters and black oriel windows are in counterpoint to the gothic of Big Ben next door. The distinctive roof chimneys are like stovepipe hats on Puritan divines, breaking the roofline in what might seem an architectural satire. The wheel of the London Eye peers jokily down on the scene.

The Palace of Westminster was commissioned after the old parliament burned down in 1834. It was to be in a 'gothic or Elizabethan style', a bold revolt against the still-prevalent Georgian classicism. Designed by Charles Barry and adorned by Augustus Pugin, the composition is the world's most bravura work of gothic revival, a balanced series of elevations whether seen from the river or the square.

The bell tower of Big Ben is largely Pugin's, its profile so familiar its oddity defies analysis. Pevsner found it 'completely unorthodox, a fairy tower of no archaeological precedent'. Pugin took its design from Scarisbrick Hall in Lancashire, which today looks like a pastiche. Its free gothic was to be imitated in public buildings across the land, as if a medieval clock-tower should serve as totem of the new Victorian dynamism.

Historic structures now crowd the scene. The roofline of old Westminster Hall is just visible to the right of Big Ben through the trees. It was begun by William Rufus in 1097 and was probably the largest secular building in Europe in its day. In front of it we have a clear view of St Margaret's, the old parish church of Westminster, once crowded about with buildings but now exposed in its churchyard. It might still be dreaming itself in a quiet Middlesex village. The church is of little architectural interest, which makes it the more endearing in such company. Sir George Gilbert Scott's adjacent north transept of Westminster Abbey aims a kick in its direction, as if trying to bully it off the site.

We now turn to the abbey's west front, an old friend but to me rather sad. Its forecourt has been ruined by traffic engineers refusing to divert the Sanctuary road out of the square nearer to the QE II Centre. This forces the monarch, statesmen, processions, horses, carriages, cars and coaches to manoeuvre their ceremonial way to the cramped west door round an effete Victorian monument to the dead of Westminster School. I sometimes wonder who rules modern Britain, traffic or democracy.

The abbey facade is mostly medieval, much restored and with twin towers added by Hawksmoor in the 1730s. They are ostensibly gothic but have anachronistic baroque windows and classical cornices. We know them so well this no longer seems absurd. A proposed central tower for the abbey, which might have acted as a visual focus to the square and echoed Big Ben, has been suggested, most recently by the composer Andrew Lloyd Webber, but has never been built.

Immediately to the right of the facade we see the conical roof of the abbey Chapter House, containing its loveliest medieval interior. Next to it rises the dramatic return of Westminster Palace in the shape of Victoria Tower, strong and confident in its gothic but delightfully penned in by the roofs of Westminster School.

The Sanctuary is closed to the right by Scott's building over the entrance to Dean's Yard. It was designed not to compete with the abbey but to defer to its surroundings in unobtrusive Bath stone, with what Scott called an 'accidental' arrangement of 'gabled fronts . . . parapets and dormers'. Such deference would be inconceivable in a modern architect. The yard behind is an oasis of ecclesiastical calm, its cloisters even more so.

PRIMROSE HILL

Primrose Hill competes with Parliament Hill, Alexandra Palace and Shooter's Hill to offer the best distant viewpoint over central London. Of these it has the widest panorama and the best foreground. I lived nearby for most of my life, and from the summit watched London's skyline changing by the year. A grassy slope runs gently downhill to the Zoo where Regent's Park still offers a dignified entry to the metropolis.

The hill's survival is fortuitous. It was crown land, originally a hunting forest, left isolated to the north of St Pancras by the creation of Regent's Park in the 1820s. The Eyre estate was building villas to the west in St John's Wood and Eton was building to the north in Belsize Park. The hill had been a place of resort in the eighteenth century and was now threatened with new buildings. In

Westminster from Primrose Hill over the Zoo, Big Ben just visible

1829 a mausoleum was proposed, turning the slope into a giant ziggurat, with ninety-four tiers of profitable burial vaults.

With pressure mounting to save London's 'northern heights' from development, an act was secured in 1842 to keep Primrose Hill as open space. Much was made of the need of Londoners for exercise and an 'outdoor gymnasium' even survives at the foot of the hill. On the summit a grove of trees lasted until the Second World War, when it was cut down for an anti-aircraft battery and the hill used to graze sheep.

Primrose Hill acquired a mystical personality when William Blake saw it as the location of 'Jerusalem's pillars of gold', where he had 'conversed with the Spiritual Sun'. Welsh cultural revivalists here founded their Gorsedd of the Bards, leading to the Eisteddfod movement that later moved to Wales. It has since featured in many films and in the writings of Alan Bennett, Margaret Drabble, Martin Amis and other local residents. The footpath to the top has been inscribed with a lyric by the group Blur, 'And the view's so nice'.

The prospect of London from the summit spans 180 degrees. To the east are the Holloway flats crowned by the campanile of the old Caledonian Road market. The turrets of St Pancras are in the middle distance, with the once prominent view of St Paul's, notionally 'protected' but increasingly enveloped in high buildings. The Shard beyond looks peculiarly incongruous at this distance, seeming to dwarf even the towers of Canary Wharf.

The view south across the Thames basin is weakened by the lie of the land. The old royal suburb of Westminster was located on swampy ground next to the abbey, leading the Stuarts and Hanoverians to flee to drier Kensington and Windsor. As a result only the tops of Big Ben and Victoria Tower are visible, looking half submerged. Beyond are the heights of Sydenham and Crystal Palace, forming the southern rim of the London basin. The palace itself was moved to south London after the closure of the Great Exhibition. Its conflagration in 1936 is still recalled by elderly residents who watched from the top of Primrose Hill.

At our feet lies a restful contrast, John Nash's Regent's Park. Its stucco villas and terraces were originally located amid clumps of trees, such that each could believe itself alone in the country, an ideal of *rus in urbe* that in summer is still almost plausible. On the left of the park are the stately facades of Cumberland and Chester terraces, like palaces dropped in from St Petersburg. In the foreground on the canal bank lies the Snowdon aviary, with the Zoo's Mappin Terraces and elephant house behind, now empty of elephants. Regent's Park is still one of Europe's great urban set pieces.

Primrose Hill is a place where Londoners come to watch over their capital, mingling private pains and pleasures with those of the city as a whole. There is always a knot of spectators on its summit, discussing the view as if it were a book club. I know every zigzag of these footpaths, the warmth of its summer grass, the lengthening tree shadows in autumn, the toboggan runs in winter. For me this will always be a special view.

RICHMOND HILL
The Thames towards Twickenham

The view from Richmond Hill has been lauded ever since Henry VII built a palace here in 1501, named after his seat of Richmond in Yorkshire. Under his granddaughter, Elizabeth, it became a popular resort, the tidal river being a faster and safer thoroughfare than any road. Londoners would even take trips to see the queen hold audiences on the terrace. On the hill was a beacon, recalled by Macaulay when describing the Armada signal: 'The sentinel on Whitehall gate looked forth into the night/ And saw o'erhanging Richmond Hill that streak of blood red light.'

Greater celebrity came with the Hanoverians, yearning to escape the fog and politics of London. They brought with them poets, artists and essayists (as journalists were then called) who declared Richmond Arcadia, a landscape fit for Claude or Poussin. The Thames was London's Tiber, its liquid history. Here the gods of the river sported with the muses, and Old Father Thames watched local maidens flirting with courtiers on the towpath.

Soon aristocrats and artists were taking houses to be near the court. Reynolds lived on the hill and Turner near by. Gainsborough and Constable came here to paint. The Virginian city of Richmond was so named because its founder, Colonel William Byrd, thought the site reminded him of home. As for the folk song 'The Lass on Richmond Hill', the lass herself is strongly contested between Surrey and Yorkshire.

From the Victorian period there were pleas for the view's protection, probably the first in this book to enjoy such an accolade. The Richmond shoreline belonged to court families who had held property since the eighteenth century or before: Buccleuchs, Cardigans, Ladbrokes and Tollemaches. Conservationists fought profiteers. By the 1890s Petersham Ait, also known as Glover's Island, was threatened with a large Pears soap advertisement, the day being saved only when a local philanthropist bought it. An act passed in 1902

The serpentine Thames: Richmond Hill *by JMW Turner, 1825*

specifically protected Richmond from development, though this did little to halt the battles.

The chief casualty was the old Star and Garter pub on the hilltop. It was bought as a home for disabled veterans after the First World War and ponderously rebuilt in 1924 by Sir Edwin Cooper. It was specifically located on the hill to honour the wounded with 'the finest view in London'. The benefit to the few was thought to outweigh the offence to many.

The view from Richmond Hill today differs from its Georgian past chiefly in the growth of trees. They pleasantly conceal the spread of suburban estates over the western reaches of London, but conceal also the distant course of the river and the courtly mansions along the Twickenham shore. But the river's curve immediately below the hill remains clear, its water reflecting the changing mood of the sky, white, blue, grey, silver and blood red at sunset.

To Hogarth, this Richmond curve perfectly evoked the S-shaped 'line of beauty' of the rococo, signifying liveliness and 'calling the attention', in contrast to 'static and inanimate' straight lines. To Plato such serpentine curves were 'eternally and by their very nature beautiful, and give a pleasure of their own quite free from the itch of desire'. Here the curve is broken only by the positioning of Glover's Island, free of hoardings but still a beauty spot on the face of the river.

On the left, Surrey, bank is Petersham Meadow, complete with ruminating cows, now under what amounts to a cow-preservation order courtesy of the National Trust. Beyond is Petersham and the seventeenth-century gem of Ham House, home of the scheming Stuart courtier the Duchess of Lauderdale. A ferry once crossed the river to Twickenham at this point.

The Middlesex bank offers glimpses of Marble Hill, built for the Countess of Suffolk, mistress of George II, with whom his dalliance appears to have comprised little more than games of cards. It borders the grounds of Orleans House, named after French aristocrats who sought fashionable refuge from revolution.

Upstream was Alexander Pope's home and grotto, and Horace Walpole's Strawberry Hill. Here, wrote Pope, 'barges as solemn as barons of the Exchequer move under my window, and Richmond Hill and Ham Walks bound my prospect'. It was, he wrote, 'the Muses' fav'rite seat . . . the Graces' lov'd retreat'. His house has gone but the grotto survives. Walpole's Strawberry Hill has been restored to its 'Gothick' splendour and opened to the public.

We can only imagine what Pope might have said of the towers rising over Kingston in the distance and of an office block erected in Twickenham itself, not to mention the looming bulk of the rugby ground. The Victorians fought to protect the view from Richmond Hill, and largely succeeded. We struggle to do so and fail. Yet the outlook from Richmond Hill is still mostly as painted by Turner and others. In a city of lost prospects, that surely is worth preserving.

WATERLOO BRIDGE
Towards the City of London

'Earth has not anything to show more fair' wrote Wordsworth of the view of London from Westminster Bridge. 'Dull would he be of soul who could pass by/ A sight so touching in its majesty.' Wordsworth was writing from abroad and from memory, recollecting London at dawn, 'all bright and glittering in the smokeless air'. He was inspired by his sister Dorothy's observation that a man-made spectacle could compete with his favoured works of nature. She was right, but Wordsworth was recalling London at dawn with its fires not lit.

Views of London from the Thames are both celebrated and vulnerable. They offer the charm of the river, variety and a rare opportunity to see the city at street level from a distance of more than a few yards. A mild curiosity of Wordsworth's sonnet is that it tends to be illustrated by Canaletto's view of the City of London from Somerset House. Westminster Bridge does not offer this view with St Paul's and most of the City's spires being invisible round the Lambeth bend. Today the Westminster view is also impeded by Hungerford Bridge. I therefore prefer the 'Canaletto' view of the City, from the Somerset House end of Waterloo Bridge.

Until the Second World War this view was little changed from the nineteenth century. It was a scene of riverside wharves and warehouses, with behind them the business houses of the City rising uphill. St Paul's was dominant and some of Wren's spires still visible. This survives along the north bank. It plays host to the dignified

Touching majesty: The Thames from Somerset House, *Canaletto, 1746–50*

St Brides to the Shard: the new London from Waterloo Bridge

facade of Somerset House, its ground-floor arcades once descending into the pre-Embankment river and giving access to Admiralty barges. To its right lies the oasis of the Temple, protected enclave of the legal profession. The old City of London school then carries the eye past the former mouth of the Fleet river to the rise of Ludgate Hill and the newly roofed Blackfriars Bridge over the river.

Here London sits on what is still recognisably a hill, but all other echoes of the past die away. The view of St Paul's has been compromised, its portico obstructed by a glass box. The visually coherent,

indeed exciting, policy of once clustering towers on the crest of the City hill has failed, as has the hope of retaining 'sky penetration' through the towers behind the cathedral. The bulbous Walkie-Talkie appears to have slid downhill in an effort to join its soul-mate, the adjacent Shard.

We do better to blot out comparison with Paris, Rome or Berlin and regard the new London as a place of the times, given over to raw speculative building. This is best demonstrated on the south bank from Waterloo Bridge, in the line of office and residential towers now emerging along the Southwark shore. To some, this abandonment of skyline design is visually stimulating, a symbol of a metropolis of uncompromising vitality, ready to embrace any market and go where it leads even if the result is a mess.

The scene is most exciting at night, when illumination replaces bulk and colour is reflected by water. On the north bank, lights line the Embankment and climb the City hill to where the subtle illumination of St Paul's holds sway. Brightly lit office blocks blaze across the water, to find reflection in the garish primary colours projected onto the National Theatre, the Hayward Gallery and County Hall. Advertising was once banned along the Thames – hence the device of the Oxo Tower grilles – but is now permitted even on the National Theatre facade. The southern approach to Waterloo Bridge may yet rival Piccadilly Circus. The view is vulgar or vital according to taste.

Day or night, London from the Thames displays the visual anarchy that is the new landscape of London. I doubt if Wordsworth would cheer, but he would surely agree that 'dull would he be of soul' who could remain unmoved.

EPILOGUE

How safe are my hundred views? Efforts to conserve both urban and rural England go back to the earliest days of urban expansion. There were battles over common land round London, when Octavia Hill lost the fight to keep Swiss Cottage open as a park, but others won the fight for Hampstead Heath. The Victorians passed specific acts to safeguard the Malverns and the view from Richmond Hill. The National Trust was founded in 1895, protecting almost all the great landscapes in the Lake District and others on Exmoor, the Vale of the White Horse and the Long Mynd in Shropshire. The Campaign to Protect Rural England was founded in 1926. After the Second World War came the national parks, and with them town and country planning legislation more extensive than anywhere in Europe. These lawmakers knew what they were doing, deploying taste and determination to safeguard what they felt was England's visual heritage. What we most value about that landscape today is their memorial.

These moves have always been popular. The 'English countryside' is embedded in the national personality. At the time of the London Olympics, polls by YouGov, Demos, Royal Mail and British Future ranked it above or on a par with the royal family, the NHS and Shakespeare as what people prized most about England. One in five Britons belong to the National Trust and a majority are involved in walking, bird-watching, field sports, cycling and climbing.

Almost all my views are within 'designated' national parks, areas of outstanding natural beauty, green belts or, in the case of town views, urban conservation areas. So too is much of the rural landscape visible from them. In the countryside, designation covers roughly fifteen per cent of England's land area. Between that and the fifteen per cent already under some form of development is some seventy per cent of mostly farmed land that is at the mercy of local planning, but under increasingly strict central government guidelines (the total is nearer ninety per cent over the whole of theUnited Kingdom).

Until recently, county and district planning regulations laid down the parameters for the development of this seventy per cent. The measures have broadly worked. England is the sixth most crowded country in the world, with 400 people per square kilometre, topped only by Asian states such as Bangladesh and South Korea and in Europe by the Netherlands. Yet half a century of primacy given to distinguishing woods, commons and farmland from built-up areas has left a landscape that belies this density. Firm planning control has mostly prevented the sprawling municipalities familiar elsewhere in the world, while embracing urbanisation the size of Bristol every decade. Planning is an English success.

By the turn of the twenty-first century, changing patterns of work had rendered this framework increasingly unstable. Town centres and industrial zones were emptying and derelict. Market forces, chiefly the attraction and lower cost of greenfield sites, were pushing building to the urban fringes and beyond. In the country new farming methods destroyed woods and hedges and erected barns, silos and warehouses. Subsidies to energy companies meant wind turbines proliferated. Lobbying from landowners, house-builders and leisure promoters put every unprotected acre 'in play'. England was displaying Mark Twain's maxim, that land is valuable 'because they are not making it any more'.

By 2010 this pressure led to a relaxation of control by the coalition government. All land became subject to an ubiquitous requirement for more building, even in designated areas such as green belts. Where there was no plan in place, government inspectors should show a 'presumption in favour of sustainable development', a term that came to mean little more than economic viability. There was a chorus of dismay at this change.

The blanket nature of the new relaxation, with universal targets for building emanating from Whitehall, made it hard to calculate just where the pressure to develop would manifest itself. Most of my entries are vulnerable to insensitive intrusion. In the south alone development targets for undesignated land could materially affect views from the Chilterns at Coombe Hill, the North Downs above Wye, the South Downs at Arundel and Ashford Hangers, and White Horse Hill in Berkshire. Equally at risk are distant views of Corfe Castle, Dartmouth, Carrick Roads and Tintagel among many others. There are proposals for turbines or pylons in Dedham Vale, the Wye valley and the Bristol Channel opposite Exmoor. Of course not all the land now affected might be regarded as scenically important, but no effort was made in the new regulations to identify landscape quality as such. Housing developers naturally favour areas of existing scenic beauty for their estates.

The most glaring difference is between emerging practice in urban and rural parts of the country. Sensible conservation has always meant guiding but not freezing the market in land. In cities its disciplines are now respected. Property owners sacrifice value to retain the amenity and historic character of their surroundings. They quibble over details, but rarely over the principle of conservation as such. Graduated status is given to historic buildings, areas and settings. Most of my urban views are safe other than from high buildings intrusion.

This does not mean no change. I served as chairman of English Heritage's historic areas committee for five years, hearing and often granting appeals for easement from conservation control. The point of control was not to stop development – plainly it does not – but to consider it in the light of the aesthetic and historic quality of an area and in the public interest, often fiercely expressed, in its protection.

I believe the same principles should apply to the countryside. Rural landowners should accept the cardinal planning principle that public interest in the aesthetic quality of the environment requires them to sacrifice value without compensation from the state. The owners of London's West End are not permitted to build multi-storey blocks in its squares and gardens. The owners of the Vale of Aylesbury should be treated in the same way.

In country as in town, private property rights should not override the public interest in a protected landscape, any more than in matters of pollution or nature conservation or the right to roam. Rural landowners argue that land has always been 'managed' for profit and that building is merely another crop. We no longer say the same of Durham, Bath, Richmond or Greenwich. The entire surface area of England has in some sense to be managed to make money. But where money is the sole criterion, land has often ended up wasted and derelict.

In modern built-up areas, highest rental values tend to be where conservation has been most stringently applied, not just in Westminster and Kensington but in the residential suburbs round Birmingham, Manchester and Sheffield. The conserved mill town of Hebden Bridge in Yorkshire, one of my views, is a model of urban revival, while the largely demolished mill settlements round it languish in recession. The widespread opinion of planners after the Second World War was that small market and manufacturing towns had no future. They were wrong. The most expensive property is usually the most beautiful, and such beauty has external value to residents and visitors alike. Obviously not everyone can live in a picture village in the Cotswolds any more than they can live in Belgravia, but everyone can enjoy these places and would feel regret if they were no more.

England's landscape has become a battleground between those who wish to guard its intrinsic beauty and the commercial pressures placed on it. This is not new, but it is newly intense. Those such as myself who put fine landscapes alongside art galleries and cathedrals in the tally of national assets can find these battles heart-rending. The arrival of colossal wind turbines on formerly protected hills is an extraordinary intrusion. They are bigger, more mobile and more noticeable than any railway, road or quarry.

The release of swathes of rural England for building – the new planning regime stipulates no limit or even concept of limit – would transform much at least of southern England. It would replace true rurality with a landscape everywhere pockmarked with small estates and fields of houses. There is no secret of what this would look like. It can be seen along the coast of pre-war Essex and Kent, in southern Ireland or Portugal or in suburban New Jersey. Indeed it is emerging in Yorkshire in the Aire and Calder valleys, omitted from designation when the adjacent Peak and Pennine parks were formed.

This would mean a specific shift away from the present sweeps of untrammelled nature visible in most of my views towards a landscape in which humanity was everywhere noticeable. Such a process is invariably one way. The free market never restores countryside (except after the Black Death). Even in the derelict and depopulating areas of Durham and Lancashire, abandoned settlements do not go 'green', any more than they do in devastated Detroit. They simply go to ruin.

There is said to be a 'price to pay' for the preservation of the countryside. The only price is sensible planning. Certainly it appears to mean the more intensive building of urban communities, although those in England are among the least densely populated in Europe (even when density overall is high). But the real answer is the imaginative reuse of an urban England fashioned for the industrial revolution and, in large measure, under-used ever since. Deindustrialisation has left more serviced acres unproductive than ever in history. In 2010 urban land already allocated for over a million houses was reported to be lying fallow. The concomitant waste of infrastructure, materials and energy is senseless. There is no shortage of land for building, only of the will, the incentive and the physical planning to bring appropriate land to market.

Clearly, the first task in protecting rural England falls to those who live in it and care for it. I have never understood the objection to Nimbyism. If local people do not value and fight for where they live, others are unlikely to do so. Sometimes the national interest must rule, forcing through a road or rail line or requiring a port or power station. Equally, the national interest may override local demands for housing, as in parks and along coasts. There is always a tension over land use, between the varying demands of owners, neighbours, tourists and 'the nation'. Such tension lies at the heart of politics.

Rural planning should be on the same lines as urban planning. The countryside outside designated areas should be classified and protected for its scenic quality, as it is for purposes of nature conservation and agricultural productivity. Little extra work is involved here. Almost all the fields and woods in England are listed on Whitehall computer maps for subsidy purposes. All I am proposing is that the concept of outstanding natural beauty should be widened to protect areas of countryside that we want to remain predominantly agricultural and not subject to 'peppering' with random buildings and estates. The overwhelming majority of the seventy per cent of land that is currently neither designated nor developed would be so listed. But the lists would be graded.

After the top grade of designated parks and green belts would come land enjoying a total ban on building outside existing structures. This would be the England most people recognise as constituting valued countryside. Lesser grades of land would enjoy declining degrees of control, such that change of use would be permitted, including to such marginal uses as playing fields, golf courses and allotments. The lowest category would be rural land to which no landscape value could reasonably attach. As open space, it might retain a presumption against development, but that would be subject to review or local override.

Whenever I have discussed such ideas with planners, the conclusion is that such listing could be achieved easily within the existing law. It would yield the immense benefit of certainty, that some land would be safeguarded virtually for ever while the release of marginal land would allow developers to know where to concentrate their activity and resources. Since the decay of local planning after 2010, countryside almost everywhere, not just in the south-east of England, has become enveloped in conflict, appeal and dilatory litigation. It has torn communities apart and led to bad planning decisions. Almost certainly it has led to less land being released for building than were land specifically listed as appropriate for such building.

There must be a better way than at present. As I said at the start of this book, a view is not a picture. It is a contract between people and nature, nature harnessed to the needs of humans. I have seen and described a hundred such contracts. Some are scenes of intense loveliness, evoking Coleridge's ecstasy, that 'he on honey-dew hath fed/ And drunk the milk of Paradise.' Most I have just marvelled at, marvelled that somewhere in England I could gaze over so much we have inherited from the past that remains so beautiful. Like ninety per cent of Britons, I live and work in a town but value the countryside. Like them I yearn to know that someone is guarding it. The countryside offers a oneness with nature that is the essence of public sensitivity to the wider environment. That oneness is terribly vulnerable.

ACKNOWLEDGEMENTS

─────

My thanks go to all those kind friends who suggested views, corrected entries or offered hospitality on my travels. There are dozens of them, too many to list here, and they stretch the length and breadth of England. I can only apologise for not always including their favourite views. I thank Andrew Goudie for help with geology and John Wright with botany. Daniel Crewe at Profile, Trevor Horwood and my brother Tom were astringent editors of the text, fighting to keep my enthusiasm in check and my occasional anger at bay. They were the embodiment of rigour.

I was greatly assisted in my travels by the National Trust and its local staff, and by its ever fertile photographic archive. The Trust remains the best repository of knowledge and concern about the landscape in Britain. I also thank *Country Life* and its photographer Paul Barker for being, as often before, a keen and helpful collaborator. The magazine is a true bastion of all that matters in England's countryside. May it last forever! Cecilia Mackay was a superb picture researcher.

Books on England's landscape are legion. I cannot include those on individual sites or regions (other than the unmissable Wainwright), though they are sometimes mentioned in the text, but I found these more general works helpful:

Bryson, Bill, et al., *The English Landscape*, London, 2000

Burke, Edmund, *A Philosophical Enquiry into the Origins of the Sublime and Beautiful: And Other Pre-Revolutionary Writings* [1757], Harmondsworth, 1998

Clark, Kenneth, *Landscape into Art*, London, 1949

Drabble, Margaret, *A Writer's Britain: Landscape in Literature*, London, 1979

Fortey, Richard, *The Hidden Landscape*, London, 1993

Goudie, Andrew and Rita Gardner, *Discovering Landscape in England and Wales*, London, 1985

Hardyment, Christina, *Writing Britain: Wastelands to Wonderlands*, London, 2012

Hoskins, W. G., *The Making of the English Landscape*, Leicester, 1955

Mabey, Richard, *The Common Ground*, London, 1980

Mabey, Richard, *Flora Britannica*, London, 1998

Macfarlane, Robert, *The Wild Places*, London, 2007

Mount, Harry, *How England made the English*, London, 2012

Muir, Richard, *Reading the Landscape*, London, 1981

Rackham, Oliver, *The Illustrated History of the Countryside*, London, 2003

Sinclair Iain, *Lights out for the Territory: 9 Excursions in the Secret History of London*, London, 1997

Wainwright, A., *Memoirs of a Fellwanderer*, London, 1993

PICTURE CREDITS

4Corners Images: 236–7 (Colin Dutton), 263 (Olimpio Fantuz/SIME); Alamy: 15 (V&A Images), 28–9 (JLImages), 31 (Kevin Britland), 77 (James Osmond), 122–3 (Tony Watson), 132–3 (Tony Peacock), 145 (Greg Balfour Evans), 158 (Andalusia Plus), 170 (Blackout Concepts), 189 (David Martin Hughes), 201 (Peter Barritt), 215 (Barry Morgan), 258–9 (Nick Bodle), 281 (Darryl Gill), 334–5 (Stephen Chung); Ashmolean Museum, University of Oxford, on loan from a Private Collection: 125; Paul Barker: 35, 74, 108–9, 165, 186–7, 207, 228–9, 247, 253, 272, 283, 286, 327; Bridgeman Art Library: 33 (Butler Institute of American Art, Youngstown, Ohio), 38 (Agnew's, London), 53 (Ashmolean Museum, University of Oxford), 58 (Victoria Art Gallery, Bath and North East Somerset Council), 88 (Private Collection © The artist), 96 (Private Collection), 154 (National Gallery, London), 156 (Stapleton Collection), 212 (Devonshire Collection, Chatsworth / Reproduced by permission of Chatsworth Settlement Trustees), 330 (Lady Lever Art Gallery, National Museums Liverpool), 333 (The Royal Collection © 2011 Her

Majesty Queen Elizabeth II); Adam Burton: 82–3; Calderdale Metropolitan Borough Council: 234; Chris Ceaser: 10, 270; Roger Clegg: 302–3; Anna Dillon/www.annadillon.com: 115 (Oil on Board. From *The Ridgeway Series*); Collections Photo Library: 63 (Brian Shuel); Corbis: 43 (Radius Images), 71 (Peter Lewis), 128–9 (Pawel Libera), 243 (Quentin Bargate), 264–5 (Anthony West), 279 (Image Source); Joe Cornish: 244, 250; Penny Daniel: 118, 318–19, 323; Kris Dutson/www.southernscenicphotography.co.uk: 90–91; Thomas Endlein: 150; Simon Fraser: 294; Edward Fury: 178, 190–91; Getty Images: 20 (James Osmond), 46 (David Wall), 51, 102–3 (Matt Cardy), 204–5 (Guy Edwardes), 267 (Keith Wood), 314–15 (Oli Scarff); James Grant/www. jamesgphotography.co.uk: 220–21; Hovis Marketing Archive at The History of Advertising Trust/www.hatads.org.uk: 99; Penny Hurt LRPS: 180; J. Paul Getty Museum, Los Angeles: 299 (Thomas Girtin, *Durham Cathedral and Castle, c.*1800, watercolour over pencil heightened with gum arabic, 37.5 x 48.9 cm); Rhys B M Jones: 183; Angie Latham/www.celtic–photography. co.uk: 194–5; Mary Evans Picture Library: 217 (ILN), 240 (Francis Frith Collection); © McCoy Wynne: 288–9; National Trust Images: 60 (Charlie Waite), 80 (Joe Cornish), 139 (John Millar), 152–3, 306–7 (Arnhel de Serra); New Forest National Park Authority: 136 (James Brown); Norfolk Museums & Archaeology Service, Norwich Castle Museum: 162; Peter Noyce: 111; Ben Pipe: 68–9; Alan Ranger: 40–41; John Robinson: 276–7; Michelle & Jonathan Rousell: 117; Scala, Florence: 316 (Metropolitan Museum of Art/Art Resource); Science & Society Picture Library: 49 (NRM/Pictorial Collection); Shutterstock: 93; Stephen Spraggon: 86; Betty Stocker: 174; Peter Styles: 198; © Tate, London 2013: 141, 231; Christopher Ward: 296; Richard Wheeler: 218, 223; Andrew Whitaker/Northern Horizons: 309; Terry Yarrow: 65, 173.

Endpapers: *Chalk paths* (1935), by Eric William Ravilious (1903–1942). (Photo by DeAgostini/Getty Images) by: DEA PICTURE LIBRARY.

INDEX

A

Abbotsbury 66–70
Adam, Robert 138
Airedale 246–9
Aldeburgh 164
Alfred the Great
    73, 141, 143
Allen, Ralph 57–61
Alnwick 293
Arlington Row 169
Arthur, King 50, 52–3,
    73–5, 85, 141
Arts and Crafts
    movement 112,
    175–6, 297
Arundel 88, 107–10
Ashbee C. R. 175–6
Ashford Hangers
    110–13
Ashness Bridge 266
Austen, Jane 57, 94,
    211, 242
Avon gorge 62–4
Aylesbury, vale of
    113–15, 340

B

Bamburgh 305
Barna Barrow 78–81

Barnsley, Edward 112
Bassenthwaite 265
Bath 57–61, 75
Bax, Arnold 54
beech woods 112,
    113–18
Beeston Castle 197–9
Bempton Cliffs 227–30
Berkeley Castle 206
Berkshire downs
    140–43
Betjeman, John 54
Bibury 169–71
Bideford 34, 41
Big Ben 324–5, 328
Black Mountains 179
Blackdown hills 84
Blackheath 313–17, 320
Blackpool 269
Blake, William 16, 328
Blenheim Palace 211
Borrowdale 19, 257–61,
    268
Botallack 27–30
Bowland, Forest of 269
Bradford 247–9
Bragg, Melvyn 261
Brecon Beacons 81,
    178, 181, 196
Bredon hill 173, 196

Brettenham, Matthew
    155
Breidden hill 184
Brent Knoll 84, 87
Brighton 57
Brill 115
Bristol 62–4
Britten, Benjamin
    144–6
Broadway Tower
    171–4, 206
Brown, Capability 15,
    61, 137, 172, 213–14
Brunel, I. K. 62–4
Bruton 75
Burke, Edmund 16
Buttermere 261–3
Byron, John 315

C

Cadbury 73–5
Cade, Rowena 45–7
Cambridge 127, 149–51
Campaign to Protect
    Rural England 337
Canaletto 313, 333
Canary Wharf
    317–20, 328
Cannock Chase 216
Cape Cornwall 27–30

Carrick Roads 30–32

Castle Combe 64–6

Castle Howard 211

Castlerigg 264–6

chalk downs 116,
118–24, 131–4,
140–43, 227–30

Chatsworth 211–14

Chepstow 196, 202

Chesil Beach 66–70

Chesterton, G. K. 142

Cheviots 246, 293–8,
304

Chilterns 113–17, 339

Chipping Campden
174–6

Clark, Lord 12

Clee hills 177–9, 184

Cleveland Way 244

Clifton 62–4

Clifton-Taylor, Alec 241

Clovelly 32–5

Clyro 179–81

Coalbrookdale 62,
184–8, 193

Coleridge, S. T. 81, 83,
261, 266, 268, 343

College Valley, Cheviot
296–8

Coniston 267, 269

Constable, John 16,
95–8, 151–4

Coombe Hill 113–15

Coquetdale 293–5

Corfe Castle 70–73

Cornwall 27–47

Cotswolds 21, 65, 75,
115, 169, 171–4, 176,
190, 206–8

Country Life 176, 305,
344

Creech Hill 73–6

Croome Court 172

Crummock Water 262

Cuckmere Haven 131–4

Culbone 79–81

D

Dartmoor 35–7

Dartmouth 37–9

Defoe, Daniel 221

Derwentwater
16, 21, 257, 260,
264, 266–8

Docklands, London
313–17

Dover 118–21

Duddendale 280–82

Durdle Door 89, 92

Durham 298–300

E

Edale 219–22, 285

Eden valley 269, 282–6

Elgar, Edward 196–7

Eliot, T. S. 248, 320

English Heritage 54,
120, 339

Eskdale 280

Essex 22

Eton 146

Evesham, vale of 172

Exmoor 36, 37, 79–84

F

Falmouth 30–32

Farne Islands 305–8

field patterns 114, 116,
249–51, 273

Fiennes, Celia 142

Flamborough Head
227–30

Flatford 151–4

Flitcroft, Henry 104

Forest of Dean 196,
203, 206

Forestry Commission
203

Fortey, Richard 189

Frost, Robert 110

G

Gibbs, James 130, 137,
160

Gifford, William 314

Gilpin, William 14, 21,
202–3

Gimson, Ernest 112,
175

Girouard, Mark 197

Girtin, Thomas
299–300

Glastonbury 76, 85–7

Gold Hill, Shaftesbury 98–100

Golden Cap 95

Golden Valley 181

Goodwood 109

Gordale 231–2

Gowbarrow Hill 274–7

Grand Tour 14, 155

Gray, Thomas 257

Greenwich 21, 313–17

Griggs, F. L. 176

Grigson, Geoffrey 38, 52–4

Grimshaw, Atkinson 252–4

Gummer's How 19, 268–71

H

Hadrian's Wall 285, 300–305

Halifax 233, 248

Hampshire downs 110–12, 118

Hardy, Thomas 47, 70, 91

Hardknott Pass 280–82

Hartland 19, 34, 40–42, 91

Hartside 282–6

Hawksmoor, Nicholas 173–4, 177–9

Hawkstone 181–4

Hay-on-Wye 179–81

Haytor 35–7

Hazlitt, William 12

Hebden Bridge 233–5, 249, 340

Helvellyn 269, 270, 274–7, 284

High Cup Nick 285–6

Hill, Octavia 337

Hockney, David 227

Hogarth, William 331

Holkham 155–7, 161

Honister Pass 260, 261–2

Hope valley 220–22

Hopkins, G. M. 274

Hoskins, W. G. 17

Housesteads 301–4

Housman, A. E. 174, 177–9

Hughes, Ted 234

I

Ice Age 119, 121, 200, 269

Iron Age 75, 119, 140–43, 178, 206, 222

Ironbridge 184–8

Isle of Wight 135–7

J

James, Henry 150

Jekyll, Gertrude 305

Johnson, Samuel 182

Jurassic Coast 37, 92–5

K

Keats, John 16, 266

Kent, William 14, 100, 137–40, 155–7

Keswick 260, 264, 266–8

Kinder Scout 216–20

King's College, Cambridge 149–51

Kingston Lacy 72

Knight Payne 161–2

Kynance Cove 43–4

M

McEwan, Ian 67

Macfarlane, Robert 12

Malham Cove 231

Malvern hills 193–7

Mam Tor 217, 219–22

Manifold valley 215

Mendip hills 75, 85–7

Michelin guide 18

Minack Theatre 45–7

Mont St Michel 50–51

Monument, The 318–22

Morecambe Bay 269, 281

Morris, William 169, 172

Mount Edgcumbe 48–9

N

Nairn, Ian 107

Nash, John 162, 310, 328

National parks 17, 214, 233, 337–8, 341

National Trust 16, 43, 51, 61, 78, 84, 101, 138, 139, 163, 171, 267, 271, 331, 337

Needles, The 135–7

Newcastle 318–10

New Forest 136

Newlyn 50–52

Newton, Isaac 151

North Downs 113, 118, 121–4, 142, 339

O

Offa's Dyke 179

Oswald, Alice 39

Oxford 125–30, 149

P

Palladio 61, 155

Palmer, Samuel 16, 53

Paxton, Joseph 313–14

Peak District 214–22

Peckforton castle 184, 197–9

Pennant, Thomas 257

Pennine Way 231, 284–6, 298, 304

Pennines 19, 235–8, 244, 249–51, 269, 282–6

Penzance 50–52

Petrarch 14

Pevsner, Nikolaus 61, 104, 157, 193, 298, 325

planning 17, 326–9

Plymouth 47–9

Polden hills 87

Poole 71–2

Pope, Alexander 14, 61, 137–8, 146, 169, 332

Porlock 82–4

Porthcurno 45–6

Portland Bill 60, 67, 89–90

Potter, Beatrix 16, 268, 271

Poussin 14, 101

Pre–Raphaelites 16, 44, 53, 172

Prior Park 59–61

Purbeck, Isle of 72–3, 80–90, 135

Q

Quantock hills 84, 87

R

Rackham, Oliver 114

Radcliffe Camera 127–30, 149

Ransome, Arthur 268

Ravilious, Eric 141

Rawnsley, Hardwicke 16, 267

Repton, Humphrey 15, 157, 160–63

Ribblehead 235–9

Richmond, London 329–32

Richmond, Yorks 239–41, 330

Rievaulx 15, 241–44

Ridgeway 113–14, 143

right to roam 218

Roaches, the 222–4

Romans 13, 84, 114, 119, 196, 280–81, 295, 300–304

Romney Marsh 121–4

Roseberry Topping 244–6

RSPB 203, 227–30

Ruskin, John 16, 266–8

S

St Aldhelm's Head 90

St Just 27–30

St Michael's Mount 50–52

St Paul's cathedral
319–20, 333–4
Salisbury 95–8
Saltaire 238, 246–9
Salvin, Anthony
78, 198
Scafell 257, 262, 268,
269, 275, 278–80
Seven Sisters 94, 95,
131–4
Severn, vale of
84, 172, 178–97,
182, 188, 193, 196,
200, 206–8
Shard, The 320–21,
324, 328, 335
Shaftesbury 98–160
Shakespeare, William
119, 131
Shenstone, William 15
Sheringham 160–63
Simonside 293–5
Skiddaw 260, 264,
265, 284
Snape marshes 154,
163–6
Solent, The 135–7
South-west coast path
45, 92
Somerset Levels 73–6,
85–7
South Downs
107, 110–12, 118,
131–4, 339

Stanage Edge 219–20,
222
Stevens, Wallace 18
Stiperstones 184,
199–200, 206–8
Stonehenge 266
Stonor 116–17
Stoodley Pike 234
Stourhead 15, 73–5,
100–104
Stowe 100, 137–40, 155
Swaledale 249–51, 273
Swift, Graham 164
Symonds Yat 202–5

T

Talman, William 212
Teesside 244–6
Telford, Thomas
62, 185
Tennyson, Alfred Lord
44
Thames, The 144–6,
313–15, 329–36
Thomas, Edward
110–13
Tintagel 52–4
Titterstone Clee 177–9
Traherne, Thomas 19
Trelissick 31–2
Trevelyan, G. M. 175
tors 36–7, 84, 87, 177,
200

Turner, J.M.W.
316, 330
Turville 116–17
Tyndale Tower 206–8

U

Uffington 141
Ullswater 265, 274–7
Undercliff, Lyme 95
UNESCO 288, 290

V

Valley of the Rocks 79
Vanbrugh, Thomas 137
Virgil 15

W

Wainwright, Arthur
260, 262, 269, 279
Wales 83–4, 85,
178, 179, 184, 189,
192, 200
Walpole, Horace
14, 332
Wasdale 278–80
Waterloo Bridge 332–6
Weald 121–4
Wells 85–7
Wenlock Edge 184, 189
Westminster 322–6
Westminster Bridge
332–3
Whin Sill 285, 301, 305

White Horse hills
140–43
Whitby 252–4
Widecombe-in-the-
Moor 37
wind turbines 143–4,
340–41
Windermere 261,
268–71

Windsor 143–6
Wordsworth, Dorothy
279, 332
Wordsworth, William
16, 18–19, 22, 84,
232, 260, 271,
274–7, 279, 282,
332–3, 336
Wormsley Park 117

Wrekin 173, 184, 189
Wren, Christopher 129,
313–17, 320–21, 333
Wrynose Pass 280–82
Wye valley 14, 16,
179–81, 193, 196,
202–5, 339